The Brontës and War

Emma Butcher

The Brontës and War

Fantasy and Conflict in Charlotte and Branwell
Brontë's Youthful Writings

palgrave
macmillan

Emma Butcher
University of Leicester
Leicester, UK

ISBN 978-3-319-95635-0   ISBN 978-3-319-95636-7   (eBook)
https://doi.org/10.1007/978-3-319-95636-7

© The Editor(s) (if applicable) and The Author(s) 2019
This work is subject to copyright. All rights are solely and exclusively licensed by the Publisher, whether the whole or part of the material is concerned, specifically the rights of translation, reprinting, reuse of illustrations, recitation, broadcasting, reproduction on microfilms or in any other physical way, and transmission or information storage and retrieval, electronic adaptation, computer software, or by similar or dissimilar methodology now known or hereafter developed.
The use of general descriptive names, registered names, trademarks, service marks, etc. in this publication does not imply, even in the absence of a specific statement, that such names are exempt from the relevant protective laws and regulations and therefore free for general use. The publisher, the authors and the editors are safe to assume that the advice and information in this book are believed to be true and accurate at the date of publication. Neither the publisher nor the authors or the editors give a warranty, expressed or implied, with respect to the material contained herein or for any errors or omissions that may have been made. The publisher remains neutral with regard to jurisdictional claims in published maps and institutional affiliations.

Cover illustration: © The Bronte Society

This Palgrave Macmillan imprint is published by the registered company Springer Nature Switzerland AG
The registered company address is: Gewerbestrasse 11, 6330 Cham, Switzerland

To Valerie

PREFACE

The Brontë men have fascinated generations of readers and researchers. This book stemmed from a simple question that was once put to me. Why are the men in the Brontë books so awful, so violent? Although there are more dimensions to it than that, this book traces the siblings' fascination with authority and violence back to their juvenilia, opening up future territories in Brontë research that have previously been unexplored.

This is the first full-length book dedicated to a theme in the Brontë juvenilia. Much of the groundwork has been laid by encyclopaedias, edited collections and transcription notes, which are detailed and plentiful. This book is the first result of those labours, which have enabled future generations to access a toolkit and explore important undercurrents within the narratives.

This book was born from my Ph.D. thesis, 'The Brontës and the Military', which was generously funded by the Arts and Humanities Research Council at the University of Hull. Gratitude in plenty is given to the Brontë Parsonage Museum, especially Ann Dinsdale and Sarah Laycock, for access and use of their collections, as well as the exciting opportunity to translate my research into an exhibition, 'The Brontës, War and Waterloo' in 2015. Thanks also to Patsy Stoneman and a warm dedication in memory of Sarah Fermi. Thanks are owed to my thesis examiners, Christine Alexander and Catherine Wynne; the British Association for Victorian Studies committee; and the board members of the Juvenilia Press. Special thanks to Chawton House Library and

Tony Yablon for awarding me with the Tony Yablon Visiting Fellowship. Thanks also to Jessica Cox and Valerie Sanders, this would not have happened without you. Final thanks to my colleagues, family, friends, and loving partner, Andrew.

Leicester, UK   Emma Butcher

CONTENTS

Abbreviations

Tales: Tales from Glass Town, Angria and Gondal. Edited by Christine
  Alexander
Angria: Tales of Angria. Edited by Heather Glen
EEW (I, II, III): Edition of the Early Writings of Charlotte Brontë. Edited
  by Christine Alexander
WPB (I, II, III): The Works of Patrick Branwell Brontë. Edited by Victor
  Neufeldt
PCB: The Poems of Charlotte Brontë. Edited by Victor Neufeldt
Blackwood's: Blackwood's Edinburgh Magazine

LIST OF FIGURES

CHAPTER 1

Introduction: Youth Writing War

Charge on the enemy
Victory leads
Capture their battery
Footmen or Cavalr'y
He shall be conqueror
Fastest who speeds

Think not of danger now
Enter the breach
Dream not of cannon-ball
Mount by the shattered wall
Soon shall their banner-staff
Bend to your reach

War is an ecstasy
Risk is wild
What though their battlements
Stand like a rock[1]

Charlotte's youthful poem, 'Charge on the Enemy' (1837), is not situated within her other Angrian writings, acting as a stand-alone example of her interest in war. Throughout, the verse's exhilarating, progressive form captures the essence of war, demonstrating multidimensional knowledge of militarism ranging from battlefield terminology to feelings of near-death

© The Author(s) 2019
E. Butcher, *The Brontës and War*,
https://doi.org/10.1007/978-3-319-95636-7_1

1

experience. It is heroic and patriotic, yet also dark: 'risk is wild'. It is playful and euphoric, yet considered and poignant. It is a deeply multifaceted response to the experience of war.

Like this poem suggests, young people are integral witnesses to history, yet, over time, their voices have been marginalised in the grand scheme of authoritative adult narratives. Even in the nineteenth century, when childhood became a social category in its own right, young people were caught in a passive consumer culture where their identity was shaped by the literature written *for* them, rather than *by* them. By returning to the past and analysing events through the lens of youthful penmanship, it is clear that youth's imaginative agency captures previously (un)interrogated moments of history. In the instance of war, it is the uninhibited, inquisitive nature of youth that paints a vivid canvas of some of the most important military events in history. This is the case in regard to the focus of this book, which examines Charlotte and Branwell Brontë's youthful writing partnership in the years following the Napoleonic Wars.

The Brontës contribute to a legacy of young people writing war in the nineteenth century. Samuel Coleridge's son, Hartley Coleridge, reworked the Napoleonic Wars into his imaginary war-gaming kingdom, Ejuxria. His map, drawn between 1804 and 1810, is the only surviving material of this kingdom from his hand, yet surviving family correspondence confirms the kingdom's content. His brother Derwent, writing of the kingdom after Hartley's death, stated that, after declaring that he had letters from Ejuxria, he [Hartley] would launch into his kingdom's news, which regularly revolved around wars fought between sovereign powers.[2]

Hartley Coleridge is just one example. Other notable authors such as George Eliot, Robert Louis Stevenson and Iris Vaughan wrote war narratives as children.[3] The Juvenilia Press has published numerous volumes of child authors, highlighting the sophisticated, interesting and playful forgotten content of important writers. The war stories and accompanying drawings written by these young prodigies tend to rework and play with past military periods; their tales usually revive or reimagine historical wars. Although these writings do not demonstrate the same sophisticated level of sustained content as the Brontë juvenilia, or perhaps Hartley Coleridge, they do, however, highlight the importance of war in the creative development of well-known authors, demonstrating early understandings of conflict, death, heroism and military masculinity.

Charlotte and Branwell Brontës' collaborative writings take the form of a war-fuelled fantasy world, first titled Glass Town (1829–1834) and then evolving into Angria (1834–1839). Over the course of approximately ten years, Charlotte, aged 13–23, and Branwell, aged 12–22, constructed an elaborate encyclopaedia of characters, places, and events, which are a complex conflation of real-life influence and imaginative play.[4] A majority of the literature does not fall under the usual category of 'child author', as, technically, these are 'coming of age' or 'teen' writings. Yet, with the Brontës, there has become a clear divide between the siblings' adult published works and the labyrinth of youthful writings they produced in the safety of their tight family unit. Childhood, despite its categorical placing in legal and social circles, is a fluid, abstract concept that is relative to the process of 'growing up'. Both Charlotte and Branwell's saga is often in line with youthful nature, it is experimental, imitative, and playful.

Despite its youthful execution, their saga demonstrates an ever-evolving recognition of one of the most adult topics that a young writer could tackle: war. As this book will go on to demonstrate, this was an exciting time in war writing, with British soldiers and journalists putting pen to paper and trying to make sense of a particularly conflict-riddled period, ranging from large-scale wars and their legacies—namely the Napoleonic Wars—to other colonial conflicts around the globe, such as the First Anglo-Ashanti War. The Brontë children were part of this nationwide conversation, using writing as an outlet to process and evaluate the varying post-war opinions they were exposed to through the material they read. The following chapters demonstrate that both siblings read widely and had a strong knowledge of formal and opinion-based war histories gained from canonical texts, biographies, newspapers and periodicals circulating in the 'adult world'. Using these texts as their source material, both brother and sister created a fantasy theatre of war, spending over a decade crafting their worlds of Glass Town and Angria. Within, they built a playful, alternative military history. The sagas draw on conflicts ranging from the ancient to the recent past and go further to consider and imagine wartime feeling and sensation. In sum, their writings offer an important socio-historical reading of war's impact on the social and artistic climate of Britain in the post-Waterloo years. Ultimately, this book shows that, if listened to, youthful voices are a rich spectrum of sources for understanding military mentality; the young mind occupies a twilight zone that responds and is sympathetic to the most serious real-world situations, yet is also emotionally intuitive enough to tap into wartime states of feeling and create uninhibited, imaginative war commentary.

CELEBRATING THE BRONTË JUVENILIA

The Brontës' early writings remain a complex and uncertain, yet fascinating, area of scholarship. The majority of manuscripts were written deliberately in miniature hand, almost illegible to the naked eye. The siblings' saga was a private microcosm constructed by a shared imagination, which was mutated and adapted through various forms. It began with three different play sagas—Our Fellows' Play, Young Men's Play and Islanders' Play—the latter two morphing into the Glass Town saga in 1829. Finally, this fully formed saga evolved into Angria in 1834. This trajectory goes some way to explain why confusion exists between who wrote what and when parts were written. It is still unknown how many undiscovered fragments of juvenilia exist and how much content has been destroyed, either by the Brontës themselves or posthumously. The main focal worlds of this book, Glass Town and Angria, appear to be fairly complete, yet even in recent years, more manuscripts are being discovered. In 2017, a Glass Town manuscript—retrospectively titled *A Visit to Haworth*—written by Charlotte was discovered when a book previously belonging to the Brontë family was sold by a private collector in America. In 2019, a little book by Charlotte turned up at an auction house in Paris. Although finding new Brontë material is rare, the extensive nature of the Brontë universe leaves extra stories and layers of detail open to discovery and interpretation.

Emily and Anne were involved in the Plays and Glass Town writings (1825–1832). The early Brontë sibling unit—Charlotte, Branwell, Emily and Anne—acted as a form of collaborative, playful 'think tank'. It is well known that the Reverend Patrick Brontë gave Branwell a set of toy soldiers in 1826, and each of the four siblings picked one, named him and used him for their creative collaborative stories. Emily and Anne's soldiers—Parry and Ross—make appearances in the early stories but have less involvement as the saga goes on.[5] Despite Emily and Anne's evident presence within these early stories, no manuscript is written in their hand. Emily and Anne's non-vocal, marginal role in the Glass Town saga is potentially why, in 1832, the two younger siblings made a decisive move away from Glass Town and distanced themselves from the Angrian writings. They formed their own saga, Gondal, which was separate yet in-keeping with their shared writing tradition. Emily and Anne's move away from Glass Town consolidated Charlotte and Branwell's writing partnership and confirmed them as the primary owners of their ever-evolving Glass Town and Angrian events and characters.

The Glass Town and Angrian manuscripts are notoriously difficult to navigate. Within these private spaces, Charlotte and Branwell had the freedom to discuss explicit, problematic content in an uncensored literary environment, without any intention for it to be shared with a public audience. The result of this is, however, a problem for future critics. Unlike published material, the saga is an organic, ever-changing conversation between the sibling unit and therefore signposting and clarity in regard to direction and any last-minute character changes is often omitted.

Christine Alexander and Juliet McMaster's *The Child Writer* offers detailed explanations as to the patterns and practices of the child writer during the long nineteenth century. As well as erraticism, the child's desire to imitate material they have read is often a reason why children's voices are seen to lack authenticity. Alexander and McMaster advocate that this regressive interpretation misunderstands the juvenilias' intrinsic value. Alexander quotes Robert Browning:

> He saw imitation as vital to the development of genius: 'Genius almost invariably begins to develop itself by imitation. It has, in the short–sightedness of infancy, faith in the world: and its object is to compete with, or prove superior to, the word's already–recognised idols, at their own performances and by their own methods'.[6]

Although this quotation opens up various avenues of discussion, it primarily captures the fast-paced methods of the child writer, whose writings boast an air of authority, yet are unstable in their structures, content and allegiances. Charlotte and Branwell's juvenilia fleetingly touch upon different events, opinions and histories: in short, what captures the siblings' immediate attention and imagination. Much of the juvenilia discards information that was a focal point only a story ago or changes the narrative to construct an alternative chain of events, even completely changing the identity of a character. This, which Browning terms, 'short-sightedness', exudes negative connotations as to the unreliability of the child narrator, yet, Browning's comments on the 'development of genius' celebrate the skill of the child in recognising and rewriting the adult world around them. At a fundamental level, the fluid and uninhibited nature of juvenilia make it fun and playful. In fact, Sara Lodge suggests that the Brontë juvenilia goes further with play, mimicking 'the rhetorical play of contemporary magazine culture: it is an arena of repartee, slang, drunkenness, political one-upmanship, challenge and reply that fully enjoys the freedoms accorded to men in the outside world'.[7] Lodge suggests that the siblings' immersion in the magazine culture around them allowed them to pause and reflect on the more sinister aspects of war. Charlotte and Branwell's war world is a meta-meta space of play and reflection, where fact and fiction are fused together to form a responsive alternative history through which we can interpret the attitudes and feelings generated within the post-Napoleonic moment.

In a broad sense, the siblings' inclusion of societal attitudes within their writings could fall under sociological criticism. Michael Rossi defines this approach as looking 'at how a literary work, as a product of a society, has been shaped by these forces [accepted attitudes and values] and how it, in turn, supports them'.[8] There is a problem with this, however, in the sense that the Brontë juvenilia deliberately evades this mainstream rhetoric of social response by existing as a separate, private space of experimentation. It is one-sided: their juvenilia are founded on societal attitudes, yet it overtly contributes nothing back to society itself. Instead, rather than brand this complex mode of reading the juvenilia within one broad critical framework, this book has also been influenced by the work of Laurie Langbauer, whose research addresses reading social history through juvenilia. Although Langbaur mainly relates her argument to the Romantics' youthful writings, she argues that prolepsis enabled child writers to imagine rhetorical events as if they have already happened. This, in itself, gives rise to an alternative, creative way of imagining the past, and the potentials of that past. As Langbaur states: 'Recovering juvenility matters, first of all, because it recasts history'.[9] Langbaur goes on to say that this act of prefiguring and reworking produces 'incisive meta-critical reflections: their supposed prematurity required that they actively engage with questions of identity and meaning-making and ruthlessly interrogate preconceptions of causality and development'.[10] It is, then, the status of the writer as a youth that allows for an alternative critical model of history to arise, where history runs parallel with the development and growth of the self and is reconfigured as both imitation and creative play. In the case of Charlotte and Branwell, the foundations of their saga are built on real-life war and conflict, yet it is their reinvention of reality through both imitation and interrogation of others' opinions that formulates an alternative method of reading the past. Their fantasy world exists as a dimension in which history and fantasy collide, creating a new record of past that is not just concerned with factual events, but the emotions and commentary generated by these events.

The Brontës' experimentation with the literary adult world allowed them to deconstruct, critique and rework content to suit their own saga. It is through this play and adaptation of the adult world that the child writer refreshingly highlights and interrogates contemporary adult opinion. The Brontës' openness to exploring and expressing different opinions of the period allows for a mosaic of perspectives regarding war to come through and creates a multi-layered, sophisticated case study of the period. As well as giving a general overview of contemporary public opinions that were in vogue—exhibited through various modes of literature, especially the periodical press—this book primarily captures the Brontës' own authorial voice and paints an alternative military history comprised of fact and fiction, but confidently rests in a hazy twilight zone of subjectivity and creativity.

GROWING UP IN THE SHADOW OF WAR

The Brontës' parents, Maria and Patrick Brontë, lived through the Revolutionary and Napoleonic Wars. Maria, born in 1783 in Penzance to a merchant father, saw first-hand the impact the Napoleonic Wars had on Britain, which disrupted trade and fishing and brought great hardship to the commercial trade centre in Cornwall and beyond. Likewise, Patrick lived through the anxiety and threat generated by the wars. Whilst studying for a curacy at the University of Cambridge, he joined the volunteer corps, which had 154 members by February 1804. Patrick joined in the wake of fresh fears of French invasion, as Napoleon's Grand Army was ready to march across the English Channel. As well as participating in a drill once a day and parading, Patrick was taught how to handle and use arms. After the end of his degree and preliminary curacy appointments in Essex and Shropshire, he was stationed in Yorkshire, where he would remain as a parish curate for the rest of his life. His first position was in Dewsbury where, as David Harrison remarks, 'He visited distant cottages, held services in working-class areas, and showed sincerity and compassion for their [the working class] plight during the hard times of the cloth industry during the disruptions caused to trade by the Napoleonic Wars'.[11] Later, whilst stationed in Hartford—his fourth appointment—Patrick was fully aware of the attack on Rawfolds Mill by the Luddites, the impact of which remained with him for many years. When both Brontë parents married in 1812, they united their experiences of war. Both had personally witnessed how the Napoleonic Wars impacted their local communities, and both understood how international warfare could damage and shape the fabric of British society.

The Brontë children were born into this climate: a nation affected and scarred by war. The eldest surviving child, Charlotte, was born in 1816, a year after the decisive battle of Waterloo. This meant that, unlike their parents, the children did not carry any immediate memories of large-scale war. Instead, the siblings were faced with growing up in a post-war climate. Although the landed gentry felt some immediate post-war economic benefits in the years following Waterloo, a majority of the population faced economic hardship and an unstable social climate. Although the war was over, the civil, often violent, conflict in Britain raged on. The Brontë children saw the problematic effects generated by the introduction of the Corn Laws in 1815, which provoked a reactionary campaign from radicals who regularly met and distributed pamphlets and petitions. Henry Weisser goes as far to say that the rise of philosophic radicals in the 1820s—headed by Jeremy Bentham and James Mill—even created an age of accepted radicalism, which saw a number of reforms pushed through Parliament.[12]

As well as experiencing an economic, political and social climate in flux, the Brontë children were born into an age where the literary trade flourished through rapid expansion. Although the popularity and wide distribution of periodicals meant that the British population received regular updates of the radical post-war changes that blighted local communities, it also meant that the previous wars could be memorialised and relived through conversational articles, opinion pieces and storytelling.

Despite living through the war's hardship, Patrick enjoyed keeping up-to-date with this eclectic mix of war material. As a staunch Tory and Catholic sympathiser, he related to and hero-worshipped the Duke of Wellington. The Brontë family owned various commemorative goods that celebrated Wellington's military career including portraits, biographies, busts and a medallion case that states that he was the 'most noble and exalted hero in the annals of history'. Patrick subscribed to *The United Service Journal* and borrowed other magazines, such as the Brontë family's favourite periodical, *Blackwood's*, which promoted Wellington's military achievements and perpetuated the rhetoric of heroism, despite his waning popularity as a politician in the years following Waterloo. Patrick's infatuation with Wellington was passed on to his children, especially Charlotte. She also remained a loyal supporter of Wellington throughout her life.

Patrick and Charlotte's hero worship of Wellington is just one example of how the media was central in shaping the opinions and imaginations of the parsonage's occupants. It is these opinion pieces, reviews and biographies that take centre stage in this book. Although newspapers such as *The Leeds*

Intelligencer, *Leeds Mercury* and *John Bull* are important sources of con-temporary commentary, especially in documenting the unstable post-war climate in and around Haworth, periodicals such as *Blackwood's*, *The New British Novelist* and *The United Service Journal* combined both current events with the arts. Each offered the siblings access to a shared national conscious that was obsessed with reading and writing about war. Within each issue the Brontë family read features, memoirs and discussions relat-ing to wartime accounts and figureheads, providing a mosaic of plot and character ideas they could adopt and recreate.

In addition to the mass media that swept through the parsonage, the family also had access to their own home library. The parsonage held a vari-ety of books that would have been available to the Brontë children from a young age. These include numerous titles with military content, such as *The Works of Virgil* (1824)—with an annotated copy of the *Aeneid*—John Mil-ton's *Paradise Lost* (1797), The Bible,[13] annuals such as *Friendship's Offer-ing* (1829), Lord Byron's *Childe Harold's Pilgrimage* (1827), and Walter Scott's poetry and prose, such as *Lay of the Last Minstrel* (1805). Beyond the parsonage, the family managed to acquire and read many other classics that contained military content, including Romantic poetry, the plays of William Shakespeare and Ben Jonson, *Arabian Nights* (1706), James Rid-ley's *Tales of the Genii* (1764) and the full nine-volume set of Scott's *Life of Napoleon* (1827).

Speculation as to where the Brontës accessed their reading material is still contested. Evidence of their extensive literary intake is evident throughout the collected siblings' juvenilia and later works, however, it is difficult to track down their reading or borrowing base. Bob Duckett has conducted the most extensive research as to where the Brontës borrowed their books. First, it is likely that they visited and read books at Ponden Hall. Duckett has recorded details of the Ponden Hall Catalogue of Books, auctioned in Keighley in 1899, which goes some way to uncovering what books the Brontë family were exposed to.[14] This collection includes biographies of eminent men, such as Leiut Sarratt's *Life of Buonaparte* (1804), historical military memoirs that are of interest yet unrelated to memoirs discussed in this study—such as William Thomson and Robert Beatson's *Military Memoirs Relating to Campaigns, Battles and Stratagems of War Ancient and Modern* (1803) and *Naval and Military Memoirs of Great Britain, from 1727 to 1783* (1804)—national magazines, such as copies of *The Oxford Review* (1807), and various books relating to geography, grammar, and songs and hymns.

Aside from this private collection, the siblings' father joined Keighley Mechanics' Institute in 1833, giving him access to their well-stocked library. This does not, however, account for the siblings' early reading as their father's membership coincided with the existence of an already fully formed saga. In fact, during the Brontës' younger years, Haworth had no library. There were numerous circulating libraries around the Yorkshire area, however, Charlotte maintained that she did not have access to one. Nevertheless, by studying the subscription and circulating library lists, such as Misses M & S Laycock's in Sheffield and Widdops' Circulating Library in Manchester, it is clear what kind of materials the reading public had access to, which included numerous traditional titles and themed content found within this study. As Duckett attests, Haworth, despite its primitive stereotype, was a cultural centre: 'the Brontës lived amongst educated and creative people many of whom may have loaned books and discussed literature [...] Joseph Hardacre [...] John Nicolson, "the Airedale poet", Abraham Wildman, John Milligan, Isaac Constantine, John Jowett, J. Oldridge, John Kitson, James Mitchell and the ubiquitous Revd. Theodore Drury'.[15] This is in addition to the Revd. Jonas Driver who lent *Blackwood's* and *John Bull* to the family until his death in 1831. Despite the Brontës' limited access to resources, the type of reading conducted by Haworth's creative types would have contributed to the general literate atmosphere of the community, which the siblings may have contributed to or been inspired by. Regardless of sources, it is clear that the siblings' knowledge of war was well rounded and varied, gathered from national and international literature with the encouragement of their father. By the time both Charlotte and Branwell wrote their first war story, they were already important consumers in the post-war literary landscape.

Soldiers in Haworth

Here lies a true soldier who all must applaud
Much hardship he suffered at home and abroad
But the hardest engagement he ever was in
Was the Battle of Self and the Conquest of Sin.[16]

A constant reminder of the Napoleonic Wars dominated the skyline of Haworth. The summit of Stoodley Pike housed a monument, erected in 1815, to commemorate the dead of Waterloo. Although housing in our present day has interrupted the view from Haworth and other villages in the valley, it was a visible and poignant part of the landscape as the Brontë children were growing up: a constant reminder of the consequences of conflict and a symbol that the previous wars were very much alive in local memory.

There is no evidence that the Brontë siblings interacted with soldiers whilst growing up in Haworth. In fact, the family did not have any direct ties with the military with the exception of William, the Revd. Patrick Brontë's brother, who took arms in the 1798 rebellion in Ballynahinch, Ireland. Nevertheless, it is highly likely that the Brontës would have known of Haworth's military connections as their father, as curate, would have been familiar with the parish and its people. Despite the siblings growing up in an era before the national census listed individuals and their occupations—rather than household—there are clues as to the military residents of Haworth. There is no information that is relevant in the 1841 census, however, in 1851 the Chelsea Pensioners, Joseph Fletcher, aged 79, and John Farrar, aged 62, are living in and listed as being born in Haworth. Interestingly, the census also reveals an army pensioner, John Crabtree, aged 75, living as a lodger in Haworth. The Revd. Patrick Brontë's letters show that this pensioner and Patrick had disagreements about money.[17] Although these records are clearly past the period of focus for this book and there can be no evidence that these ex-military men were living in Haworth whilst the siblings were growing up, the entries demonstrate that returning soldiers made Haworth their home after Napoleonic Wars and continued to make it their home long after.

Other sources give clues as to Haworth's military residents. In the parish's baptismal registers in 1813 and 1816, respectively, a William Firth is listed as a 'Militia Man' and John Appleyard as a 'Militia Sergeant' under 'father's occupation'.[18] Similarly, the headstones in Haworth churchyard reveal their graves' military occupants. Although most are not applicable to the timeframe of this book, like the epitaph that opens this section, one reads:

IN Memory of John Bland late Sergeant in the 1st Dragoon Guards. Served in the Army 30 Years. He died Octr 3rd 1821 Aged 68 Years.
    ALSO Sarah his Wife. She died July 12th 1847, Aged 96 Years.
    ALSO Michael Bland late in the 1st Dragoon Guards Served 20 Years. He died Novr 16th 1811. Aged 53 Years.
    Farewell vain World thou shop of toil and pain With our Redeemer now we hope to reign.

> Welcome sweet death thou entrance into bliss A place of rest O what a change is this
> ALSO of JOHN CLAYTON, late of Bradford, grandson of the above named JOHN BLAND, who died July 4th 1886 in the 86th Year of his Age.[19]

Although John Bland died before the Brontë siblings were little more than babies, his family remained long-standing residents of Haworth. Again, although it is unclear whether the Brontë family engaged with them on a personal level, with John's 30 year's service there could well have been stories shared verbally through the pulpit or in everyday conversation.

Lastly, the Diary of John Kitson, a working-class labourer, acts as an unusual source in regard to the soldier residents of Haworth. Although the timeframe, again, falls outside the focus of this book, the opening lines reveal a poignant connection between Kitson and the military: 'I John Kitson was born September 1781 at Bell hile [sic] a little below Haworth of poor parents in yorshire [sic] and my father went to be a soldier when I was but a child so as I could not tell on him going but he left my mother with three lads'.[20] Kitson continues this remarkable diary until his death, where he talks of his inability to work or eat due to poor health. Although the diary does not go into further detail about his father, it provides emotive imagery of war disrupting the local landscape as soldiers leave their homes and families behind. In the post-war climate, with many surviving soldiers returning to their families with war-induced physical and mental injuries, the Brontë children would likely have seen these same heads of family, but altered, return to their local landscape, or perhaps seen bereaved families in times of hardship. Although these local sources do not provide much substance for this book, they evidence that soldiers were part of Haworth's social fabric in the post-Waterloo era and, alongside the siblings' military reading, their presence and legacy may have provided mood music for the siblings' imaginative understandings of war and the everyday soldier.

The Major Wars and Conflicts in Glass Town and Angria

The siblings' juvenilia may have originated from childhood play, but play soon grew into an imaginative empire. This section provides a useful introduction to the wars and conflicts that consistently rage through the

Glass Town and Angrian saga. The following summaries are primarily con-structed from Branwell's writings, which concern themselves with the linear chronology of Glass Town and Angria's history. Whereas Branwell typically constructed sweeping battle scenes, Charlotte's war writings responded to how these battles impacted their shared characters' personalities and identi-ties. Her stories play a major role in highlighting the societal impact of war on their kingdom, especially during the Angrian post-civil war years (1837–1839). Therefore, in different ways, both siblings establish themselves as authoritative war writers.

The main wars in the saga are as follows:

The Twelves War (1829–1830)
Rogue's Insurrection of Glass Town (1830–1832)
The Wars of Encroachment and Aggression (1833–1834)
The Angrian and Glass Town Civil Wars (1835–1837)
Post–War Angria (1837–1839)

The Glass Town and Angrian saga was born out of war gaming. Their early pre-Glass Town manuscript titled *History of the Rebellion in my Fellows* (1828) showcases the logistical talents of an eleven and twelve-year-old, imagining and reenacting a large-scale battle with their toy soldiers, headed by the Duke of Wellington and Napoleon Bonaparte. This type of militant play laid the foundations for the first series of wars, written in the following year (1829) that brought Glass Town and its history to life. The saga begins with **the Twelves War**, with the Twelves sailing to and colonising the West Coast of Africa. The Twelves consist of notable military names, such as the Duke of York and the Duke of Wellington, who act as the chiefs of this adventurous band. After sailing from England to the African coast, they engage in a battle against the Dutch on Ascension Island, before sailing to the coast and successfully establishing a colony. After a short period of peace, war erupts between the colonisers and the Ashanti. The war culmi-nates with the Battle of Rosendale Hill, which is often elevated to the status of myth in future Glass Town narratives. The battle results in the death of the king of the Twelves, the Duke of York, which then leads to Wellington's subsequent coronation.[21] Before he takes his crown, however, Wellington travels back to Europe to fight in the Napoleonic Wars, refusing to take up this position until he has vanquished Napoleon. He succeeds, returning to Africa as both hero and sovereign.

Although military characters and discussions remain integral to the fabric of the Glass Town Federation, which incorporates the provinces and capital city, Verdopolis, large-scale conflict next arises in **Rogue's Insurrection of Glass Town**. By this point, the two main protagonists of the Glass Town and Angrian saga, the Royalist son of Wellington, Zamorna, known in these early tales at the Marquis of Douro, and his Republican friend and rival, Alexander Percy, then known as Rogue, emerge as Charlotte and Branwell's chosen alter egos. Rogue, Glass Town's leader of Republicanism, terrorises Verdopolis by staging an insurrection based on the French Revolutionary model. This is described in detail throughout Branwell's series *Letters from an Englishman* (1830–1832) in which the historian, John Flower, documents his imprisonment and impending execution after being charged for lending the government money. The Twelve's forces, however, manage to recapture the city and save the prisoners. Flower's narrative picks up again with him witnessing Rogue's attempt to rally his supporters, resulting in another battle in which, at one point, Rogue mercilessly executes prisoners of war. Finally, the narrative concludes with Rogue's defeat by Wellington's forces and his subsequent execution.[22]

After a year of relative peace, the Glass Town Federation faces its largest conflict yet. **The Wars of Encroachment and Aggression** rage through the Glass Town saga between 1833 and 1834. Branwell, narrating again as John Flower, documents this.[23] These series of conflicts begins with Talleyrand—the fictitious statesman of Frenchysland based on the real-life French diplomat—travelling to Glass Town with news that Napoleon, the leader of The Glass Town Federation's neighbour state, Frenchysland, has been overthrown and demands that the Federation accept their new republic. In the meantime, Napoleon takes back power and demands that Sneakiesland, a province of the Glass Town Federation, should be given to him or the Federation will face war. The Federation rejects this request and war ensues. In addition, other enemy groups, such as the Arabs and Ashanti, join allegiances with the French, which generates widespread hostility and racially aggravated tensions. War begins in a ceremonious manner, Branwell listing regiments and describing a lavish military spectacle. Following this, the war takes a dark turn. The Federation faces a series of difficult and damaging battles including: Little Warner, the Battle of Angria, the Bridge of Guadima and the Battle of Veleno. Finally, in the opening pages of *An Historical Narrative of the War of Aggression*, the Duke of Wellington, now a retired member of state, steps in to save the day. After meeting with the other Twelves, who do not wish to invest any more in the war, Wellington distances himself and sets about funding further supplies as head of the army. In short, it is now the government versus the army. After securing a defeat against the French, the army storm the government building and force the representatives to sign Wellington's agreement, which sets out an economic and military course of action. After their previous defeat the French rally, but are finally defeated by the Federation thanks to Wellington's injection of energy and funds.

After the Glass Town Federation's victory, the hero of the war, the Duke of Wellington's son, now known as Zamorna, is gifted his own kingdom of Angria. Alongside his band of noble followers, Zamorna chooses Alexander Percy—formally Rogue during the insurrection, now known as Northangerland—to be his new nation's prime minister. Whilst the spirit of coronation is still sweeping the nation, especially in the new Angrian capital, Adrianopolis, tensions between the two leading men quickly escalate resulting in violent parliamentary proclamations and Alexander Percy's suspicious absences. Nevertheless, attention from this is diverted by a conflict between Angria and the Ashanti tribe.

Henry Hastings, Branwell's pseudonymous soldier poet, who fought in the previous wars, takes over the narration and becomes one of the most central and important characters in the fantasy saga. He begins by narrating the violent, reactionary war between the Angrian army and Ashanti, the latter having recently slaughtered all the citizens of Dongola. In a racially aggravated retaliation, Zamorna orders his men to commit genocide, sending his troops into battle. Hastings recounts this ferocious conflict in detail. In the juvenilias' typical divergent fashion, however, the narrative perspective takes a turn as Zamorna loses a by-election in Adrianopolis. Distracted by this defeat, Zamorna ends the first civil conflict in Angria and Hastings is sent to report on the political turmoil in the capital instead.

The narrative is propelled forward with the victory of the Reform Party in the Verdopolitan general elections. The new party wishes for Angria to be expelled from the Verdopolitan union, causing Zamorna and Alexander Percy to temporarily unite and brace the country for **The Angrian and Glass Town Civil Wars**. Civil war against the Reform Party ensues, headed by the Verdopolitan naval captain, the Marquis of Ardrah. Hastings, once again, dominates the war narrative, documenting life on the front line as well as noting the internal wars that intensify between Zamorna and Percy. Percy begins to return to his past revolutionary 'Rogue' self, such as that seen during the 1830–1832 insurrection years, rousing his supporters to take advantage of Angria's vulnerability and enter into the confusion for the

Republican cause. Percy's vigilante group storm a meeting of the Verdopolitan cabinet, overthrow the government and declare one great Republic of Africa. The group continues to march on Zamorna's army, defeating the Royalist group at the Battle of Edwardston. Zamorna is saved by Percy from being sentenced to death and is instead banished to Ascension Isle. In the meantime, Angria suffers: horrific murders and tortures are carried out on civilians who oppose the regime, including Zamorna's son, whilst Zamorna's queen, Mary Percy, wastes away whilst grieving the absence of her husband.

Under the regime's surface, however, rumblings of support for Zamorna continue. With the news that the exiled king is likely to return, the Republican regime starts to crack, causing mass panic from the inner party. Zamorna returns from banishment and joins the Duke of Fidena's army to march on Verdopolis,[24] seizing power over the old capital. The narrative once again focuses on Hastings, who confesses to shooting his superior Royalist officer, defecting from the Royalists, and joining the Republicans. The Republicans' imminent defeat plunges him into a state of self-deprecation and he uses alcohol to curb his suffering. He emotively describes the retreating army of Republicans, who have suffered heavy casualties in the fight for Verdopolis. The Royalists retake both the capital and Angria, whilst Alexander Percy disappears into the abyss. The civil war ends.

From hereon, between 1837 and 1839, the siblings' tales focus on the problem of **Post-War Angria**. Alexander Percy and Zamorna reconcile, much to the distrust and displeasure of the Angrian citizens. Brawls in taverns proliferate alongside rumours of the nation's unstable economy, including bankruptcies, debts and stagnant trade. Moreover, the degeneration of Hastings becomes a primary focus; his compulsive drinking and violent activities—such as an attack on a farm—embody the anger and frustration of readjusting to everyday life in a war-shattered nation. As Branwell's writings devolve into a series of misdirected ramblings, Charlotte takes the lead on writing post-war Angria. Her novellas provide neat conclusions to the siblings' decade-long saga. As the final section of Chapter 4 details, trauma and alcoholism define this era of Angrian history. With tales dedicated to Zamorna and Percy's war-weary relationship, to Hastings' final stand and capture, these contributions provide an (anti)climactic finale to a nation whose landscape and inhabitants have consistently been defined and shaped by war. Whereas Branwell provides no definitive conclusion to his writings, continuing to write Angria-inspired material until his death in 1847, Charlotte bids goodbye to their collaborative kingdom in her *Farewell to Angria* (1839), where she turns away from 'full-plumed heads' and the full-faced paintings that inhabit 'the strength of manhood & the furrow of thoughtful decline'.[25] In the fallout of war, Angria is abandoned by its writing duo. The siblings leave their landscape and characters scarred, changed and beaten:

> But we must change, for the eye is tired of the picture so oft recurring & now so familiar.[26]

Chapter Summaries

This chapter has laid the foundations of this study, introducing the youthful Charlotte and Branwell Brontë as war writers. Chapter 2 of this book reviews the siblings' literary, military influences, demonstrating the siblings' awareness and interest in war literature ranging from Virgil to Walter Scott. The first three sections of the chapter are divided by time period—classical, late Renaissance to early Restoration, Romantic—with a fourth individual section awarded to Scott. These sections contextualise the Brontës' military reading, forming the groundwork for them to be considered as a domestic 'think tank' that shared a passion for war literature across all time periods. The first subchapter, 'Classicism', explores Charlotte and Branwell's Roman and Greek influences, such as Homer and Virgil. After first identifying key classical texts and wars that captured the siblings' imagination, the chapter moves on to discuss how classical models of violence—both sporting and on the battlefield—influenced contemporary archetypes of military masculinity. The following subchapter, 'Late Renaissance to Early Restoration', builds on canonical representations of military masculinity through the Brontës' reading of comedic and villainous soldier figures in works by playwrights such as Shakespeare and Jonson. The section ends with an evaluation of Milton's influence on the siblings' representations of Napoleon-like characters within their saga. The next subchapter, 'Romanticism', focuses on where the Brontës positioned themselves within the pro- and anti-war discourse of Romantic writers such as Byron, William Wordsworth and Robert Southey, in regard to the Napoleonic Wars. This subchapter considers how Charlotte and Branwell grappled with these varying opinions through their own representations and evaluations of war, linking these creative tensions to their own conflicted writings within their saga, which change between the celebration and demonisation of war. The final subchapter, 'Walter Scott', offers a separate analysis of Scott's influence on the siblings' understandings of war. Setting aside Scott's biography of Napoleon, which underpins the Chapter 3, the section explores Scott's poems and novels. It shows how Scott's representations of the powerful warrior in a historical and fantastical context influenced the siblings' understandings of how the military intersects with idealised notions of romance and chivalry. Lastly, Scott's narrative techniques are compared to Branwell's, offering new insights into how 'fog of war' stream-of-consciousness narratives were adopted by military writers and became a modern avant-garde method of representing war.

Chapter 3 focuses on military celebrity, investigating how the military rivals, Wellington and Napoleon, captivated Charlotte and Branwell's imaginations and fuelled their sibling rivalry. Studying the varying obsessions and interactions that existed between these two generals provides a new socio-historical model through which to read Charlotte and Branwell's reactions and reimaginings of masculinity. The chapter transitions from the representations of both military icons in a contemporary cultural context—especially biographies and the post-war media—through to the siblings' literal adoption of their names and characteristics within their early fantasy saga. Finally, the chapter explores how the siblings reworked the rivalry between and personalities of these influential names into their main protagonists, Zamorna and Alexander Percy, the two drivers and military heroes of the saga.

The following three chapters analyse the siblings' engagement with contemporary warfare and civil unrest, addressing how they reworked military media into their own writings. Chapter 4 focuses on the Napoleonic Wars and is divided into three sections: the rise of the military memoir, patriotism and the military spectacle, and trauma and alcoholism. First, the chapter demonstrates the siblings' engagement with and mimicry of military memoirs, many of which were published in post-Waterloo British periodicals. Using these accounts, the chapter moves on to discuss the siblings' conflicting views on war, focusing first on their patriotic writings, and then those that grapple with the darker elements of war. The final section evidences how the siblings were aware of war trauma in an age where it was not present in contemporary medical terminology. Their patriotic and traumatic understandings convey how the role of biography and the media—especially the periodical press—was instrumental in influencing their fluctuating views on war. More broadly, it also show-cases the range of personal war commentary the British public were exposed to: reading audiences were caught in a confusing double bind of post-war celebration and suffering.

The next chapter continues to discuss overseas warfare, but this time in a colonial context. Between 1823 and 1831, the First Anglo-Ashanti war broke out. This racially aggravated war, fuelled by the British colonial quest, was often discussed in the media and proved to be another formative military influence on the Brontë unit as they were growing up. Despite being a relatively low-key war compared to the Napoleonic Wars, the exotic location and brutality of this conflict tapped into the British public's and, more specifically, the siblings' imaginations. This chapter considers how racial violence was represented and replicated within their saga, both in relation to military masculinity specifically and the conduct of war more generally. Within their racial descriptions, Charlotte and Branwell fully engage with the prejudices, sensations and horrors of battle, demonstrating their problematic relationship with war and their broader interest in the dynamics of non-white warfare within the contemporary period. Moreover, this section allows for a wider discussion of themes such as Christianity and fatherhood, which are associated with racial interactions.

The final chapter of this book looks at civil warfare and unrest. It emphasises that Charlotte and Branwell were not just interested in large-scale wars, but the broader consequences of war on society. As well as analysing their early interest in famous civil conflicts of the age, such as the American War of 1812 and the French Revolution, the final part of this chapter considers how their early writings engaged with the post-Napoleonic anxieties and revolts enveloping Britain and their local Yorkshire landscape. This book, therefore, spans multiple theatres of war, both large and small scale, consolidating the siblings' varied military interests and demonstrating that the Brontë saga was a product of war in all its diverse forms.

The book concludes with a discussion that acknowledges the legacies and undercurrents of war in Charlotte Brontë's published works after her and Branwell's writing partnership ended. The findings of this book allow readers to revisit her representations of violence and masculinity in the context of war, whilst being sensitive to the influence and presence of Branwell who helped ignite and fuel her creative energy. As a whole, this book builds multiple purposes to achieve one ultimate aim. Its purposes are to showcase the Brontës' importance as child authors, to bring Branwell Brontë into the creative writing dynamic, and to demonstrate the collective power of the early Brontës as both researchers and imaginative fantasy authors. But, bearing all these points in mind, its ultimate goal is to establish the siblings as important war commentators and historians, which, in turn, gives a valuable, liberated insight into early nineteenth-century military cultures that flourished in post-Waterloo Britain.

NOTES

1. *PCB*: 221.
2. See Molly Lefebure, *Private Lives of the Ancient Mariner: Coleridge and His Children* (Cambridge: The Lutterworth Press, 2013): 246.
3. The Juvenilia Press has published scholarly editions of these works. George Eliot's short story *Edward Neville* (1995), edited by Juliet McMaster and others, is set during the English Civil War. Robert Louis Stevenson's *First Writings* (2013), edited by Christine Alexander and Elise McPherson, were concerned with biblical tales and nautical adventures. *The Diary of Iris Vaughan* (2004), edited by Peter Alexander and Peter Midgley is a first-hand account of seven-year-old Iris's experiences of colonial Africa during the Second Boer War (1899–1902).
4. Christine Alexander and Margaret Smith's detailed encyclopaedia on the juvenilia acts as a handy companion to the content discussed within this book. See Alexander and Margaret Smith's *Oxford Companion to the Brontës* (2012).
5. See, for example, the initial stories of the Twelves, *Two Romantic Tales* (1829) and *The History of the Young Men* (1830–1831) by Charlotte and Branwell, respectively, and Charlotte's *A Day at Parry's Palace* (1830). Equally, in the early tales, all four siblings take on a godlike role as Genii. From 1831, however, the Genii are removed from the forefront of the saga and only referred to in relation to Glass Town's history.
6. Christine Alexander, "Defining and Representing Literary Juvenilia," in *The Child Writer from Austen to Woolf*, ed. Juliet McMaster and Christine Alexander (Cambridge: Cambridge University Press, 2005): 78.
7. Sara Lodge, "Literary Influences on the Brontës," in *The Brontës in Context*, ed. Marianne Thormählen (Cambridge: Cambridge University Press, 2012): 2.
8. Michael John Rossi. *James Herriot: A Critical Opinion* (London: Greenport, 1997): 57.
9. Laurie Langbauer, *The Juvenile Tradition: Young Writers and Prolepsis, 1750–1835* (Oxford: Oxford University Press, 2016): 4.
10. Ibid., 6.

11. David Harrison, *The Brontës of Haworth* (Victoria: Trafford, 2002). Harrison also notes that the Revd. Patrick Brontë 'secured the acquittal of a wrongfully accused private in the army charged with desertion, a hanging offence' (5).

12. These reforms included Catholic Emancipation (1829) and the abolition of British slavery (1833). See Henry Weisser, "Radicalism and Radical Politics," in *Britain in the Hanoverian Age: An Encyclopedia 1714–1837*, ed. Gerald Newman and Leslie Ellen Brown (New York: Garland, 1997): 585–586.

13. Marianne Thormählen's *The Brontës and Religion* (1999) demonstrates the role the Bible played in shaping the lives and works of the family. As well as the Bible's use as a religious teaching tool, as enacted by their father the Revd. Patrick Brontë on a daily basis, it is also filled with dramatic stories that aroused the siblings' imaginations. From the Old Testament they would have been familiar with the battles between the Canaanites and the Perizzites, the Gileadites and the Ephraimites, and the Philistines and the Israelites. Equally the God in the Old Testament, Jehovah, is a much more violent and vengeful God as opposed to the Christian God in the New Testament. It is worth considering that the young siblings grew up immersed in this violent, divine rhetoric.

14. See Bob Duckett, "The Library at Ponden Hall," *Brontë Studies*, 40.2 (2015): 104–149.

15. Bob Duckett, "Where Did the Brontës Get Their Books?" *Brontë Studies*, 32.3 (2007): 204.

16. This epitaph is inscribed on the grave of William Foster, who died on 23 February 1807, aged 78. He is buried in the graveyard of St Michael and All Angels' Church, Haworth. This was transcribed directly from his gravestone.

17. In October 1843, the Revd. Patrick Brontë wrote a letter to an unidentified correspondent asking, 'Dear Sir, When you see John Crabtree, you will oblige me by desiring Him to pay the debt which he owes'. See Dudley Green, ed., *The Letters of Reverend Patrick Brontë* (London: Nonsuch, 2005): 152.

18. Taken from the 1813 and 1816 St Michael and All Angels' Baptism Records, West Yorkshire Archives, Bradford, 51D81.

19. Epitaph directly transcribed from gravestone.

20. John Kitson, *The Diary of John Kitson of Haworth* (Keighley: Public Library, 1843).

21. With both Charlotte and Branwell writing separate yet similar histories based on the same events, there are inevitable inconsistencies in their narratives. In Charlotte's version of events, the Duke of York does not die but rather returns to England.

22. As is commonplace for the Glass Town and Angrian juvenilia, Rogue is resurrected as a character in Branwell's following tale, *The Pirate* (1833).

23. See Branwell's two tales of the same name: *An Historical Narrative of the War of Encroachment* (1833–1834) and *An Historical Narrative of the War of Aggression* (1834).
24. Prince John Augustus Sneaky Fidena is the eldest son and heir of Sneakiesland. He is Zamorna's most respected and trusted friend.
25. *Tales*: 314.
26. Ibid.

CHAPTER 2

The Brontës' Military Reading

CLASSICISM

Idyllic visions of masculinity dominate classical literature. The Brontës' exposure to and, in Branwell's case, training in ancient texts and translations by their Cambridge-educated father facilitated their knowledge and understandings of ancient warfare whilst encouraging them to engage and interact with godlike models of muscular, warrior men. This section investigates one of the most important bygone periods in the Brontës' childhood reading, ancient Greece and Rome. By assessing the siblings' engagement with classical warfare, then moving on to how battlefield violence and physicality are transposed on to sporting events and masculine models in their saga—focusing primarily on Homer's *Iliad* (710–60 BC) and Virgil's *Aeneid* (19 BC)—it will become clear how the fabric of the siblings' saga is inextricably bound with classical ideals and customs.

It is important to note that the foundation of Charlotte and Branwell's early writings derives from Grecian, mythological models. The Brontës' own fictitious supernatural selves, 'the chief Genii', live in the Jibbel Kumri, or Mountains of the Moon, a strong allusion to the Greek gods' residence, Mount Olympus. In fact, classical references permeate the saga; all the learned, aristocratic characters are classicists. The Republican revolutionary, H. M. M. Montmorency, has a library dedicated to ancient history, and Elrington Hall, home of Alexander Percy and Zenobia Elrington, contains numerous ancient volumes. Throughout the saga, the Brontës reference all the major classical authors: Scipio Africanus, Socrates, Ovid, Virgil and

© The Author(s) 2019
E. Butcher, *The Brontës and War*,
https://doi.org/10.1007/978-3-319-95636-7_2

Herodotus. Although the siblings' reading was varied, the ancient world underpins the entire juvenilia.

As the scholar of the household, it was Branwell who was particularly interested in classical warfare. Throughout his writing life, he remained interested in the ancient world; his most notable Roman- and Greek-inspired writings are the dramatic verses 'Caractacus' (1830) and 'The Pass of Thermopylae' (1835) as well as a translation of Horace's *Odes* (1840).[1] In the former two, whereas 'Caractacus' documents the British king who armed his country against the invading Romans, 'The Pass of Thermopylae' recounts a battle between the Persians and the Greeks in a narrow coastal pass. For 'Caractacus', Victor Neufeldt has already traced Branwell's main source of information to William Mavor's *Universal History [Volume 6]* (1804), discounting the idea that Branwell used the conventional classical source of Tacitus' *Annals* (14–68 AD). Branwell would have most likely read about the latter in Book Seven of Herodotus' *Histories* (440 BC): Christine Alexander observes Charlotte's fleeting references to the Greek historian through her learned gothic bluestocking heroine Zenobia,[2] and, from Branwell's classical education, it is likely that he was even more famil-iar with his writings. The interconnecting text between 'Caractacus' and 'The Pass of Thermopylae', however, is Edward Gibbon's *The Decline and Fall of the Roman Empire* (1776). Both Charlotte and Branwell were likely to have read Gibbon's epic or would certainly have been familiar with it. In his *Angria and the Angrians (1a)* (1834), Branwell foresees that Angria's empire will become 'the Decline and Fall of Africa'.[3] Similarly, in Charlot-te's *Leaf from an Unopened Volume* (1834), Zamorna's increasing likeness to the Roman Emperor, Augustus, alongside her allusions to 'Goths in myriads',[4] is indicative of Charlotte's reading of Gibbon.[5] Both 'Caracta-cus' and 'The Pass of Thermopylae' are mentioned in Gibbon's chronicle. Gibbon talks of Britain's invasion in the first century of the Christian Æra. He commends the 'various tribes of Britain' who 'took up arms with savage fierceness',[6] one of them led by Caractacus. Moreover, Gibbon reflects on the battle between the Persians and the Greeks when theorising how the Romans may have defeated the Goths at Thermopylae:

> In this narrow pass of Thermopylae, where Leonidas and the three hun-dred Spartans had gloriously devoted their lives, the Goths might have been stopped, or destroyed, by a skilful general; and perhaps the view of that sacred spot might have kindled some sparks of military ardour in the breasts of the degenerate Greeks.[7]

Branwell adopts this language of praise, mimicking Gibbon's celebratory remarks with his: 'Arise ye Spartan heroes, rise [...] / Never did trumpet's loudest voice / Rouse the fierce soldiers to rejoice / As now will yon ensanguined pass / And that one word, Leonidas!'.[8] It is from the siblings' widespread reading about ancient Greece and Rome, both from the works of ancient and contemporary historians, that their enriched history of warfare truly becomes noticeable. Their engagement with primary and secondary material that documents and celebrates both classical models of warfare and masculinity adds an extra layer to their knowledge of different cultures, doctrines and historical genres.

As Stephen Miller notes, in classical Greece it was essential for men to excel in athletics. Sports such as boxing, swimming and armed combat contributed to the projected image of Rome as a strong, athletic dynasty.[9] Although these doctrines are discussed by an array of classical writers, Homer's *The Iliad* and Virgil's *The Aeneid* are the most noticeable texts that influenced the Brontës' writings.[10] Each narrative enforced the necessity of heightened masculinity in times of war, yet also provided vivid accounts of exercise and physical games in track and stadium environments. Prefiguring the Olympic Games, Homer and Virgil's writings provide detailed descriptions of funeral games: these games were similar in format to our present-day understanding of the Olympics but were held in honour of a recently deceased hero. Branwell's 'Ode on the Celebration of the African Games' (1832) pays homage to these early death-inspired competitions. Although his poem does not concern death specifically, Branwell aligns melancholic language with the idea of death as a catalyst for celebration. In the Olympian hall, the reader is urged to 'Haste upon this day of Gladness / Drive away the voice of sadness / And of Grim Despair'.[11] In Virgil's *Aeneid*, Aeneas commemorates the first anniversary of his father's death by offering tributes to the gods and hosting games. Although the event is something that he 'shall always find bitter',[12] his tone changes, and his positive thoughts arise: 'Once more I greet you, my divine father. I come to greet your sacred ashes'.[13] With his father's presence felt, the games begin. In Homer's *Iliad*, Achilles offers a similar tribute consisting of games and prizes in honour of his beloved comrade, Patroclus. After the congregation buries the dead in a mass mourning, Achilles makes them sit whilst he brings out the prizes for the funeral games: 'Agamemnon and you other Greek men-at-arms, these are the prizes that await the charioteers in this contest'.[14] In ancient culture, it is clear that death and grief are expressed and processed through physical activity and muscular demonstrations of manliness. The games, in turn, combat the weakness associated with death, triggering the need to display primal, masculine instincts for survival. Alexander notes that, at this point, Branwell was suffering his own loss, his sisters belittling the tyranny of the Genii—the Greek-inspired gods—within the Glass Town saga. Branwell plays with this Greek assertion of manliness in the face of death, asserting his own masculine position as brother as he experiences a death-like moment through his decline of imaginative control in the face of his sisters: 'These are the powers that rule our land / Nor can we hope their fetters to release'.[15]

In classical literature, it is difficult to distinguish the language of the arena from that of battle, affirming the close union between sport and war. In Virgil's *Aeneid*, the narrator describes how 'they [the contestants] charged and turned and charged again, winding in circles now in one direction now in the other, fighting out in full armour the very image of battle',[16] emphasising the warlike atmosphere in the arena. In Homer's *Iliad*, Achilles describes how the games' contenders and the military are one and the same: 'Achilles then gave order for his war–loving Myrmidons to put on their bronze armour and every charioteer to yoke his horses [...] The charioteers led off and after them came a cloud of infantry one could not count'.[17] In 'Celebration', Branwell fixates on this connection, revealing the bloodthirsty natures of the Genii: 'Round their huge jaws the red foam churning / Their souls for blood and battle burning [...] still again impatient to begin'.[18] This terrifying roar of the Genii is accompanied by anthems of war: the 'trumpets loud and shrill' mimic the patriotic, warlike anthem of Branwell's later poem 'Sound the Loud Trumpet' (1834),[19] written under his pseudonym, Henry Hastings. As ancient warfare is purposefully and intimately bound with visions of masculine power and pugnacious dominance, so is Branwell's vision of Glass Town, its celebrations and physicality revolving around the glorification of war.

One of the most popular physical sports in classical culture was boxing, which also happens to be the most fashionable masculine activity for all classes in Charlotte and Branwell's decade-long saga; characters ranging from aristocrats to criminals partake. This is unsurprising, given the nineteenth-century cross-class obsession with pugilism.[20] The Brontës were not immune to this obsession; their heroes, Lord Byron and John Wilson, the latter a writer for *Blackwood's*, practised the sport, and Branwell became a member of the local Haworth boxing club. Moreover, Branwell kept up to date with the latest pugilist news and features: discussions about boxing regularly featured in late Georgian periodicals and publications. Extracts from Pierce Egan's ongoing series *Boxiana; or Sketches of Ancient and Modern Pugilism*, pervaded the pages of the siblings' *Blackwood's* between 1819 and 1822. Maintaining links with its classical origins, another article titled 'Boxing Match at Wimbledon', written in Greek and Latin, appeared in *Blackwood's* in March 1818. It is clear that these contemporary accounts and commentaries influenced Charlotte and Branwell's characterisation. One notable champion mentioned in the *Boxiana* series, Pratt, is reimagined as Pratee, or Maurice Flannagan, in Charlotte and Branwell's writings. In Charlotte's 'Corner Dishes' (1834) he is given the position of private secretary to Zamorna so that they can box at any time. Another Glass Town boxer, Molyneux, who is patron of the ring, is similarly named after a *Boxiana* character, Tom 'The Moor' Molineaux, a famous black boxer celebrated by Egan for his warlike form and courageous spirit. In his last unfinished novel, *And the weary are at rest* (1845), Branwell demonstrates his continued interested in pugilism. His protagonist, Alexander Percy, alludes to the popular sporting chronicle *Bell's Life in London*, published between 1822 and 1886: 'I can be as sharp a shot and as stalwart a walk as any one but when I am out o' the vein I will not brag of performances worthy of being registered in any column of Bells Life in London',[21] verifying that Branwell continued to hold the sport in high esteem until the end of his life.

Although it is clear that, contextually, the art of boxing played a major role in nineteenth-century masculine and sporting discourse, the late Georgian reader is often reminded that the origins and values of this activity are much indebted to ancient society. In Egan's *Boxiana*, he notes:

> It was sanctioned by those distinguished nations [Rome and Greece], in their public sports, and in the education of youth, to manifest its utility in strengthening the body, dissipating all fear, and infusing a manly courage into the system [...] the manly art of Boxing has infused that true heroic courage, blended with humanity, into the hearts of Britons, which have made them so renowned, terrific, and triumphant, in all parts of the world.[22]

Both Branwell and Charlotte, like the ancient world, make boxing a well-respected profession for their protagonists, Alexander Percy and Zamorna. In *Life of Alexander Percy, Vol. I* (1834), a biography of Percy's youth, his education in pugilism—amongst other sports—is named as being directly responsible for his 'masculine strength':

[mornings were] generally spent at the proffessors [sic] of boxing fencing and such athletic exercises in whose rooms he learnt all the art of Defence acquirred [sic] ideal skill and strength and repaired or warded off the inroads which the life he led was making on his naturally strong and springy constitution.[23]

Like Percy, Zamorna is also passionate about the sport. Inspired by bawdy pugilist names circulating in the period such as Jem Belcher, Tom Tring and Ikey Pig, Charlotte brands her prizewinning fighter with a number of pugilist nicknames: Young Wildblood, the Swashing Swell, Handsome Spanker and the Fancy. Branwell encouraged his sister's interaction with the sport, celebrating their mutual interest in his tale, *Real Life in Verdopolis, Vol. II* (1833). Although there are a number of the siblings' writings—*Letters from an Englishman, Vol. II* (1831), *Something About Arthur* (1833), *The Green Dwarf* (1833) to name a few—that deal with an outbreak of fisticuffs, this particular story keenly demonstrates their protagonists' pugilist upbringings. After Zamorna brings in governmental troops to quell a prison riot started by Percy, Percy arrives at an aristocratic gentleman's club, Elysium, and goads his rival into participating in a boxing match. Branwell's lust for violence and bloodthirsty battles manifests here: 'a toucher on Rougues [sic] smeller which brought out a beautiful stream of claret [...] soon their eyes became black as the Midnight their lips red as coral'.[24] This descriptive passage is, furthermore, interspersed with warlike language: 'first blood was cried', 'the battle displayed perfect sience [sic]'.[25] Although similar language is used in *Boxiana*—in one instance, Egan explains boxing's 'most hurtful blows': 'the blood often runs from his ears, mouth and nose'—some of the most bloodthirsty descriptions of physical combat would have come from Branwell's classical reading.[26] For example, in Homer's *Iliad*, a gory match occurs between the champion boxer, Epeius, and the nobleman Euryalus:

When the two men had kitted themselves out, they stepped into the middle of the gathering, put up their massive fists and fell on each other. Heavy blows were exchanged; cheek–bones cracked fearfully; and the sweat began to pour off them. Then, as Euryalus was looking for an opening, godlike Epeius, leaping in, caught him on the cheek. Euryalus remained upright no longer, and his whole body sagged.[27]

Moreover, in the fifth book of Virgil's *Aeneid*, an equally gory fight is recounted between the Trojans, Dares and Entellus. It is so violent that the match has to be called off when it culminates with Entellus beating a bull's brains out.[28] The use of gruesome language in these classical texts clearly aligns itself with the contemporary appeal of sensationalising violence, be it in the periodical press, or in the Brontës' imaginations: it facilitated a connection between past and present understandings of unrestrained, red-blooded forms of masculinity, forms that the Brontës admired and adopted.

A less violent, but equally competitive activity that was popular in ancient Greece and Rome was archery, a sport associated with the oracular god Apollo in Greek and Roman religion and mythology. Within Charlotte and Branwell's juvenilia, Charlotte's protagonist is repeatedly likened to Apollo in both physical appearance and character. Despite maturing in his identity—evolving from the Marquis of Douro to the Duke of Zamorna—and changing in his manner and physical appearance, he is consistently compared to the classical god throughout the saga. In Charlotte's early tale, *Albion and Marina* (1830), the Marquis of Douro [Zamorna] is described as follows: 'His stature was lofty; his form equal in magnificence of its proportion[s] to that of Apollo'.[29] It is also demonstrated, however, through Charlotte's drawings and early writings, that her hero was feminine in appearance. This is something that Zamorna is often teased about in Charlotte's later juvenilia: in *The Spell* (1834), the narrator remarks how 'the Duke of Zamorna was once like a girl!'.[30] Although his original, physically effeminate self may appear to contradict doctrines of bodily power, especially godlike physicality, the Marquis of Douro's soft features further justify his likeness to Apollo: Apollo is repeatedly described as the ideal figure of the *kouros,* an athletic youth that was inextricably bound with classical visions of homoeroticism and physical perfection. Literally trans-lated as 'young man', this celebrated, archetypal model of manliness was mainly represented in sculpture, the *kouros,* as described by Ian Jenkins and Victoria Turner, possessing 'developed biceps, and pectoral muscles; wasp waist; flat stomach; a clear division of torso and pelvis; powerful but-tocks and thighs'.[31] It is not surprising that this erotic vision of manliness captured the imagination of the young Charlotte Brontë, the sensual and physical ideals available to her making a deep impression on her maturing, sexually active imagination.

In *Something About Arthur*, Charlotte's idealised vision of masculinity becomes blurred and slightly confused. After Mina Laury, the Marquis of Douro's admirer, nurses Douro back to health in the mountains following a local conflict, the narrative describes how he had:

reached that lofty heroic stature and free, bold chivalric bearing which he now possesses. His features also assumed a richer and sunnier tone of colouring in exchange for the delicate, transparent complexion which had before given him a very effeminate appearance.[32]

From hereon Charlotte's new 'purely physical' model of ideal masculinity is complete, sculpted militant muscle essential for her ideal soldier rather than youthful athleticism. Her artwork of 1833–1834 confirms that this was not an easy transition, however, the tension between brawny Byronism and youthful beauty is clearly evident. Although her hero is shown broad chested and in full regimentals, he still retains his soft features, showing Charlotte's difficulty in breaking from classical ideals.

Charlotte's inability to separate the Marquis of Douro's masculine identity from Apollo's made an impression on Branwell. In his *Angria and the Angrians I(a)* (1834), despite his transformation from feminine beauty to Byronic hero, Zamorna, now King of Angria, is introduced as possessing 'an Appollo [*sic*] like form which his close white dress so noble set off. added a countenance whose rich curls marble forehead and an eye. which spurned creation'.[33] Regardless of his changing physical appearance, as demonstrated through Branwell's sketch of Zamorna in 1835, his association with Apollo had become an integral part of Zamorna's (self)representation. Although Branwell's harsh sketch visually departs from classical masculine imagery, it is clear that the association cannot be undone. This associative legacy is emphasised through the siblings' literature. Zamorna's new Angrian kingdom becomes an extension of himself. An image of the sun—another divine attribute associated with Apollo, the sun god—becomes a nationwide emblem of the Angrian dynasty and Zamorna's leadership.[34] In her *Peep Into a Picturebook* (1834) Charlotte celebrates Zamorna's new extension of his classical identity; the narrator remarks on a portrait of the new King: 'Fire and light! What have we here, Zamorna's self, blazing in the frontispiece like the sun on his own standard!'[35] As this extract suggests, the image of the sun also becomes imperative for warmongering propaganda. Branwell's *Angria and the Angrians I(a)* proves that Angria is, if nothing else, a militant land that uses classical ideals of strength and power to rally its people (Figs. 2.1 and 2.2):

'your Sky shall never be clouded your Land shall never be invaded your sun shall never set and your reign shall never end will be and shall be the determination and care of your King Arthur Wellesley [Zamorna] […] and

Fig. 2.1 Brontë, Charlotte (1833–1834). *Young Military Man* (Image used courtesy of the Brontë Parsonage Museum)

by this I will abide so help me God'. The Earl of Northangerland [Percy] stepped darkly forward and stretching forth his hands he cried in the loudest and most warlike voice. God save the King'[36]

With the figure of Apollo bound first to Zamorna's personal, then national, identity, it is clear that classical imagery is initially important in the siblings'

Fig. 2.2 Brontë, Branwell (1835). *Zamorna* (Image used courtesy of the Brontë Parsonage Museum)

construction of masculine form and selfhood, then becomes an integral part of the saga's core values and their kingdom's performativity.

In the juvenilia, the siblings' interest in ancient sporting and wartime culture adds an important foundation to a host of references and allusions made to historical battles and past models of masculinity. It is important to note that a multifaceted classical backdrop supports their narratives, which are crowded with military history stretching back for approximately one thousand years. By uncovering and exploring these origins, the historical foundations upon which the Brontë juvenilia are built can be understood and their complex, multidimensional understandings of military men and landscapes—both in youth and adulthood—can be traced.

LATE RENAISSANCE TO EARLY RESTORATION

Writers from the late Renaissance to early Restoration period—such as William Shakespeare, Ben Jonson and John Milton—shaped the Brontës' understandings of different versions of soldierhood. Although the siblings' interest in certain writers—such as Jonson—was short-lived in their early years, their interpretations of these sources continued to resonate throughout their juvenilia. The siblings used Renaissance models and their Romantic legacy to tackle and exaggerate the characteristics of their most problematic military characters. It is through this multi-layered analysis that Charlotte and Branwell successfully appropriate a conflation of historic masculine models, allowing their juvenilia to give a well-balanced and sagacious overview of past military masculinities. Using representations of the late Renaissance and Restoration soldier, Charlotte and Branwell were able to envisage past and present connections between the military and masculinity, and comedy and evil, incorporating these elements into their imaginary worlds.

Thus far, Brontë scholarship has frequently compared Shakespeare's 'Moorish' soldier Othello to Charlotte and Branwell's fictitious chief Ashanti warrior, Quashia Quamina. A notorious villain, Quamina follows a similar narrative to Othello; Christine Alexander notes that he 'takes on all the European clichés [...] and degenerates into a drunken murderer'.[37] Alexander also recognises the similarity between Othello and Iago, and Quamina and Alexander Percy's relationship. Both are nurtured in a homosocial military environment, yet, despite their allegiance to the same cause, Iago and Percy choose to betray their black comrades, provoking them to unleash their inner savage. Referring to Percy's false promise to grant permission for Quamina to marry his daughter, Mary Percy, the reader is reminded of Iago's duping of Othello regarding his wife, Desdemona's, infidelity; both black soldiers are described as reacting violently and pursuing their white female objects.[38]

Although race—with a military subtext—has been discussed in relation to the Brontë juvenilias' adoption of Shakespearean themes, little attention has been extended to other late Renaissance military models the Brontës recognised and adapted in their early literature. A prime example of this is the Elizabethan literary and theatrical portrayal of the comic soldier, a common component of the Elizabethan stage. Paul Jorgenson emphasises that, amongst other intentions, the common soldier provided a 'comic sub-stratum' for serious plays and added an extra layer of box-office appeal.[39] Shakespeare is known for his humorous military characters, with their wit-ticisms, scheming plots and alcoholic tendencies; Falstaff, Pistol and Nym feature in *Henry V* (1600), *The Merry Wives of Windsor* (1602) and the former two also make an appearance in Shakespeare's two-part *Henry IV* (1600). In *Othello* (1604), Iago interacts with this stereotype, Branwell par-ticularly taken with a drinking scene in which Iago, according to Buckner Trawick, 'plays to the common stereotype of the 'bluff, honest, fun-loving soldier. Calling for wine he sings a rollicking drinking song'.[40] Branwell transcribes this song in his *Letters from an Englishman, Vol. II,* this strong image of frivolity and drunkenness influencing Branwell's early conceptions of soldierly buffoonery and comradeship. Drunken imagery, however, also paved the way for Branwell's characters'—especially Henry Hastings'—more sinister faults, his later juvenilia exploring the continuous, and dan-gerous presence of military alcoholism within Angria's military.

For both Charlotte and Branwell, the most pervasive image of the sol-dier buffoon derives from Jonson's *Every Man in His Humour* (1598); Jonson captured the siblings' imagination with his satirical representation of the boasting, cowardly soldier Captain Bobadil. A popular character in nineteenth-century literary circles, Bobadil was equally celebrated by Charlotte and Branwell within their juvenilia. Their interest in the flawed military figure prefigured other prominent literary figures' fascination with him. Although notable Victorian writers such as Robert Browning, Alfred Tennyson and Edward Bulwer–Lytton wrote of their fondness for Jonson's character, it was Charles Dickens who fervently adopted the role, playing Bobadil numerous times alongside his company of literary amateurs during the 1840s. An audience member at an 1847 benefit event exclaimed: 'Dick-ens was glorious. He literally floated in braggadocio. His air of supreme conceit and frothy pomp in the earlier scenes came out with prodigious force in contrast with the subsequent humiliation which I never saw so thoroughly expressed before'.[41] As well as acting the part, Dickens also had portraits painted as Bobadil and signed his letters with the soldier's name. The character of the comic soldier had a powerful hold upon his and his contemporaries' literary imaginations.

A decade earlier, Bobadil had a similar effect on the childhood imaginations of the Brontë siblings. Although not integral to the Glass Town plot, Bobadill [*sic*] appears in Charlotte's early bawdy tales amongst body snatchers and rare lads, a slang term for the criminal underbelly of Glass Town. Besides briefly appearing in her *An Interesting Passage in the Lives of Some Eminent Men of the Present Time* (1830) as a 'tall, ugly man' who interacts with the Duke of Wellington,[42] he also makes a cameo appearance in Charlotte's *The Poetaster* (1830). In this tale, he is served justice from the whip of Hume Badey, the Glass Town physician—and real-life physician to the Duke of Wellington—who at this point is no more than a dissector of stolen bodies.

> *General Bobadill:* May it please you, my lord, Sir Alexander Hume Badey has with the most consummate insolence horse-whipped me while in the discharge of my duty.
> *Duke of Wellington:* Well, it certainly does please me, Bobadill.[43]

The passage's correlation between justice and humiliation is taken from Jonson's original play. In Act IV sc. V, Bobadil is defeated in a duel after continuously boasting about his military prowess under the facade of gentlemanly chivalry: 'I could have slain them all, but I delight not in murder'.[44] When Justice Clement is called in the final scene to expose and rectify the characters' flaws and deceits, Bobadil's 'humour' is revealed in his lament over his attack. Clement responds: 'O, God's precious! Is this the soldier? Lie there, my sword,'twill make him swoon, I fear'.[45] By adopting Bobadil's bawdiness and failure as a soldier, Charlotte shows her early understanding of how soldierhood can be problematic. Along with Branwell, who, in his *The Liar Detected* (1830), lists Bobadill amongst fifteen others charged with criminal offences—Bobadill's crime is having 'an ugly count[e]nance'—[46] Charlotte's formative impressions of military masculinity are fluid; her comprehension of soldierly character not just limited to her idealisation of warlike figures such as the Duke of Wellington. Her own and Branwell's presentation of Bobadill as 'ugly', both physically and morally, paved the way for more sinister representations of mobilised men.

Charlotte and Branwell's use of Bobadill is limited to these three tales, their interest in comic military figures diminishing as their writing matured;

his presence is more an insight into their important early influences rather than a recurring central personality. Nevertheless, traces of his characteristics can be seen in Branwell's flawed protagonist, Alexander Percy. Both a gentleman and a soldier, Percy often boasts of his devotion to Angria, writing heartfelt commentaries about his position as a speaker for the people. This is, however, often coupled with cowardice. In 1834, he retires to Stumpsland whilst Angria is on the cusp of civil war, orchestrated by Percy himself. In *Angria and the Angrians I(b)* (1834), he writes from a safe zone: 'I am here now suffering in exile in Stumpz land [*sic*] that you may awaken to your welfare I regard my self as < indeed > a temporary Martyr to your cause but how my Countrymen do you regard me'.[47] Again, in *Angria and the Angrians II(b)* (1836), when Angria looks to be losing in the civil war against Ardrah's Reform Party, Percy abandons his army and goes into hiding with his mistress, Louise Vernon. Like Charlotte and Branwell's early readings of Bobadil and other problematic soldiers, Percy becomes the epitome of the flawed soldier, not necessarily like the comic figure of Bobadil, but still exhibiting the same characteristics that contribute to a more dysfunctional image of military masculinity. If anything, Charlotte and Branwell appear to adapt the superficial comic elements of Bobadil's character and layer it with more sinister undertones: Percy has a darker, more threatening countenance, reminiscent of Shakespeare's Iago. Percy's mixture of manly, militaristic boastfulness alongside his characteristics of cowardice and deceit demonstrates the complex levels of analysis the siblings conducted through reading late Renaissance literature. Their construction of Percy's unusual, multidimensional personality is, in part, formed from these early, dysfunctional military models.

There is, however, another layer to Percy's personality: his similarity to Romantic representations of Napoleon Bonaparte, carried through from Restoration literature. Percy's Napoleon-like associations with power and evil adhered to Restoration-Romantic models that were firmly embedded in early nineteenth-century culture. To clarify, Branwell's fictitious Napoleon (Boney)—who morphs into Percy—is primarily constructed in the Emperor's image, which was, in turn, largely shaped by Romantic revivals of Milton.[48] During the mid-seventeenth century Milton's work was part of a post-civil war Republican discourse. In turn, Napoleon advocated Republicanism, even publishing a pro-Republican pamphlet entitled *Le souper de Beaucaire* in 1793. The siblings recognised and adopted this tone, feeding this representation into Percy: he is a combined reincarnation of Napoleon and the Miltonic Lucifer. As Nigel Smith notes, 'The first readers of *Paradise Lost* knew well that here was a Republican [...] speaking. The poem was read as an extensive critique of the ceremony and spectacle that greeted the return of the monarchy'.[49] Like Satan and his fallen angels who, as Smith argues, vocalise their lost Republican liberty, the Brontës' Percy leads a troubled existence, his Republican utopia brought to ruins, much like Oliver Cromwell's and Napoleon's. Branwell attempts to rationalise the origins of this Miltonic, Republican image by imagining his protagonist's backstory through the lens of another writer who explored the nature of evil and power, Shakespeare. Branwell's *Life of Alexander Percy, Vol. II* (1835) ultimately follows a similar narrative to *Macbeth* (1606), Percy's first love, Augusta di Segovia [Lady Macbeth], scheming with Percy to kill his father, Edward Percy [Duncan], in order to obtain his wealth and assets: in one instance, Montmorency, Percy's associate, refers to the couple as Lord and Lady Macbeth.[50] By affiliating his protagonist with Macbeth, the valiant soldier turned power-hungry murderer, Branwell conceptualises Percy as a dangerous military figure who is mentally unstable and morally corrupt.

As well as developing Percy's character within a Shakespearean discourse, Branwell—and Charlotte—frequently envisage him as the fallen angel Lucifer from Milton's *Paradise Lost*. In the *Macbeth*-inspired narrative of Percy's youth, Percy recalls the second book of Milton's epic, where Hell is connected with Earth and spirits 'pass to and fro / To tempt or punish mortals'[51]: 'The Devil tempted me day and night, and—Now!—I have arrived on landing full into the midst of a vast conclave of Demons'.[52] The Brontës' comparisons between military figureheads and the Devil mimic contemporary Romantic trends that directly place Napoleon amidst satanic imagery. George Cruikshank's satirical engraving *Boney's Meditations on the Island of St Helena—or—The Devil Addressing the Sun* (1815) epitomises the Miltonic association between France's leader and Hell. The exiled Napoleon is transformed into the Devil and addresses the sun: 'I hate thy beams, that bring to my remembrance from what state I fell'.[53] In a broader cultural sense, Simon Bainbridge notes that Romantic radical thinkers and 'the conservative Lake poets, saw the Napoleonic contest in Europe as a re-enactment of the Miltonic epic struggle'.[54] Bainbridge goes to lengths to list a number of wide-scale media representations of Napoleon dressed as Satan, emphasising that this analogy 'was by this time well established in newspapers, pamphlets, poetry and caricatures'.[55] As well as widespread print mediums—such as *The Times*—frequently drawing comparisons between the two, poets the Brontës read and admired regularly used Milton's Satan to illustrate the threat, genius and Byronism of France's Emperor.[56] William Wordsworth adopted Milton's style, form and tone in a number of poetical works. Published alongside 'View from the Top of Black Comb' (1813), which Branwell imitated in 1840, Wordsworth's 'Look now on that Adventurer' (1813) directly comments onNapoleon's ambition, the military leader surveying his kingdom from a sublime height: 'And so hath gained at length a prosperous height, / Round which the elements of worldly might / Beneath his haughty feet, like cloud, are laid'.[57] Brook Thomas notes this parallel, observing that both Milton and Wordsworth describe Lucifer as 'the great adventurer'.[58] Cohering to this Restoration–Romantic tradition, Samuel Taylor Coleridge frequently referred to a Miltonic Napoleon in his pre-Waterloo essays published in *The Morning Post* and the *Courier*,[59] and Robert Southey's 'The Poet's Pilgrimage to Waterloo' (1816) graphically describes Napoleon 'Like Satan rising from the sulphurous flood, / His impious legions to the battle plain'.[60] From this exposure to Romantic representations of Napoleon, and its pervasive image in early nineteenth-century popular culture, it is unsurprising that the young Brontës formulated Alexander Percy from its ashes.

The Miltonic Percy often troubled Charlotte and Branwell, with his demonic physicality and presence. Although there are a number of narrative moments that linger upon his destructive, repellent character, the most detailed description lies in Charlotte's *A Peep Into a Picturebook*:

> The [Percy's] expression in this picture is somewhat pensive, composed, free from sarcasm except the fixed sneer of the lip and strange deadly glitter of the eye, whose glance – a mixture of the keenest scorn and deepest thought – curdles the spectator's blood to ice. In my opinion this head embodies the most vivid ideas we can conceive of Lucifer, the rebellious Archangel: there is such a total absence of human feeling and sympathy; such a cold frozen pride; such fathomless power of intellect; such passionless yet perfect beauty – not breathing and burning and full of lightning blood and fiery thought and feeling like that of some others whom our reader will recollect [Zamorna].[61]

Referring to Percy and her own Byronic protagonist, Zamorna, Charlotte effortlessly conjures imagery of the same Miltonic Napoleon featured in

Romantic literature and popular culture. Despite Percy's character specifically evolving from Napoleon, Charlotte was also attracted to the dark elements of the Republican rebel. Her teenage writings, therefore, transformed the classical, feminine image of her childhood protagonist, the Marquis of Douro, into the Devil-like Zamorna, rival only to Percy. In addition to Charlotte's damning description above, Branwell's *Angria and the Angrians III(d)* (1836) responds to Charlotte's reinvention: recounting an instance when Percy and Zamorna swapped identities. After admitting defeat in the Angrian and Glass Town Civil Wars of 1835–1837, Zamorna is captured and banished to Ascension Isle by Percy, much as Napoleon was exiled on St Helena following Wellington's victory at Waterloo.

In Charlotte's *Four Years Ago* (1837), which now only exists in transcript format, Zamorna's devilish qualities are explored to their full potential when he studies himself in the mirror:

> My little partner said, 'what a lovely night it was.' 'Yes,' said I, abstractedly, for my eyes were fixed on the mirror. It reflected [...] myself leaning against one side of the porch, and the devil, the exact shadow of myself, against the other [...] The devil began to talk to Honor and tell her she was a very pretty girl, a wild, gentle, being, fit to be born and reared in the woods of the West. He told her she was his country–woman, and she coloured and flashed a look of enthusiasm upward, so as to meet fully the glance of his royal highness [...] 'Oh my lord, all who are born in my country love it, but there is no country ruled by you which I should not adore,' the devil looked satisfied, grim evil shade! How he winked and nodded at me, who stood so quietly, gentlemen, so innocently listening to the great deceiver making love, very much scandalized at him, but not thinking it right to interfere [...] 'Your Grace is the devil,' concluded Castlereagh. 'I am' was the solemn answer, accompanied by a sigh so contrite, so humble.[62]

Although much of Charlotte's conceptualisation of the Devil here is informed by James Hogg's exploration of split-personalities in *The Memoirs and Confessions of a Justified Sinner* (1824),[63] it also recalls an instance in *Paradise Lost* where the Devil creates a passageway to Earth to tempt mortals into sin.[64] In Charlotte's case, her passageway is substituted for a mirror. Moreover, just as Milton's epic revives the tale of Eve and the Devil, the latter posing as a serpent to illustrate sin and temptation, Zamorna's charm and persistence with a vulnerable woman named 'Honor' assumes similarities to Eve's fall from grace.

The image of the serpent is most pervasive when Zamorna and Alexander Percy are at war with one another. It is common in the juvenilia for their military-based brotherhood to break down; Charlotte and Branwell's later Angrian tales recount the climactic civil war that matures from their politically charged rivalry. In a series of speeches, written consecutively in a collaborative effort by the two siblings, Charlotte [Zamorna] refers to Percy as a serpent.[65] In *Adress* [*sic*] *to the Angrians By his Grace The Duke of Zamorna* (1835), she states: 'Still the toad personified by his delegates lies crouched at the ear of Eve', a close transcription from Milton's *Paradise Lost*: 'Him there they found / Squat like a toad, close at the ear of Eve, / Assaying by his devilish art to reach / The organs of her fancy'.[66] She similarly brands him as a serpent in her *From the Verdopolitan Intelligencer* (1835): 'it was the infliction of my venomous fang, the utterance of my own threatening hiss'.[67] This is reminiscent of Book X of *Paradise Lost*, when God finds that Eve has eaten from the Tree of Knowledge, and now, with the release of Sin and Death on Earth, there sounds 'a dismal universal hiss' followed by God turning all the devils in Hell into snakes who hiss 'through the hall, thick swarming now'.[68] By introducing Miltonic serpent imagery within their warmongering language, Charlotte and Branwell conceptualise a threatening display of militarism, much as the Romantics conveyed the threat of France's Napoleon. By using graphic representations of evil and sin generated in the Restoration period, Charlotte and Branwell were able to convey a troublesome image of power and military masculinity, one that treads a fine line between seductive, Byronic appeal and satanic, power-driven ominousness.

Charlotte and Branwell's early obsession with satanic military models, shared through an indistinct portrayal of their protagonists, Percy and Zamorna, is significant when considering the development of the Brontës' early fixation with heroic role models. What Charlotte and Branwell's—and Romantic society's—reading of late Renaissance and early Restoration literature has shown is that both siblings did not engage with a one-dimensional model of militarism, but a wealth of literature that presented the soldier as comic, dysfunctional and even demonic. Their evaluation and adoption of Shakespeare, Jonson and Milton helped shape their multidimensional understandings of the soldier. Zamorna and Alexander Percy embody military qualities of the Early Modern period and personify the darker, problematic models of wartime masculinity.

ROMANTICISM

The Napoleonic Wars spanned a majority of the Romantic era, generating a torrent of political and military verse that exemplified wartime feeling and opinion. By the post-war period, the first- and second-wave Romantic poets were equally critiqued and celebrated nationwide. A majority of Charlotte and Branwell's verse—fraught with pro- and anti-war tensions—adopted the changing views of their favourite Romantic poets. Although it is likely that the siblings were exposed to a considerable amount of verse imitating the canonical Romantic style, their inspiration derived mainly from William Wordsworth, Samuel Taylor Coleridge, Robert Southey and, most prominently, Lord Byron.[69] This subchapter explores how these canonical poets' conflicting stance on war is embodied within Charlotte and Branwell's juvenilia, the first half considering their negative viewpoints and the latter half, positive. Although the first-wave Romantic pattern regarding British militarism—initially pro- and then moving to an anti–war position—is not repeated in the siblings' early writings, there is evidence that Charlotte and Branwell's narratives reflect the same fears as their Romantic influences. Issues such as morality and the recognition of individual suffering haunt their saga much like the first- and second-wave Romantics' writings. Moreover, like Wordsworth, Coleridge and Southey, Charlotte and Branwell's opinions of war are fluid and nowhere near consistent. Regarding Byron, the siblings' favourite poet, his negative views on Napoleonic combat resonate in Charlotte and Branwell's poetic creativity and characterisation. Unlike his Romantic predecessors, Byron was a consistently harsh critic of the Napoleonic Wars, although he did not promote anti-militarism altogether, later joining the Greek War of Independence (1821–1832). It is, however, his post-Waterloo laments in *Childe Harold's Pilgrimage* (1812–1818) and *Don Juan* (1819) that dwell on the conscience of the siblings in their later battles: their more mature ideas on death and suffering come to the fore as their saga suffers the brunt of Branwell's relentless conflicts.

Neil Ramsey has observed that, despite the colossal impact of the Napoleonic Wars on Britain, little scholarly attention has been given to Romanticism and warfare. He argues that many 'critics of Romanticism viewed the period's major authors as having evaded contemporary politics following their disillusionment with the progress of the French Revolution'.[70] Critics such as Betty Bennett, Simon Bainbridge, Gillian Russell, Philip Shaw, J. R Watson and Jeffrey N. Cox, however, have all attested to the impact of war on the Romantic writers' imaginations and poetry.[71] By the late 1820s, when the Brontës were beginning to write, they would have been familiar with the political allegiances of their celebrated poetic heroes. Wordsworth, Coleridge and Southey had all rejected their anti-war sentiments and developed into patriotic, pro-military conservatives. Byron remained a spokesman for the dead, poetically vocalising the war as a terrible tragedy. Throughout their adolescence, it is likely that the Brontë children were exposed to most of the poets' public works.[72] Through characters such as Henry Hastings, the national poet and song writer of Angria, Charlotte and Branwell experimented with the Romantics' different opinions on war: sometimes they glorified it through patriotic verse, other times they used verse as a means to reflect. The siblings, detaching themselves from their previous patriotism, occasionally realise the more negative or poignant aspects of battle, using poetry as a distinct moment of awareness. Unlike the Romantic poets, however, Charlotte and Branwell offer a collage of viewpoints that fail to reach a definitive opinion. Whereas Wordsworth, Coleridge and Southey followed a similar path that first opposed then supported the war, Charlotte and Branwell continued to wrestle with both views. War is superficially presented as exciting, yet—in an epiphanic fashion—philosophically positioned against trauma and death, a subject that the siblings were continuously grappling with.

Although their opinions were by no means steadfast, Charlotte and Branwell, as they matured, gradually became more aware of the negative aspects of war. Through their Romantic readings, they are likely to have read numerous protest poems about war that Wordsworth, Coleridge, Southey and Byron had composed, the former three in their radical years. Charlotte's later poems 'Deep the Cirhala flows', in *Stancliffe's Hotel* (1838), and 'She was alone that evening' (1837) retain the ecstatic language of war yet are permeated with a distinct moment of realisation regarding the unnatural death that conflict inevitably brings. The former talks of 'Trump and triumphant drum / The conflict won', yet equally lingers on the dead 'Beneath a foreign sod, / Beside an alien wave'.[73] The latter sees Zamorna's wife, Mary Percy, lamenting over the separation from her husband; the setting is the closing hours of a summer's day on the eve of battle. Despite the romantic backdrop, the poem ends with an omniscient premonition: 'The last ray tinged with blood – so wild it shone / So strange the semblance gory, burning given / To pool & stream & sea by that red heaven'.[74] Mary Favret proposes that suffering is addressed by the Romantics through the figure of the war widow.[75] Paula Guimarãs alludes to the Brontës' use of war widows and female abandonment in her essays on feminine memory, travel and imagination. Guimarãs, however, does not link suffering and widowhood to a Romantic tradition.[76] Mary's lament, 'She was alone', characterises the Romantic displacement of soldiers' suffering on to widows. Charlotte emphasises Mary's violent grief and bodily torment: 'She scarce had seen a face, or heard a tone [...] Wearied with reading books, weary with weeping / Heart-sick of Life'.[77] Wordsworth's early poem 'Salisbury Plain' (1793) generates this same image of protest through the imagery of widowhood, accentuating the suffering that war brings:

> But human sufferings and that tale of woe
> Had dimmed the traveller's eye with Pity's tear,
> And in the youthful mourner's doom severe
> He half forgot the terrors of the night,
> Striving with counsel sweet her soul to cheer,
> Her soul for ever widowed of delight.
> He too had withered young in sorrow's deadly blight[78]

It is through female distress and sorrow that Romantic poetry secured a sentimental means of criticising war. Joining this rhetoric, Southey also emphasises the suffering of those left behind in his 'The Soldier's Funeral' (1799): 'Her tears of bitterness are shed: when first / He had put on the livery of blood, / She wept him dead to her'.[79] Like Southey and Wordsworth, Charlotte's choice of melodramatic, feminine rhetoric joins a legacy of women's violent protest poetry; she emulates and adopts an early anti-war Romantic stance, exhibiting a woman's awareness of war's mortality.

Male characters in the juvenilia, such as Henry Hastings and Alexander Percy, also respond in a traumatic, poetic way to war and death. Instead of engaging with women's experiences of war, Branwell grapples with first-hand, masculine experiences of injury and death. In Branwell's 'Misery Part II' (1836), Percy is shown reflecting his—and by proxy Angria's—recent defeat at the hands of Ardrah's Reform Party during the civil war. Percy connects with collective soldierly suffering, expressing a vivid image of post-battle trauma through the rhetoric of death:

> The Battle is done, with the setting sun;
> The struggle is lost, and the victory won [...]

And they who survive in their agony
Now stiff and spent and speechless lie,
Their dim eyes wander towards the sky
Yet seek, and see, no comfort there;
For here, upon this stormy Heath,
The laboured faintness of the breath,
The chill approach of Iron Death.[80]

Through the language of mortality, Percy lingers in the hazy, traumatic moments between life and death. Loss of mobility and speech coupled with 'dim eyes' that see no comfort in heaven generate distressing imagery of the battle's impact. Despite a literal death of the body, Branwell also suggests, through the reminiscences of Percy, a paralysis or death of the mind; that first-hand combat is both bodily and mentally traumatic.

Hastings also suffers mental anguish in the face of war. Although he is usually known in the saga for his patriotic anthems, an unsettling poem in Branwell's *Angria and the Angrians I(d)* (1834), written during Hastings' service in the 1833–1834 Wars of Encroachment and Aggression, reveals his raw confession of fear and suffering:

But that worn wretch who tosses night away
And counts each moment to returning day
Whose only hope is dull and dreamless sleep
Whose only choice to wake and watch and weep
Whose present pains of body and of mind
Shut out all glimpse of happiness behind[81]

Hastings suggests that this poem was intended as another war anthem—'it [the poem] is quite different from what when I began I meant it to be'–[82] but instead it forms a new path. In Branwell's battle narratives, conscious moments such as these lend the saga a sense of poignancy; patriotism is permeated by philosophic moments of awareness about war's hardship and mortality.

Branwell's poetry aligns itself with Romantic war poetry. As has been made clear, not all Romantic poetry was evasive of war; Adrian Caesar observes, 'in order to create, in order to authenticate the [Romantic] 'self' one has to suffer'.[83] This is true of Coleridge's and Southey's early poetry, which engaged with death and warfare in a direct fashion. In Coleridge's

'Fire, Famine, Slaughter: A War Eclogue' (1798), Slaughter boasts 'I have drunk the blood since then / Of thrice three hundred thousand men' and 'I stood in a swampy field of battle; / With bones and skulls I made a rattle'.[84] This rhythmic disturbing vision of death is also present in Southey's 'To Horror' (1797) where he calls on 'Horror' to transport him to scenes of death and suffering; Bainbridge notes that, 'the battlefield is crucial to this imaginative tour'.[85] Southey laments: 'let me trace their way, / And hear at times the deep heart–grown / Of some poor sufferer left to die alone, His sore wounds smarting with the winds of night'.[86] Like Branwell's engagement with mortality on the battlefield, Coleridge and Southey's early protest poetry would have offered early inspiration for this troubled blurring between ornate poetry and harsh reality.

In *Angria and the Angrians II(g)* (1836), a particularly poignant moment of awareness is communicated by Branwell, who adapts two stanzas from Byron's *Don Juan* to reflect on the sublimity of battle and death after Angria's climactic civil war in 1836:

> Here pause we for the present as even then
> That awful pause dividing life from death [...]
> The march the Charge the shouts of either faith
> 'Reform' or 'Angria' and one moment more
> The death cry drowning in the battles roar.[87]

Using Byron as a mouthpiece, Branwell momentarily contemplates war's terrors, imitating Byron's intentions in *Don Juan* to make the British consider and critique the recent Battle of Waterloo (1815). Shaw notes, 'Byron still felt sufficiently outraged by Waterloo to address the Duke of Wellington directly and ask: 'And I shall be delighted to learn who, / Save you and yours, have gained by Waterloo?'.[88] Similarly, Bainbridge notes:

> In his dedication to Wellington at the start of Canto IX of *Don Juan*, Byron describes war as a 'brain–spattering, windpipe–slitting art, / Unless her cause by Right be sanctified' (IX. 4) and throughout the poem he insists upon the factual nature of his 'true Muse' and 'true portrait of one battlefield' (VIII, 1, 12), emphasizing the shocking physicality and gory nature of martial combat when describing Juan and Johnson 'trampling' over 'dead bodies' and 'wallow [ing] in the bloody mire / Of dead and dying thousands' (VIII. 19–20).[89]

Branwell attempts to convey similar emphasis by including Byron's words in his own narrative. By interrupting the relentless, violent shock resonating throughout Angria, Branwell's reproduction of Byron offers himself and the reader a moment's pause to reflect on the horrors of war.

Charlotte also gave thought to Byron's laments of war in her final Angrian tales. By 1838–1839, her kingdom had been ravaged by civil war, betrayals and deaths. Her last novella, *Caroline Vernon* (1839), is particularly preoccupied with the subject of acceptance and reconciliation in a landscape and community traumatised by war. In one section, she recalls Byron's *Childe Harold's Pilgrimage*. In a letter from Quashia Quamina, Charlotte aligns his sobriety with a passage from the battlefield: 'Sober I am, and sober I have been, and by the bleached bones of my fathers, sober I mean to be to the end of the chapter'.[90] Not only does this sentence associate alcoholism with the aftermath of war, it also subtly conjures a lurid description of death seen in *Childe Harold*: 'Let their bleached bones, and blood's unbleaching stain, / Long mark the battle-field with hideous awe: / Thus only may our sons conceive the scenes we saw!'.[91] This transcription, like Branwell's use of *Don Juan*, provides a latent yet significant moment of awareness in Charlotte's narrative. The effect of Europe's recent conflicts appears to have had an increasing effect on the siblings the more they chose to fully engage with death and destruction in their own work.

By the time the Brontës were born, Wordsworth, Coleridge and Southey were staunch conservatives, anti-revolutionaries and pro-nationalists. Many critics believe their sudden adoption of opposing beliefs stemmed from a fear of French invasion. P. M. S. Dawson writes that, on top of changing attitudes to British mob violence and French tyrants such as 'Robespierre', 'the imminent prospect of French invasion in the early 1800s completed their transformation into English Patriots'.[92] Throughout their saga, Charlotte and Branwell generate patriotic language through stirring songs and poetic laments, imitating the Romantics' later nationalistic stance. Wordsworth's *Poems, in Two Volumes* (1807), Coleridge's 'France: An Ode' (1798) and 'Fears in Solitude' (1798), and Southey's poetry and prose such as 'The Poet's Pilgrimage to Waterloo' and *History of the Peninsular War* (1823–1832)—the latter Branwell transcribed—furnished the Brontë siblings with the *other* side of Romanticism. This side was less radical, and more in line with the conservative values that were held at the parsonage.

Wordsworth's poems in *Two Volumes* such as 'Rob Roy's Grave' (1807) and 'Glen-Almain, or the Narrow Glen' (1807) recall eminent wartime figures and reanimate romantic, militaristic morale. Celebratory poems such as 'To the Men of Kent, Prove your Hardiment' and 'Ode to Duty' prefigure the siblings' stirring patriotic—and fantastical—poetry of their colonial empire such as 'Merry England, Land of Glory' (1829) and 'The Glass Town' (1829), which describes the army as 'glorious and mighty'.[93] Additionally, Wordsworth's poetry draws parallels with the nostalgic warrior verse of Walter Scott, which is discussed in the following section. Verse such as 'And, far and near, through vale and hill, / Are faces that attest the same; / And kindle, like a fire new stirr'd, / At sound of ROB ROY's name' provides visions of patriotism; Wordsworth's poetic voice celebrates Scotland's celebrated outlaw, using poetry and folklore to resonate with the mass public.[94] By using history as a platform, Wordsworth could successfully ignite sentiment from the British people who wanted to mobilise. As Richard Cronin notes:

> *Poems*, 1807, is written to a people who have learned once again to experience the 'ancestral feeling' that united them with the past of their nation, and, in consequence, with the nation's literary heritage. They have become once more a nation 'who speak the tongue / That Shakespeare spake'.[95]

Charlotte and Branwell emulate Wordsworth's method of reviving ancestral nostalgia in times of war. Charlotte's early poetry regularly evokes visions of knights, castles and battles. In her 'On Seeing an Ancient Dirk in the Armoury' (1830) she inspects a dagger: 'Hast thou the glorious blood of the martyrs spilt / Or torn the mighty warrior's lofty chest'.[96] Charlotte's anthemic language is intensified through Branwell's war songs. In his battle chant, *Angria and the Angrians (Ia)* (1834), Branwell deliberately evokes the language of the people: 'Sound the Loud Trumpet oer land and oer sea / Join tongues hearts and voices rejoicing to sing / Afric arising hath sworn to be free / Glory to Angria and GOD SAVE OUR KING'.[97] By imitating Romantic patriotism both siblings use nostalgic models and vocabulary to impose nationalistic values on their imaginary world.

Another pro-war Romantic attitude the Brontë siblings adopted was Coleridge's and Southey's opinions of France, once heralded by them as a place of revolutionary liberalism and now denounced in their wartime and post-war writings. Coleridge's 'Fears in Solitude', which muses on the threat of invasion implores:

> Stand forth! be men! repel an impious foe
> Impious and false, a light yet cruel race,
> Who laugh away all virtue, mingling mirth
> With deeds of murder; and still promising
> Freedom, themselves too sensual to be free,
> Poison life's amities, and cheat the heart.[98]

Coleridge's verse is fraught with anxiety and anger, emotions that also resonate within Southey's post-Waterloo poem, 'The Poet's Pilgrimage to Waterloo': 'Remorseless France had long oppressed the land, / And for her frantic projects drained its blood'.[99] It is this opinion of Napoleonic France that provoked Southey to justify his changed militaristic beliefs in his *History of the Peninsular War* (1823): 'it was as direct a contest between the principles of good and evil as the elder Persians, or the Manicheans, imagined in their fables: it was for the life or death of national independence'.[100] These alarming representations of France as bloodthirsty, false and evil helped construct Charlotte and Branwell's fictitious enemy kingdom, 'Frenchysland', which acted as a critical caricature. Throughout the saga, the country is shown to conspire with foes such as Alexander Percy, the native Ashanti tribe and the Arabs at all given opportunities. Its connections are dubious and licentious: Pigtail, a menacing tavern owner, sells and tortures children, Montmorency, a Verdopolitan nobleman and French émigré, possesses the qualities of a gothic villain and, sweepingly, Charlotte stereotypes the Frenchwoman as a 'callous and hackneyed and well–skilled flirt'.[101] As this book demonstrates in Chapter 6, despite the Napoleonic threat of French invasion having passed, the trauma of the French Revolution amidst the post-war rumblings of unrest around Europe still made France an anxious topic of conversation. Although the article 'French Poets of the Present Day', published in the May 1832 edition of *Blackwood's*, suggested 'France was humiliated but still respected',[102] the Romantics' verse contributed to the siblings' general unease surrounding the country and its occupants, which they were able to adopt and manipulate through playful humour.

This section has established the influence the Romantic poets held over the adolescent imaginations of Charlotte and Branwell. The poets' commentaries on war, amidst their philosophical perceptions on conflict and death, had a profound impact on the siblings as their kingdom and characters become more embroiled in war. The siblings' perceptions of war were bound within the canonical poetic environment to which they were exposed. The ever-changing perceptions of the Romantics allowed the siblings to evaluate war from an objective platform, encouraging them to explore and develop their pro- and anti-war sentiments.

WALTER SCOTT

'For fiction—read Scott alone; all novels after his are worthless'.[103] Charlotte's bold statement, written to her friend Ellen Nussey in 1834, exemplifies Walter Scott's influence on the Brontës in their formative years. In the parsonage, Scott was a household name, the whole Brontë family avid readers of his wide-ranging publications. Yet, the Brontë family were not alone in their hero worship of Scott; his novels, verse, plays and other diverse mediums of writing were celebrated across Britain. On his death in 1832, *The Times'* obituary declared that he was 'the greatest genius and most popular writer of his nation'.[104] Scott's influence on Emily Brontë's writings has been made known in recent scholarship, parallels found between both *Wuthering Heights* (1847) and *Waverley* (1814). It is clear, however, that Scott also had a profound impact on Charlotte and Branwell's young writings. This section addresses Charlotte, Branwell and Walter Scott within the framework of war, occasionally extending analysis to Scott's contemporaries and imitators. I begin by analysing Scott's displacement of present conflict in favour of Scottish folklore and the fantastical warrior, considering how his portrayal of legends and the supernatural shaped Charlotte and Branwell's own creativity. I then lead into a discussion of Scott's revival of chivalry and military romance before, finally, finishing with Branwell's adoption of Scott's literary technique, 'fog of war'.

The majority of Scott's poetry and prose captures contemporary wartime feeling through past romantic parameters. Throughout the Napoleonic Wars, leading into the aftermath of European civil violence, Scott revives Scottish folklore and stereotypes of chivalric knighthood in an attempt to reassociate romance with war and heroism. Scott's literature has much to do with Charlotte and Branwell's mythological exaggeration of Scottish war history. The backstory of Branwell's protagonist, Alexander Percy, remains grounded in Scottish legend, his name associated with Alnwick, a town in Northumberland on the periphery of Scotland. For many years, its castle was the principal seat of the powerful Percy dynasty, a lineage familiar to the Brontës through Shakespeare and Scott's works. Scott's *Tales of a Grandfather* (1828) associates their name with a Scottish war legend:

There is a silly story told of Malcolm [III of Scotland] being killed by one of
the garrison of Alnwick, who, pretending to surrender the keys of the castle
on the point of a spear, thrust the lance–point into the eye of the King of
Scotland, and so killed him. They pretend that this soldier took the name of
Pierce–eye, and that the great family of the Percies of Northumberland were
descended from him.[105]

Although he admits that this is a fable, Scott's mythical militarisation of
the Percy name had a profound impact on the imaginations of the young
Charlotte and Branwell. It is this conflation of war and folklore that influenced Branwell to conceptualise soldiers having both historical and aristocratic legacies, providing two classes of military men in Glass Town and
Angria. Although Charlotte and Branwell do engage with foot soldiers,
such as Henry Hastings, they primarily show interest in military masculinity descended from nobility. Their characters' wealthy lifestyles become the
focus of Charlotte and Branwell's more domestic scenes. Percy's ances-
try is of special appeal to both siblings, some of their most unsettling and
atmospheric scenes occur in his 'gothic' country estate.

Scott's most explicit blend of war and the fantastical can be found within
his *A Legend of Montrose* (1819). In this work, he intimately describes
the 'Children of the Mist', the popular name for the warmongering clan,
Gregor of the Trossachs, who feature in both of these juvenile narratives.
The historical clan was known for their incessant roaming of the Scottish
landscape, free from any domestic constraints and following the commands
of the famous outlaw Rob Roy MacGregor:

> The clan [...] was a small sept of banditti, called, from their houseless state,
> and their incessantly wandering among the mountains and glens, the Chil-
> dren of the Mist. They are a fierce and hardy people, with all the irritability,
> and wild and vengeful passions, proper to men who have never known the
> restraint of civilised society. A party of them lay in wait for the unfortunate
> Warden of the Forest, surprised him while hunting alone and unattended, and
> slew him with every circumstance of inventive cruelty. They cut off his head,
> and resolved, in a bravado, to exhibit it at the castle of his brother–in–law.[106]

These vagabonds—who have a ghost-like quality due to their evasive
nature—are adopted by Charlotte and Branwell and used within Branwell's *Letters from an Englishman, Vol. V* (1832) and Charlotte's *The Green
Dwarf*. Both siblings endow these men with a supernatural quality. In *The

Green Dwarf, Charlotte presents the leader, Ape of the Hills, as a god-like immortal that possesses overbearing and heroic physical qualities. She describes him as a 'gigantic warrior, whose snow-white hair and beard proclaimed advanced age, while from his erect bearing, herculean frame, and sinewy limbs, it was easy to perceive that he retained unimpaired all the vigorous powers of youth'.[107] Branwell reiterates this physical description of the 'Ape' in his *Letters from an Englishman, Vol. V*. He, however, goes further in gifting the clan explicit mythical qualities:

> They came trooping up file after file dark Gigantic, Savage, Beings more like Genii than men. I saw not one of them much lower than 7 feet. several reached the enormous height of 8 or 9 feet!! They were magnified and exaggerated resemblances of the most northern Highlanders of the 17th century. like them their rough long ragged and matted Hair hung over their shoulders and visages mixing with as rough and ragged a Beard But not so as to conceal a pair of huge dark glaring eyes. which wandered about from every object. with an expression of ferocious delight and wonder natural to all savages.[108]

Branwell and Charlotte's descriptions epitomise their successful mimicry of Scott's historicism and fantasy. Rather than treating history as solely fact, the siblings were able to understand the multidimensional nature of history that blends both reality and mythology. Their imitation of Scott's writing enabled them to tread the line between fact and fiction, allowing truths to be exaggerated and manipulated. Their saga is a conflation of textbook history and folklore; and a regurgitation of bygone fiction already based around an indistinct synthesis of both historical truth and myth.

Another major part in Scott's displacement of war resides in his deliberate revival of both the chivalric warrior and romanticised landscapes of war. Simon Bainbridge and Neil Ramsey have discussed Scott's blend of war and nostalgia. Bainbridge analyses Scott's intentions at length, arguing how his popularity during the Napoleonic Wars stemmed from his ability to displace time and militaristic subject matter: 'at a time when war had become modern, it could be experienced imaginatively through the more appealing forms of Scott's romances'.[109] Additionally, Ramsey observes how Scott's aesthetics 'enabled his writing to reflect war's violence yet distance his reader from the effects of horror, detailing glory rather than misery'.[110] *Lay of the Last Minstrel* (1805) is just one poetic example of Scott's literary achievement of the military 'picturesque': 'Nine-and-twenty yeomen tall

/ Waited, duteous, on them all: / They were all knights of mettle true, / Kinsmen to the bold Buccleuch'.[111] As this example demonstrates, Scott reimagines the soldier as a sentimentalised, warrior figure, reestablishing past heroic ideals of courtly love and military brotherhood.

Charlotte and Branwell's juvenile poetry draw from Scott's historical displacement of war, Charlotte through her engagement with knightly romance, and Branwell through battlefield heroics. Whereas Scott formulated a soldierly ideal to boost public spirit, Charlotte's verse is purely self-driven, her imitation and adoption of the romantic warrior model a means of satisfying her own girlhood fantasies. Poems such as 'On Seeing an Ancient Dirk in the Armory' and 'The Red Cross Knight' (1833) are written under the pseudonym of the Marquis of Douro, the young, impressionable soldier-son of the fictitious Duke of Wellington, and are used to reflect on knightliness and its inherent values. In the former, Douro reminisces about Scotland's Jacobite rebellions (1688–1746), an era frequently reimagined by Scott and Robert Burns, another early influence on the Brontë children. In Scott's case, novels such as *Waverley* transported the reader to Scotland's riotous highlands, whilst Robert Burns' poetic ballads such as 'Ye Jacobites by Name' (1791) and 'The Battle of Sherramuir' (1790) combined contemporary wartime feeling with Jacobitical romance. Aspiring poets in the Brontës' favourite periodical, *Blackwood's*, mimicked both Scott and Burns. For example, 'Verses' (1817) and a review of 'Poems by a Heavy Dragoon' (1819) hark back to olden times, replacing the realities of war with nostalgia. The former laments: 'Auld Scotland!—land o'hearts the wale! / Hard thou hast fought, and bravely won: / Lang may thy lions paw the gale, / And turn their dewlaps to the sun!'.[112] Charlotte's 'Seeing an Ancient Dirk' emits comparable wistfulness: 'Ages on Ages long have passed away / Since thou wast ruthless in the battle plain, / Since chieftains clad in polished war array / Have with thee triumphed o'er the blood slain'.[113] This elegiac tone is repeated in much of Charlotte's verse.[114] Her fixation on Scotland's past and landscape not only allowed her to revive medieval codes of honour but to reassert soldierly doctrines of chivalry and nobility through the Marquis of Douro [Zamorna], her juvenile version of idealised masculinity.

Charlotte's 'The Red Cross Knight' is tightly bound with Scott's literary interest in the Crusades (1095–1291), a series of military campaigns sanctioned by the Catholic Church during the middle ages. Although the historical grounding of the poem resides in Scott's literature—Richard I

'Cœur de Lion' is mentioned in *Ivanhoe* (1820), *The Betrothed* (1825) and *The Talisman* (1825)—Scott and, in turn, Charlotte, take their imagined figure of the Crusader from Edmund Spenser's *The Faerie Queene* (1590). Spenser's hero is the epitome of knight errantry, defending the image of God and gallantly saving damsels in distress: 'So forward on his way (with God to friend) / He passed forth, and new adventure sought'.[115] This description is similar to Scott's model of knightliness in *The Talisman*: 'A Christian soldier, a devoted lover, could fear nothing, think of nothing, but his duty to Heaven and his devoir to his lady'.[116] Emulating this, Charlotte's knight is equally chaperoned by God: 'Through blood, through fire, through carnage, wade. / Led by that high and heavenly gem, / The living star of Bethlehem'.[117] Despite Charlotte's general image of the Crusader originating from Spenser, she was drawn to Scott's historical employment of the Crusades within his poetry. Unlike Spenser's knight, who not only lives in the chivalric realm but the mythological, the Marquis of Douro's hero is also modelled on real-life Crusader figureheads. Scott repeatedly glorifies Richard I's involvement in the Crusades in his novels and verse. For example, 'The Crusader's Return' in *Ivanhoe* states, 'High deeds achieved of knightly fame, / From Palestine the champion came; / The cross upon his shoulders borne, / Battle and blast had dimm'd and torn'.[118] Like Scott, Charlotte lingers upon Richard I's significance, grounding herself in military historicism in amongst her fantastical visions.

Although Branwell's historical poetry typically reflects his classical training,[119] his 'The Fate of Regina' (1832) reanimates the image of the warrior, using chivalric discourse to transform his rebels into gallant knights: 'O Connor down the Mountains brow / Pours his fierce warriors on the plain below'.[120] Whereas Charlotte's verse attempts to satisfy a girlish ideal, Branwell instead attempts to emulate Scott and his contemporaries in order to achieve maximum atmospheric effect. Although, as Neufeldt notes, Branwell's form in this poem is influenced by *The Iliad* (750 BC) and *Paradise Lost* (1667), his reference to battlements and gates 'towering high above the stormy rain' suggests similarities with Scott's *Marmion* (1808),[121] in which, depicting the Battle of Flodden Field (1513), the 'bastion, tower, and vantage–coign; / Above the booming ocean leant / The far–projecting battlement'.[122] It is from these linguistic parallels that the reader can understand the contemporary popular practice of restructuring wartime experience. Branwell succeeds in grounding his own fictitious battles within a past context. Much as Napoleonic writers attempted consciously to distract the public from war's horrors by displacing time and location within their literature, Branwell succeeds in establishing his imaginary insurrection within a historical and literary canon, glorifying his brutish lust for war by tempering violence with picturesque imagery and epic language.

Moreover, Scott's description of combat in *Marmion* showcases a pioneering literary technique that Samuel Baker titles 'fog of war'.[123] The technique was used to emphasise the chaotic nature of war by plunging the reader into the centre of battle. In this same *Marmion* passage, Scott writes: 'They close in clouds of smoke and dust [...] O life and death were in the shout, / Revoil and rally, charge and rout [...] And plumed crests of chieftains brave, / Floating like foam upon the wave'.[124] Baker recognises, from its introduction into the literary world, 'fog of war' has been repeatedly imitated. This is certainly true for the military memoirs of the period. George Gleig's *The Subaltern* (1825) and Lieutenant Spencer Moggridge's 'Letters from the Peninsula' (1827–1828), serialised in *Blackwood's*, are just two examples that have sections narrated from the claustrophobic thick of combat. Whereas memoirs used the technique to vividly relate the immediate experience of war to a disinvolved audience, Scott used it within a historic context. This passage from his *The Tale of Old Mortality* (1816) demonstrates Scott's use of the technique whilst describing a Jacobite rebellion:

> The front ranks hardly attempted one ill-directed and disorderly fire, and their rear were broken and flying in confusion ere the charge had been completed; and in less than five minutes the horsemen were mixed with them, cutting and hewing without mercy [...] the whole field presented one general scene of confused slaughter, flight and pursuit.[125]

Whilst reading this passage, the reader experiences the confusion of battle: the rhetoric of blindness that is conjured by Scott causes the reader to feel as if they are in a metaphorical fog.

Scott's evocation of discord and chaos is emulated within Branwell's descriptions of combat. As early as 1830, Branwell appears to recognise the personal horrors of battle. His detailed drawing of a Roman battle scene titled *Terror* (1830) depicts crazed soldiers in the midst of conflict. Moreover, in his poetry, Branwell turns to 'fog of war' to emphasise disorder, panic and the enveloping nature of first-hand combat. In 'The Fate of Regina', Branwell uses the technique to describe the military's rebellion during the insurrection of Glass Town (Fig. 2.3):

Fig. 2.3   Brontë, Branwell (1830). *Terror* (Image used courtesy of the Brontë Parsonage Museum)

Thick wreaths of smoke blot out the rising sun! [...] At every gate the storm increasing roars, While oer the rout Mars wrapt in terror soars [...] On bursts he [Zamorna] then his white plume waving far / Now seen now hidden as mid clouds a star.[126]

As in Scott's verse, imagery of blindness pervades this short extract with references to smoke and clouds. Loss of sight is also repeatedly replicated in Branwell's battle prose. The tale *Letters from an Englishman, Vol. VI* (1832), portrays Branwell's narrator, John Flower, relating the details of Percy's [Rogue's] insurrection of Glass Town. In the midst of the confusion and carnage, Flower recounts, 'the crush and hurry around us was terrible lances and bayonets were constantly darting round us in multitudes [...]. a mist came across my sight and I fell'.[127] In his later manuscript *An Historical Narrative of the War of Encroachment* (1833–1834), which sees the Glass Town Federation band together in pursuit of war against the French, Arabs and Ashanti, Branwell also presents a battle scene of discordant horror. Flower notes that the army was in 'a huge heap of confusion rolled on by instinct. bewildered and. struck as if by lightning I saw Douro [Zamorna] and Elrington [Percy] in rain amid the tumult and darkness endeavouring to restore some slight appearance of order'.[128] Finally, in Branwell's later tale, *Angria and Angrians I(d)*, the protagonist, Henry Hastings, recounts a 'trivial' war fought between the Angrian army and the Ashanti, a conflict that foreshadows the following year's civil war between the Angrian army, and Ardrah's Reform Party. In one instance, Hastings remarks that darkness 'seemed to come over my sight and my ears allmost [*sic*] lost the power of distinguishing sound we drew back and then [...] in fighting we trampled remorselessly upon freind [*sic*] an[d] enimy [*sic*]'.[129] In another similarly disturbing excerpt, Hastings asserts how he:

<shot > up for my eyes seemed scared by a terrific flash of lightning it was broadly and resistlessly bright I glared into the Night wildly and in < dreamy > agony of apprehension Listen what a roar. Hideously broken and rattling and Deep and trembling [...] I closed my eyes fast in horror [...] the strange impression was on me that I was alone and a hundred of miles from any one but I was so confused between sleep and cold and horror [...] all was like a nightmare.[130]

From these examples it becomes clear that Branwell, like other writers of the period, adopted Scott's 'fog of war' style, reconstructing chaotic and dramatic scenes of war within his own battle narratives. Branwell's descriptions of conflict in his and Charlotte's Glass Town and Angria demonstrate the changing nature of writing war, conveying a more personal approach in which readers are encouraged to respond to soldiers' experiences. The novel idea that the reader could be immersed within the thick of battle paved the way for new reactions and responses to war: no longer were its horrors a completely alien concept.

It is evident that Scott's historical fiction and literary style inspired Charlotte and Branwell, a majority of their juvenilia imitating and adapting his poetry and prose. Not only did the siblings utilise his models of war—ranging from warrior folklore to chivalric knighthood—they imitated and adopted his modern techniques of writing war. Overall, Scott's writings provide the final contextual layer necessary for this book to enter a deeper textual analysis of both Charlotte and Branwell's juvenilia and the post-war print culture that influenced it.

The four sections within this chapter have built the foundations that introduce Charlotte and Branwell Brontë as historians of and commentators on war. It is clear that the reading material they were exposed to at an early age was instrumental in shaping their understanding of war, but also their multidimensional representations of soldiers, ranging from the fantastical, muscular warrior, to the demonic, cowardly villain. Equipped with this mosaic of images, opinions and histories, the siblings were able to observe, process and rework this array of material into their own play and fantasy works.

NOTES

1. Branwell's personal challenge to copy out Horace's militant odes in 1840 only serves to prove that his interest in classical warfare did not diminish. His translations cover the themes present in this section—sports, war and idealised masculinity—but appear too late for us to know for certain that they had a strong bearing on the siblings' juvenilia a decade or so previously. I will treat them solely as further supportive evidence that the siblings were exposed to a very particular image of strong, masculine classical culture, one that captivated them well into adulthood.
2. *EEW I*: 301.
3. *WPB II*: 221.

4. *EEW II*: 325.
5. Ibid.
6. Edward Gibbon, *The History of the Decline and Fall of the Roman Empire Volumes I–III*, ed. David Womersley (London: Penguin, 1998): 4.
7. Ibid., 583.
8. *WPB II*: 7.
9. See Matthew Dillon and Lynda Garland's, *Ancient Rome: From the Early Republic to the Assassination of Julius Caesar* (London: Routledge, 2005).
10. The Revd. Patrick Brontë was awarded his own copy of Homer's *Iliad* for keeping in the 'first class' at Cambridge University. The family also owned a copy of Dryden's translation of Virgil's *Aeneid*.
11. *Tales*: 327.
12. Virgil, *The Aeneid*, ed. David West (London: Penguin, 2003): 92.
13. Ibid., 93.
14. Homer, *The Iliad*, ed. E. V. Rieu (trans.) (London: Penguin, 2003): 403.
15. *Tales*: 326.
16. Virgil, *The Aeneid*, 106.
17. Homer, *The Iliad*, 403.
18. *Tales*: 326.
19. *WPB*: 204.
20. In *Boxing and Society: An International Analysis* (1996), John Sugden remarks that 'Pugalism was an especially attractive target for bourgeois reformers because it brought together both of their class enemies: a decadent and dying aristocracy and an ill-disciplined, pre-industrial labour force'. See John Sugden, *Boxing and Society: An International Analysis* (Manchester: Manchester University Press, 1996): 21.
21. *WPB III*: 429.
22. Pierce Egan, *Boxiana: From the Days of the Renowned Broughton and Slack, to the Championship of Cribb* (London: Sherwood, Jones & Company, 1823): 3.
23. *WPB II*: 125.
24. *WPB II*: 294.
25. Ibid.
26. "Boxiana," *Blackwood's Edinburgh Magazine*, June, 439–443.
27. Homer, *The Iliad*, 414.
28. Virgil, *The Aenied*, 103.
29. *Tales*: 56.
30. Ibid., 125.
31. Ian Dennis Jenkins and Victoria Turner, *The Greek Body* (Los Angeles: Getty Publications, 2009): 11.
32. *EEW II*: 39.
33. *WPB I*: 219.

34. From their detailed knowledge of France's history, it is also possible that the Brontës were additionally alluding to Louis XIV (1638–1715), France's ruler and also known as the 'sun king'. Although no direct relationship is made between Zamorna and Louis, this loose connection continues to promote the Brontës' multi-layered understanding of and engagement with history.

35. *EEW III*: 92.

36. *WPB II*: 203.

37. Christine Alexander, "Autobiography and juvenilia," in *The Child Writer from Austen to Woolf*, ed. Juliet McMaster and Christine Alexander (Cambridge: Cambridge University Press, 2005): 165.

38. *Tales*: 566.

39. Paul A. Jorgenson, *Shakespeare's Military World* (Berkeley: University of California Press, 1973): 82.

40. Buckner B. Trawick, *Shakespeare and Alcohol* (Amsterdam: Rodopi, 1978): 20.

41. J. B. van Amerongen, *The Actor in Dickens: A Study of the Histrionic and Dramatic Elements in the Novelist's Life and Works* (London: Ardent Media, 1926): 20.

42. *EEW I*: 173.

43. *EEW I*: 185.

44. Ben Jonson. "Every Man in His Humour," in *The Roaring Girl and Other City Comedies*, ed. James Knowles (Oxford: Oxford University Press, 2008): 203.

45. Ibid., 217.

46. *WPB I*: 95.

47. *WPB II*: 249.

48. The evolution of Alexander Percy's character is complex. He originated from the toy soldiers the Revd. Patrick Brontë brought back for his children in around 1826; Branwell called his Boney, after Napoleon Bonaparte. Boney morphed into Rogue in around 1829–1830, Percy's criminal 'working' name, commonly associated with his time as a young Republican and a pirate. Eventually, he married Zenobia Elrington in 1833, adopting the more stable names of Alexander Percy/Lord Elrington and the Duke of Northangerland.

49. Smith, Nigel. "Paradise Lost from Civil War to Restoration," in *The Cambridge Companion to Writing of the English Revolution*, ed. N. H. Keeble (Cambridge: Cambridge University Press, 2001): 255–256.

50. *WPB II*: 162.

51. John Milton, *Paradise Lost*, ed. Stephen Orgel (Oxford: Oxford University Press, 2008): 60.

52. *WPB II*: 163.

53. Milton, *Paradise Lost*, 85.

54. Simon Bainbridge, *Napoleon and English Romanticism* (Cambridge: Cambridge University Press, 1995): 183.
55. Ibid., 185.
56. Ibid., 235.
57. Ibid., 117.
58. Brook Thomas, *Literature and the Nation* (Tübingen: Gunter Narr, 1998): 84.
59. Simon Bainbridge, *British Poetry and the Revolutionary and Napoleonic Wars* (Oxford: Oxford University Press, 2003): 125–133.
60. Southey, Robert, *Robert Southey: Later Poetical Works, 1811–1838, Vol. III*, ed. Lynda Pratt (London: Pickering and Chatto, 2012): 252.
61. *EEW II*: 87.
62. Charlotte Brontë, *Four Years Ago*, ed. C. W. Hatfield (Brontë Parsonage Museum: Hatfield Transcription): 10.
63. Robert, the protagonist of Hogg's novel, is tormented by an enigmatic stranger named Gil-Martin, who manipulates him to do his bidding. It is suggested that Gil-Martin is the Devil, yet Robert also proposes that this figure could be an extension of his imagination and self.
64. Milton, *Paradise Lost*, 60.
65. Charlotte also makes general references to Milton, mentioning the fallen angels Belial and Mammon who feature in *Paradise Lost*.
66. *EEW II*: 297.
67. Ibid., 371.
68. Milton, *Paradise Lost*, 255.
69. Other contemporary Romantic figures such as John Keats and William Blake would not have been known, or barely known to the siblings. Both poets were neglected for a quarter of a century after their deaths in 1821 and 1827, respectively. Percy Bysshe Shelley was a familiar name in the Brontë household, influencing Emily's poetry and later works. Although Charlotte often adopts Shelley's references to the sublimity of nature and classicism, his treatment of war does not appear to have overtly impacted her juvenilia.
70. Neil Ramsey, *The Military Memoir and Romantic Literary Culture 1780–1835* (Farnham: Ashgate, 2006): 117.
71. Bennett's *British Poetry in the Age of Romanticism* (1976) was one of the first academic collections to address the relationship between Romanticism, war and poetry. Since then, Bainbridge, Favret, Shaw and Cox have expanded on these themes: Bainbridge with *Napoleon and English Romanticism* (1995) and *British Poetry and the Revolutionary and Napoleonic Wars* (2003), Russell with *The Theatres of War* (1995), Shaw with *Romantic Wars* (2000) and Jeffrey Cox with *Romanticism in the Shadow of War* (2014), to name a few.

72. Although there is no definitive list of all the particular poems the Brontë children engaged with, it is likely that, from their detailed knowledge of Romantic poetry, they read widely, accumulating an extensive knowledge of Romantic concepts and doctrines. Southey, Coleridge and Wordsworth were especially admired by the siblings in their early years.

73. *Angria*: 105–6.

74. *PCB*: 247.

75. Mary Favret, "Coming Home: The Public Spaces of Romantic War," *Studies in Romanticism*, 33.4 (1994): 545.

76. See Paula Guimarãs' "'Remembrance and Forgetfulness": Feminine Memory as Identity and Death in the Poetry written by the Brontës' (2004) and "'Sunny Climes Beyond the Sea": Travel and Imagination in Charlotte Brontë's Juvenile Poetry' (2007).

77. *PCB*: 246.

78. *William Wordsworth—The Major Works*, ed. Stephen Gill (Oxford: Oxford University Press, 2008): 25. Wordsworth's lament regarding the impact of war on the domestic sphere is repeated in his 1798 poem 'The Discharged Soldier', published posthumously in *The Prelude* (1850).

79. Robert Southey, *Selected Shorter Poems c.1793–1810, Vol. V*, ed. Lynda Pratt (London: Pickering and Chatto, 2004): 332.

80. *WPB II*: 510.

81. Ibid., 287.

82. Ibid., 288.

83. Adrian Caesar, *Taking It Like a Man: Suffering, Sexuality, and the War Poets* (Manchester: Manchester University Press, 1993): 226.

84. *Samuel Taylor Coleridge—The Major Works*, ed. H. J. Jackson (Oxford: Oxford University Press, 2008): 47.

85. Bainbridge, *British Poetry and the Revolutionary and Napoleonic Wars*, 23.

86. Southey, *Selected Shorter Poems*, 103.

87. *WPB II*: 559.

88. Philip Shaw, "Childe Harold's Pilgrimage: Lord Byron and the Battle of Waterloo," *British Library Discovering Literature: Romantics and Victorians*, 2014. https://www.bl.uk/romantics–and–victorians/articles/childe–harolds–pilgrimage–lord–byron–and–the–battle–of–waterloo.

89. Bainbridge, *British Poetry and the Revolutionary and Napoleonic Wars*, 193.

90. *Tales*: 227.

91. *Lord Byron—The Major Works*, ed. Jerome J. McGann (Oxford: Oxford University Press, 2008): 51.

92. P. M. S. Dawson, "Poetry in an Age of Revolution," in *The Cambridge Companion to British Romanticism*, ed. Stuart Curran (Cambridge: Cambridge University Press, 1993): 48–74.

93. *PCB*: 7.
94. *William Wordsworth—The Major Works*, 318.
95. R. Cronin, "Wordsworth's Poems of 1807 and the War Against Napoleon," *The Review of English Studies*, 48.189 (1997): 33–50.
96. *EEW I*: 260.
97. *WPB II*: 205.
98. *Samuel Taylor Coleridge—The Major Works*, 96.
99. *Robert Southey: Later Poetical Works*, 310.
100. Robert Southey, *History of the Peninsular War* (London: John Murray, 1823): 1–2.
101. *Tales*: 274.
102. "French Poets of the Present Day," *Blackwood's Edinburgh Magazine*, May, 507–511.
103. Charlotte Brontë, "Letter to Ellen Nussey, 1834," in *The Brontës: A Life in Letters*, ed. Juliet Barker (London: Viking, 1997): 29.
104. "Sir Walter Scott, the Greatest Genius and Most Popular Writer of His Nation and His Age, Expired At," *The Times*, 25 September, 2.
105. Walter Scott, *Tales of a Grandfather* (Edinburgh: Cadell & Co, 1828): 58.
106. Walter Scott, *A Legend of the Wars of Montrose*, ed. J. H. Alexander (Edinburgh University Press, 1996): 39.
107. *EEW II*: 182.
108. *WPB I*: 219.
109. Bainbridge, *British Poetry and the Revolutionary and Napoleonic Wars*, 17.
110. Ramsey, *The Military Memoir and Romantic Literary Culture 1780–1835*, 17.
111. Walter Scott, *The Lay of the Last Minstrel* (Edinburgh: Bowhill, 1972: 52).
112. H., "Verses," *Blackwood's Edinburgh Magazine*, April 1817, 70.
113. *EEW I*: 260.
114. See Charlotte's poems: 'Written on the Summit of a High Mountain in the North of England' (1830), 'He is gone and all grandeur has fled from the mountain' (1832) and 'Death of Darius Codomanus' [*sic*] (1834) (*PCB* 1985: 25, 97, 137).
115. Edmund Spenser, *The Faerie Queene* (London: Penguin, 1987: 48).
116. Walter Scott, *The Talisman* (Edinburgh: Archibald Constable and Company, 2013): 50.
117. *EEW II*: 234.
118. Walter Scott, *Ivanhoe*, ed. Ian Duncan (Oxford: Oxford University Press, 2008): 191.
119. See Branwell's poems: 'Caractacus' (1830), 'O Mars who shakest thy fiery hair' (1831), 'And is this Greece is this the Land I Sing' (1834), and 'The Pass of Thermopylae' (1835) (*WPB I* 1997: 98, 175, and *WPB II* 1999: 3, 6), and his translations of Horace's odes (1840), some of which have militaristic content (*WPB III* 1999: 299–334).

120. *WPB I*: 203.
121. Ibid., 204.
122. Walter Scott, *Marmion* (Edinburgh: Archibald Constable and Company, 1808): 317.
123. Samuel Baker, "Scott's Worlds of War," in *The Edinburgh Companion to Walter Scott*, ed. Fiona Robertson (Edinburgh: Edinburgh University Press, 2009): 70–82.
124. Scott, *Marmion*, 356.
125. Walter Scott, *The Tale of Old Mortality*, ed. Jane Stevenson and Peter Davidson (Oxford: Oxford University Press, 2009): 338.
126. *WPB I*: 204.
127. *WPB I*: 237.
128. *WPB I*: 391.
129. *WPB II*: 320.
130. *WPB II*: 301.

CHAPTER 3

Wellington and Napoleon

O, Papa, I like a great many people! But soldiers most of all. I do adore soldiers![1]

This chapter explores Charlotte and Branwell's blend of fact and fiction in relation to military celebrity, analysing how the siblings reimagined and transmogrified the Duke of Wellington and Napoleon Bonaparte within their juvenilia. It develops points of interest in Brontës Studies, such as the psychological development of 'coming of age' authors, the juvenilia as a moment of masculine reappropriation, and the reintroduction of Branwell Brontë as a pivotal factor in this amalgam of worship, evaluation and reconstruction. Vitally, the chapter also discusses Napoleon, emphasising his equal importance to Wellington within the Brontë narrative: his presence in the media conjured from the Brontës a different form of hero worship. Furthermore, this chapter focuses on the implications of—specifically military—heroism in the post-war popular imagination. This heroism is then complicated by demonstrating how the authoritative, dangerous military man emerged as a Brontë ideal.

The first of three sections assesses the reception of Wellington and Napoleon in the media and biographical material Charlotte and Branwell read, exploring what Wellington and Napoleon meant to the Brontë family. Why was their idée fixe a product of a national, compulsive 'moment' that revelled in rivalry and masculine power? The two successive sections

© The Author(s) 2019   65
E. Butcher, *The Brontës and War*,
https://doi.org/10.1007/978-3-319-95636-7_3

then explore the siblings' transmogrification of Wellington and Napoleon into their juvenilia: first through their *literal* reconstruction of them as fictitious rulers of the Glass Town Federation and Frenchysland respectively, then as their sexualised second-selves, Zamorna and Alexander Percy. By regressing further and further into the Brontës' collaborative, creative (sub)conscious, new light is shed on how, narrowly, powerful military men were essential to their controversial masculine ideologies and, more broadly, how Charlotte and Branwell's model represents a larger cultural and historical movement that sought to process, evaluate and come to terms with the recent wars by displacing heightened emotional responses onto emerging celebrity culture.

Post-War Constructions of Wellington and Napoleon's Rivalry

With the cultural residue of Waterloo buzzing in the post-war popular consciousness, the legacy of its two celebrated adversaries equally circulated amidst the hum of contemporary war-based publications and media discussions. Although Wellington and Napoleon never physically met during the battle, or corresponded with one another, the post-war fascination centred upon these military heroes was stimulated by their mutual opinions and evaluations of one another. Andrew Roberts exposes an intense and somewhat complex relationship between these war-born heroes despite their mythical status in one another's lives:

> Napoleon and Wellington regarded each other's military ability highly by the time they met at Waterloo. Thereafter both changed their minds and slowly began to damn each other's martial prowess to the point where – in part through a series of misunderstandings – Napoleon came to loathe Wellington, and rant about his ineptitude. Meanwhile, while maintaining a public stance of great respect for his opponent, Wellington came privately to despise Napoleon both as a general and as a man.[2]

The Brontë siblings would have been acutely aware of Napoleon's opinions of Wellington. Housed at the parsonage, their favourite biography, Walter Scott's *Life of Napoleon* (1827), addresses the violent alteration in his respect for the Duke following his defeat at Waterloo. The biography reveals that, before the conflict, Napoleon spoke highly of Wellington, yet, after his subsequent defeat, had become renowned for slandering his victor. Although the following excerpt captures a moment of praise from Napoleon in regard to Wellington, it divulges the irregularity of such a statement:

'The Duke of Wellington, in the management of an army, is fully equal to myself, with the advantage of possessing more prudence'. This we conceive to be the genuine unbiassed opinion of one great soldier concerning another. It is a pity that Napoleon could on other occasions express himself in a strain of depreciation, which could only lower him who used it, towards a rival in the art of war.[3]

Scott's biography also alerts readers to Napoleon's will: the contents disclose the extent of Napoleon's bitterness directed towards Wellington and his intent to avenge his nemesis:

He bequeathed, in like manner, a legacy to a villain who had attempted the assassination of the Duke of Wellington; the assassin, according to his strange argument, having as good a right to kill his rival and victor, as the English had to detain him prisoner at St Helena.[4]

It is from this explicitly physical, violent act that the Brontë family could have comprehended the alarming degree of Napoleon's tortured psychology and all-consuming fixation: the resentment of Waterloo was for Napoleon, according to Scott, entirely encapsulated in one person.

In contrast, Wellington's true opinions of Napoleon were not revealed until after his death. His posthumous memoranda, published in George Gleig's *Life of Arthur, 1ˢᵗ Duke of Wellington I* (1862) and the third volume of the compilation *Despatches, Correspondence and Memoranda* (1867–1880), relished the opportunity to fault Napoleon's military conduct, methods and techniques. For example, Gleig's biography reveals that Wellington thought Napoleon to be a 'great actor'.[5] Additionally, Wellington's thoroughly researched memorandum of Napoleon's disastrous 1812 Russian campaign appeared as appendices in both publications. Despite documenting his honest opinions privately, Wellington built a public façade of respect for his historic opponent. As Roberts suggests, he 'had no intention of publishing and being damned',[6] choosing to maintain a dignified, honourable higher ground surrounding his military professionalism in the midst of his political unpopularity. Scott's biography emphasises this, painting the Duke in a heroic light:

The Duke of Wellington has, upon all occasions, been willing to render the military character of Napoleon that justice which a generous mind is scrupulously accurate in dispensing to an adversary, and has readily admitted that the conduct of Buonaparte and his army on this memorable occasion was fully adequate to the support of their high reputation.[7]

Looking outwards from Scott's biography, the periodical press also helped promulgate this seemingly one-sided rivalry, reinforcing the myth of Wellington and Napoleon as an inseparable, highly charged dynamic duo both in the Brontë home and beyond. Their names, spoken in unison, became commonplace in the Brontë family's favourite periodical, *Blackwood's*: an article titled 'The Military Sketchbook' dramatised them both as 'ultimate adversaries who struggled like two giants for ascendency'.[8] The compulsion of the periodical press to sensationalise and obsessively scrutinise these masculine icons is encapsulated in all contemporary popular periodicals the Brontës read or subscribed to. *John Bull*, the high Tory newspaper and *Blackwood's* follow a pattern of manipulated representation. Both periodicals present Wellington as a form of demigod by sensationalising his characteristics and repeatedly championing him as an upstanding, moral saviour. A *John Bull* contributor emphasised the stable, safe elements of his character, boasting that he remained 'unmoved and unchanged'.[9] In *Blackwood's*, Wellington's name was bathed in glory. In 'Letters from the Peninsula No. 2' Lieutenant Spencer Moggridge exclaimed that his distinction and fame 'would support a column as high and as proud as that of any warrior of modern times, whose names had been irradiated by the admiration of past ages, and will be by that of those yet unborn'.[10] Wellington's celebrity military status in British popular culture was cemented with gushing hyperbole.

Napoleon's representation is more complex. Whereas, with a few exceptions,[11] a majority of the media blindly celebrated Wellington, the British media was fascinated by Napoleon and his militaristic motivations. *Blackwood's* often presented him as a troubled, evil mastermind: an anonymous contributor in 'American Writers No. II' (1824) lamented that he was a 'character neither party [British or French] ever understood'.[12] These are similar to the terms adopted by Charlotte in her later work, *Jane Eyre* (1847), where her tyrannical, anti-hero protagonist, Edward Rochester, despite being clever and well-travelled, is simultaneously peculiar to a point that nobody could 'thoroughly understand him'.[13] Unlike Wellington, who was a steadfast war hero in a ruptured, post-war nation, Napoleon was a frightening enigma and a source of torment and confusion for the British public.

During and after the Napoleonic Wars, Napoleon was repeatedly likened to the Devil. The subchapter on late Renaissance to Restoration war literature within this book emphasises how, in contemporary Romantic poetry and the Brontë juvenilia, France's Emperor is likened to a Miltonic Lucifer. This devilish portrayal, however, spread through the contemporary media. The British public voiced a collective anxiety that struggled to come to terms with the idea that such evil ambition existed in the form of a solider and statesman who threatened the liberty of Britain and, more widely, Europe. As observed by David Snowdon, the pugilist periodical *Boxiana* invented scenes where military leaders fought head-to-head in the boxing ring, offering comfort to the British public by imagining Napoleon's defeat at the hands of its favourite boxers.[14] An 'Admired Chaunt' distributed by *Boxiana* in 1823 and reprinted by Snowdon suggests clear-cut antipathy:

> Now fill your glasses to the *brim*,
> And honour well my toast, sirs,
> "May we be found in *fighting trim*,
> When *Boney* treads our coast, sirs."
> The gallant *Barclay* shall lead on,
> The *fancy lads* adore him,
> **And *Devil* or *Napoleon*,**
> Leave us alone to *floor him*.[15]

Even after Napoleon's death, the fear of invasion from abroad still permeated cultural references, conjuring within the young, impressionable Brontës the same, if superficial, feelings that had infected the nation only a few decades previously. Just as *Boxiana* constructs Napoleon as a fearsome devil, *Blackwood's* brought his humanity into question. In an article titled 'Russia' (1826), a contributor writes that 'Napoleon was an *Evil*, and human nature may well rejoice at the extinction of its disturber'.[16] As this statement makes clear, to the public, Napoleon was much more than mortal; he was the personification of hell.

In the British media and beyond Wellington and Napoleon were presented as complete opposites, representing two versions of war: one that was wholesome and patriotic, and the other that was unjustified and tyrannical. The two words that unify them in the Brontës' life and the wider public sphere, however, are 'masculine power'. Whereas Wellington became a

symbolic manifestation of 'good masculine power', Napoleon became syn-
onymous with 'bad masculine power'. These binaries were erected by the
British press and remained instrumental in the Brontës' engagement with
concepts of masculinity and leadership. Public perceptions were entwined
with Charlotte and Branwell's juvenilia, the tales imitating contemporary
attitudes as a form of ready-made storyboard that fostered excitement and
dynamic characterisation. It is through the periodical presses' overdramatised, amplified accounts that the young Charlotte and Branwell were initially inspired to recreate their own versions of Wellington and Napoleon in
their 1829–1834 narratives. Then, with the creation of their new kingdom
Angria in 1834, they were influenced to form the intense, all-consuming
relationship between Zamorna and Alexander Percy, their two homosocial
protagonists. By reimagining and remodelling Wellington and Napoleon
into increasingly melodramatic, sensational mutations of themselves, the
siblings were able to reconstruct one of the most important associations
in military history, inventing their own past and correspondence between
two people who were ever present in each other's lives without actually
knowing one another.

Wellington Reimagined

Charlotte and Branwell's early Glass Town writings were founded on the
Wellington and Napoleon myth. When each sibling named their respective toy soldiers Wellington and Boney in 1826, they were both immediately tapping into an already established public mythology that would, in
turn, become the foundation of their fantastical world. In her first Glass
Town story, *Two Romantic Tales* (1829), Charlotte introduces her fictitious Wellington as one of twelve eminent men (the Twelves) that sail
to and colonise the West Coast of Africa. Throughout the juvenilia, she
constructs him as an ideal military model of masculinity drawn from the
Georgian press. In early Glass Town, he takes centre stage as, literally, a king
amongst men. Charlotte constructs his legendary and hierarchical status in
Two Romantic Tales based on his successes in the Napoleonic Wars, specifically Waterloo: 'The conqueror [of Napoleon] shall gain eternal honour
and glory [...] Though in his lifetime fools will envy him, he shall overcome.
At his death renown shall cover him, and his name shall be everlasting!'[17]
It is, however, Branwell who recounts the post-Waterloo fanaticism with
Wellington more thoroughly and 'matter-of-factly' in his *The History of the*

Young Men (1830–1831). In his tale, the Napoleonic Wars are incorporated into Glass Town's fictitious history, Wellington temporarily departing from his African settlement to become the champion of Europe (Fig. 3.1):

> with the title o[f] General Sir Arthur Wellesley. and dispatched with an army of 20000 British soldiers to Spain and Portugal which the French were then desolating. I need not say how gloriously he fought and beat them how he confounded Bonapartes best Generals and in the end [after] 4 years hard fighting changed the seat of war into the heart of France.[18]

Following Napoleon's defeat at Waterloo, Wellington returns to Africa. On his arrival, as Charlotte explains, his general, Beresford, relates to twenty thousand men:

Fig. 3.1 Brontë, Charlotte (1831). *Wellington Monument* (Image used courtesy of the Brontë Parsonage Museum)

Europe has been set free from the iron chain of a despot, and how the mighty victory had been achieved with which all the civilised world had rung; of all the splendid triumphs that had taken place on that glorious occasion; and how all the high sovereigns of Europe had honoured England.[19]

Then, as Branwell concludes, the current King, Frederick Duke of York, dethrones himself with the exclamation: 'I am not worthy to rule this man he is your king'.[20] Hereon, Wellington remains the sovereign ruler throughout the decade-long saga.

The spectacle of Wellington's ascension to the throne is a scene directly taken from the contemporary print media. In Charlotte's *Two Romantic Tales*, she describes how, during the coronation, the assembly had gathered with 'intense anxiety', which soon erupted into 'thundering sounds of enthusiastic joy'.[21] In a similar fashion, a melodramatic 1829 *Blackwood's* article about the Siege of Cádiz (1810–1812) uses similar sensational language to describe Wellington's arrival in the Cortes:

> His arrival in the antechamber of the Cortes having been announced, a thrilling sense of anxiety seemed to pervade the whole assembly. Every eye was directed towards the grand entrance. At length the curtains were drawn, and the Hero approached the table [...] A buzz of admiration ran through the house, in which the panting auditors joined, even with the fear of instant expulsion before them; the whole assembly spontaneously rose at once, to receive their Liberator – their OWN Hero.[22]

This extract is comparable with Charlotte's imagined scene, demonstrating the powerful, pervasive aftershocks generated by Waterloo in the periodical press. The Wellington myth solidified to such an extent that, a decade after Waterloo, Wellington the soldier (not the statesman) is remembered and reproduced as a transcendent icon. In a post-Napoleonic society, these second-hand media recollections are formulated into third-hand reimaginings. Both Charlotte and Branwell's hysteria surrounding their imagined, ceremonial event was thus part of a general movement that prefigured the advent of celebrity culture, generated by a persuasive print culture.

Wellington continued to populate Charlotte and Branwell's early stories, equipped with the characteristics imprinted on him by the Georgian press. In an issue of *The United Service Journal*, from which Charlotte was known to have transcribed excerpts, an anonymous officer recounts in his 'Sketch of the Battle of Salamanca' (1829), 'This was the first time I had seen that extraordinary man, who has since proved himself the greatest commander of the age, and justly earned the title of the Invincible Wellington'.[23] Additionally, *Blackwood's* contributors established him as a warrior of legend, affirming his 'unalterable confidence in his own powers',[24] and how he had conquered Napoleon 'by simple manly heroism'.[25] The juvenilia often sees Wellington intervening in riotous or unjust situations, executing his powers of authority in an effort to restore peace. In her early separate Islander narrative, *Tales of the Islanders, Vol. II* (1829), Charlotte introduces Wellington as head of a school. In one instance he utilises his authoritative powers when his pupils rebel against school life, forming separate battle divisions and encamping on wild parts of the island:

> He immediately went out, without speaking a word, and we followed him. He proceeded up to the place where they were encamped and called out in a loud tone of voice that if they did not surrender they were all dead men, as he had brought several thousand bloodhounds with him, who would tear them to pieces in a moment. This they dreaded more than anything and therefore agreed to surrender, which they did immediately.[26]

The Duke continued to hold a respected, resolute supportive role in the siblings' saga, acting as a constant presence of nobility and command to his family and state. Later, when Charlotte's focus gradually drifted on to Wellington's Byronic son, Zamorna, Wellington remained a respected father-like figure to his nation. For instance, in the Wars of Encroachment and Aggression in 1833–1834, it is Wellington who dissociates himself from the Twelves when they refuse to release further financial and military aid for fighting the French. Despite the opposition to his bulletproof battle plans from the Federation, Wellington single-handedly pushes through his proposal by 'choosing his opportunity and forcibly representing the Frightful urgency of the case'.[27] Without forgetting his initial promise to defend his nation, Wellington succeeds in guiding Glass Town to a successful victory.

Napoleon Reimagined

Across the sea from Wellington's Glass Town Federation, the siblings' fictitious version of a degenerate France, Frenchysland, is ruled by Napoleon. Charlotte and Branwell's representations of Frenchysland's Emperor are complex. Branwell's early writings are pervaded by a sense of ambivalence about Napoleon, reflecting conflicting and troubling viewpoints widely circulated by contemporary commentators on the recent wars, such a Lord Byron. Branwell's 1829 poems 'High Minded Frenchman Love Not the Ghost' and 'Ode to Napoleon' portray a psychologically brilliant yet destructive Byronic hero whose desire to wage war is driven by power and fury. Influenced by Byron's 1814 poem, 'Ode to Napoleon', Branwell constructs a theatrical, heroic dialogue that voices his confusion about the French leader as a literary muse. Napoleon plagued Byron philosophically, as Simon Bainbridge summarises:

> His ongoing struggle to grasp and formulate Napoleon's political and imaginative meaning played an important part in his own continuous process of self–assessment and self–representation. Napoleon dominated Byron's imagination like no other contemporary political figure, both satisfying and frustrating his characteristic craving for the heroic, famously expressed in the opening of *Don Juan* – 'I want a hero' (1,1).[28]

Like Byron, Branwell struggled to map his character psychologically. Byron's lament of 'Ill–minded man! why scourge thy kind / Who bowed so low the knee? By gazing on thyself grown blind, Thou taught'st the rest to see'[29] is mimicked in Branwell's 'High Minded Frenchman': 'For the time in his powerful mind he sees / when like a slave before him led / the kingdom of France shall bow at his knees / & gloryfy [*sic*] him as its head'.[30] Additionally, this ending also lends itself to popular biographies of Napoleon: Walter Scott's *Life of Napoleon* concludes: 'He had destroyed every vestige of liberty in France [...] and [he had] comprehended the slavery of France, and aimed at the subjection of the world'.[31] In Branwell and Byron's odes, both conclude with a decline into delusion, their heroic ideal disappearing in the aftermath of his crushing defeat. Byron writes 'Thou Thimour! in his captive's cage/ [...] Life will not long confine / That spirit poured so widely forth– / So long obeyed–so little worth!'.[32] Branwell similarly lingers on his downfall: 'I have finishd [*sic*] / and have diminishd [*sic*] / Thy most splendid height and grate [*sic*] glory'.[33] At twelve years old, the young Branwell was still forming his own opinions, and his blatant plagiarism of Byron's convictions provides a convincing example of how important rhetoric was in informing and manipulating his views on Napoleon.

Branwell's imitation of Byron's poetry corresponds to the mixed critique of Napoleon in popular publications. As the first section of this chapter demonstrates, his brilliance was generally acknowledged yet his sinister motives were condemned. For example, Scott's *Life of Napoleon* offers a typical opinion of Napoleon concluding, 'The consequences of the unjustifiable aggressions of the French Emperor were an unlimited extent of slaughter, fire and human misery, all arising from the ambition of one man'.[34] Although contributors found it difficult not to marvel at his achievements, readers were often dissuaded to consider his genius as anything but unnatural.

Despite the extensive bad press directed towards Napoleon, on rare occasions some articles made an attempt to reconsider Napoleon's bad character. Some even went as far to present him as a paternal figure. Published in *Blackwood's* an anonymous poem titled 'Napoleon's Address to the Statue of his Son' (1822) constructs Napoleon to be a sensitive family man; it is a brief, poignant anomaly when compared to other contemporary, suspicious articles concerning France's Emperor: 'Adieu! Adieu ! beloved boy! / My latest care and only joy / […] distance cannot dissipate […] / Nor quench the love, so warm and wild, / With which a father views his child'.[35] Possibly inspired by this poem, Charlotte fleetingly toyed with the idea of Napoleon as a 'good' character by reworking her fictitious Bonaparte as a restorer of domestic sanctity; helping others to build a lasting father and son relationship that he was mostly denied. In her early tale, *The Enfant* (1829), the Emperor reunites a father with his son. When soothing a dispute between a child and Pigtail, Frenchysland's notorious child abuser and killer, the Emperor proposes to a man named 'Hanghimself' that the abused child in question may be his son. After ascertaining that this is so, the Emperor 'gave them 200,000 livres, with which Hanghimself purchased a beautiful estate […] where he now lives with his Enfant, two of the happiest and most contented people in all France'.[36]

As well as these brief glimpses of paternal sympathy evoked by the British periodical press and, by proxy, Charlotte, the French specifically tried to rewrite Napoleon's notoriety. *Blackwood's* response to Las Cases' *Mémorial de Sainte Hélène* (1823) is particularly stirring. The reviewers conclude: 'We are Tories, but we have feelings. The Quarterly [another popular periodical of the day] is ever unjust when the name of Napoleon is mentioned, and sure this war of hate may cease when all political ends have been accomplished'.[37] Reviews of French war journals were also published in *Blackwood's*, one contributor noting in a review of *Memoirs of General Count Rapp* (1823) that the narrator 'represents Napoleon as mild, tender, and scarcely ever inexorable in matters of life and death'.[38] This revision of Napoleon's character paints a completely different picture from pro-Wellington, high Tory contributors.

It is likely that this outpouring of sympathetic French narrative influenced Branwell, contributing to his fluctuating opinions of Napoleon. On a positive note, his first pseudonym was coined after Napoleon's popular general, Marshal Jean–de–Dieu Soult. Nevertheless, despite this, Branwell's 'Ode to Napoleon', written by 'Young Soult the Rhymer', rebels against sympathetic French character profiles of Napoleon: the fictitious Wellington describes it in an aside as 'hatred under the mask of freind ship [sic] & if this fellow—writes any more such he shall be guilotined [sic]'.[39] After Soult concludes with Napoleon's downfall, Branwell writes a disclaimer that 'Young Soult <I> wrote it while—drunk and under the influence of passion for the Empreur [sic] had decided against him in some—cause or other—'.[40] Although distinctly juvenile in his address, Branwell may have built Soult's fictitious betrayal upon the *Blackwood's* review of *Las Cases' Journal*, which exposed damning comments made by Napoleon against Soult: 'Even of his own generals, those who had acquired fame as tacticians, he never would allow their merit [...] Soult, he says, would make merely a good *ordonnateur*, a proper minister at war'.[41] Napoleon, even though 'esteemed' by the reviewer, is then brought down in estimations by the 'spite, ignorance, and absurdity, as come from his pen, or even as slipping from him in intemperate moments'.[42] Thus, despite a generally sympathetic response to Napoleon, his revealed disposition towards others alongside Byron's disappointment at his unfulfilling heroism may have been accountable for Branwell's poetic backlash, his poetry and narratives imagining a parallel kingdom of self-absorbed history and response.

Charlotte's fictitious construction of Napoleon complements Branwell's writings. Her tale *Journal of a Frenchman* (1830) carries important reflections on Napoleon's character. The narrator, Sergeant Tree, Glass Town's novelist, bookseller and publisher, talks of his admiration of Napoleon; in spite of his father's teachings, 'he strove constantly to instil a love for the Capets into my mind [...] but secretly in my heart was captivated by Napoleon's glory'.[43] Further on in the tale, a mature narrator is seen walking through Paris in an effort to join the French army. He sees a group of soldiers ahead of him:

> While I was gazing at them in delight, they suddenly fell back in regular ranks and presented arms to a person that then passed through them, whose

appearance perfectly charmed me. He was middle–sized, attired in regimen-
tals and possessed the noblest countenance that the sun ever looked upon.
In short, he was the personification of my idea of Bonaparte. In a transport,
I threw myself at his feet and begged to be allowed to serve him. Smiling,
he ordered me to rise and asked my name. I told him and said, "Are you not
Napoleon?"[44]

In a twist, the regimental figure is actually Wellington, who chooses to save
his life after Blucher beats him repeatedly for his question. Having recently
taken control of the city, Wellington's justification for his mercy rests on
the fact that the French are now 'harmless'.

Like Branwell and Byron, Charlotte experiences crushing disillusionment that Napoleon is not a hero. The seemingly magnificent conqueror is
transmogrified into Charlotte's archetypal vision of Wellington, shattering
the misconception of Napoleon's importance and majesty. Like Branwell,
who reimagines and rewrites historical events, Charlotte reflects on a myriad
of contemporary opinions that seemed simultaneously captivated and horrified by France's enigmatic Emperor. Reacting to these criticisms, Charlotte goes some way to imagine Napoleon as an idyllic figure but retreats
into her British safe house, conforming to popular opinions that could not
consider Wellington and Napoleon under the same banner of heroism.

Mutating the Wellington and Napoleon Myth Further: Zamorna and Alexander Percy

Charlotte and Branwell's early Glass Town manifestations of Wellington
and Napoleon are indicative of a wider cultural movement that relished the
rise of military celebrity. The post-war frenzy of analysis—whether celebratory or critical—provided by both the press and biography directed towards
these two adversaries is displaced and re-represented in the Brontës' early
literature. By reading these imaginative, unassuming narratives it becomes
clear that the impact of post–war commentary embedded itself into the fabric of public consciousness. Charlotte and Branwell, as two sample citizens
in a war–affected nation, used the information at hand to form their own
opinions. Freely, they both relished the successes of Wellington, applying
his military power to fantasy landscapes and promoting him to sovereignty.
For Napoleon, they contributed to his Byronic legacy, yet simultaneously
used the medium of make-believe and play to understand his character,
knock him from his pedestal, and, for Charlotte, offer him the promise of

reconciliation (both in the private and public mind). Importantly, however, it is only as their fantasy saga progressed that they created a narrative that allowed these rivals to interact and move forward together. Whereas Wellington and Napoleon—with the exception of their (non)encounter at Waterloo—act as separate entities in the early Glass Town tales, the siblings' further displacement of them on to their invented characters, Zamorna and Alexander Percy, allows for their military antagonism to evolve into a highly sensational, personal battle. Through post-war fan fiction, Charlotte and Branwell retreat further into their imaginations to provide a powerful interaction between two men that moves above and beyond what the published press could ever achieve: a contest between two great men that transcends military competition and explores undiscovered territories of masculine friendship and homosocial tensions.

Around 1834, Charlotte and Branwell tired of their literal transmogrifications of Wellington and Napoleon. Instead they focused on developing two of their own characters, each still embodying the characteristics imprinted on Wellington and Napoleon by contemporary literature: Zamorna, Wellington's son, and Alexander Percy, known throughout the later works as Northangerland. As Drew Lamonica asserts, 'Wellington and Napoleon, the two greatest political and military rivals of then–recent history, are succeeded by the two greatest political and military rivals of the siblings' literary imaginations, Zamorna and Northangerland'.[45] Although both were regular characters in Charlotte and Branwell's early Glass Town writings, it is not until 1834 with the formation of the siblings' new kingdom, Angria, and Zamorna's subsequent marriage to Percy's daughter, Mary, that the duo's incredible dynamic is fully unleashed. After the Wars of Encroachment and Aggression, it is Percy who convinces the Verdopolitan parliament to appoint Zamorna as King of Angria. In the first of Branwell's prose written after his war narratives, titled *The Wool is Rising* (1834), Percy is shown lamenting to parliament: 'Why when I saw him in the darkest hour of battle [...] call back hope to the despairing and plant Life over death [...] I knew that I saw a son of Wellington a man destined to be a KING'.[46] After his coronation, reported in Branwell's *Angria and the Angrians I(a)* (1834), Branwell appoints Percy as prime minister, making them both the highest ranking officials in the land.

Zamorna's appointment as King of Angria revives images of his father's—Wellington's—appointment as King of the Glass Town Federation some five years earlier. The saga reminds us that both characters are first and foremost the fathers of their own retrospective nations; Wellington, of Wellingtonsland and King of the Glass Town Federation, and Zamorna, King of Angria. When crowned 'King of the Twelves' in Charlotte and Branwell's first Glass Town adventure, *Two Romantic Tales*, Wellington promises: 'Soldiers, I will defend what you have committed to my care'.[47] In reality, it is clear that Wellington also thought primarily of his nation, pushing his domestic duties out of the limelight in favour of his military career. In a short biography of Wellington, published in *Blackwood's* in 1827, the author writes:

> Perhaps there are not many individuals who, with a slender patrimony, and the prospect of a family to provide for, would not have virtually quitted the military profession altogether [...] Sir Arthur Wellesley, however, entertained very different views of things. In his eyes, a life of inaction was a life of misery [...] Above all, his heart and affections lay in the glorious profession which he had chosen; and he embraced the very first opportunity which offered of returning to the discharge of its duties.[48]

Written some years before this, however, George Elliot's preface to his biography of Wellington depicts a less neglectful family figure. Despite not presenting a first-hand account of family care, Elliot argues that Wellington's political livelihood helped advance his family's position and therefore, by proxy, made him an iconic domestic figure who prioritised his family's welfare:

> Your own great abilities as a Statesman, gave you a station in political life, which opened to your view the dignities and honors [*sic*], as well as the toils and anxieties of power; but power came recommended to your feelings by stronger hopes than the mere gratifications of personal vanity and ambition. It placed within your reach the means of advancing the prosperity of your family, and you availed yourself of those means with a purity of purpose, which will continue to reflect honor upon your name as long as domestic virtues and the ties of blood shall be respected among men.[49]

Regardless of motive, both passages generate an image of Wellington as a publicly admired figure, firmly committed to his country. Charlotte acknowledges this, replicating this intense, kingdom-driven outlook through Zamorna. Despite showing a fondness for his children, in *My Angria and the Angrians* (1834) Zamorna delivers a disturbing speech after the birth of his twin sons:

They are yours as well as mine. I dedicate them from their birth. Being born
for Angria's good, they must live for her glory, and die if need be for her
existence. I rejoice in their creation for your sakes. I love them as much for
their connection with the land whose sun is now shining on them, as I do
for the blood that runs in their veins and the flesh which covers their bones,
though that blood and flesh be my own or dearer than my own [...] I will
place them in the arms of your acknowledged representative, and in his person
all Angrians shall salute her princes.[50]

In this one passage, Zamorna embodies the inseparable bond between
fatherhood and the army promoted by Wellington: the militaristic language
embodies the tension between being father of a nation, and father of one's
family. Like Wellington, whose main 'son' was Britain itself, Zamorna confesses that empire, power and nation are more important than the sentimental emotions of one's life. Indeed, Charlotte appears to recognise that,
in a military founded kingdom, the very essence of militaristic masculinity
is embedded intrinsically within her protagonists to a point where, if need
be, domestic livelihood will be sacrificed.

After the Angrian coronation, Charlotte and Branwell play on Zamorna
and Alexander Percy's conflicted feelings for one another. In 1835, a new
political party emerges, the Reform Party, whose leader, the villainous
Ardrah, expels Angria from the Verdopolitan Union in an attempt to dis-
mantle the newly formed nation. Percy briefly redeems himself, uniting
with Zamorna's forces in defence of their nation. In 1836, however, the
Angrian army is overpowered, the capital falls, and both protagonists flee
their occupied city. Whilst Zamorna continues to fight throughout the year,
suffering his final defeat at the battle of Edwardston on 28 July, Percy abandons his friend and rouses the city to rebel against Ardrah's Reform Party.
His forces win, and thereafter his Republican army takes over the country.
Meanwhile, as punishment for his father-in-law's betrayal, Zamorna reluc-
tantly abandons his wife, Percy's beloved daughter, causing her to waste
away in the mournful ruins of her country estate.

Betrayal and revenge are paramount in the Angrian saga. After Zamorna's defeat at the battle of Edwardston, Percy spares him from death—
much as Wellington did with Napoleon after Waterloo—yet as Branwell's
Angria and the Angrians III(d) (1836) explains, he 'banish[ed] him 2000
miles off on the rocks of the Ascension Isle'.[51] Here, Branwell deliberately draws from Napoleon's real-life banishment off St. Helena, his exile

a lifelong punishment inflicted and administered by Britain after the battle of Waterloo. Interestingly, however, it is Charlotte's Byronic model of Wellington that is banished, not the wicked incarnation of Napoleon; once again, each hero's characteristics are moulded through poetic licence. The deeply moving, intensely homosocial poetic lament *And, When you Left Me* or *Zamorna's Lament* (1836), written during his sea-bound journey into exile, reflects back on better times and mourns for the friendship that had once been:

> You are a fiend, I've told you that before
> I've told it half in earnest half in jest
> I've sworn it when the furnace roar
> Of Hell was rising fiercely in my breast
> And calmly I confirm the oath once more
> Adding however as becomes me best
> That I'm no better & we two united
> Each other's happiness have fiend–like blighted [...]
> Let us consider, let us just look back
> And trace the pleasant path we've trod together[52]

Zamorna's exile, however, rather than securing his downfall, paves the way for his heroic return a year later when, once again, he rallies his troops, overpowers his enemies, and restores himself as the rightful king of Angria.[53] By 1838, Percy has once again returned to his country seat and to Zamorna's favours, much to the outrage of the Angrian citizens. Despite the repeated uprisings and betrayals he has experienced at the hands of his father-in-law, the last post-war Angrian tales show Zamorna risking his life to defend his arch-rival. In Charlotte's *Stancliffe's Hotel* (1838), Zamorna publicly defends his loyalty to Percy, mercilessly quelling a mob with military force as a violent response to their fierce protest.[54] Similarly, in one of his last writings, *Angria and the Angrians V(d)* (1839), Branwell recalls that 'there were thousands in the square and that they threatned to break the palace windows' in order to stone Percy. In the final passage, the two rivals are seen 'calmly walking down the steps', Zamorna exclaiming, 'God damn them! [...] Take my arm Percy and let them touch us who dare!'[55]

Although this imagined relationship is highly dramatised, Charlotte's description of Zamorna and Percy as 'two great drivers' in *High Life in Verdopolis* (1834) epitomises Wellington and Napoleon's relationship in the post-war periodical press.[56] Whilst Zamorna and Percy drive one another in an imaginary chronicle of retaliation and betrayal, Wellington and Napoleon's real-life battlefield and post-Waterloo rivalry continued to drive their representation in the print media. Whereas the first section of this chapter introduced this rivalry as a stand-alone narrative, it is important to now resume this discussion as the chapter concludes within the recesses of the Brontës' creative consciousness. What is clear is that Zamorna and Percy's complex narratives parallel Wellington and Napoleon's relationship in print: both public and private narratives seek to demonstrate a rivalry of military equivalence yet contrasting virtues.

As this chapter highlights, Wellington and Napoleon's rivalry was sensationalised through inflammatory commentary in the years following the Battle of Waterloo and extending posthumously. Whereas Napoleon conveyed his obsessive tendencies through literature, as Andrew Roberts exposes, Wellington secretly attempted to physically obtain Napoleon's possessions: 'Napoleon's busts, statuettes, flags, books, portraits, his sword, his watch, his cook, his sister's house, his statue, [and] two of his mistresses, amongst other objects'.[57] Although the Brontës would have been oblivious to Wellington's trophy hunting, their decision to make Zamorna and Percy mutually obsessed with one another was coincidentally accurate. It is unknown whether the Brontë children expanded their reading of Napoleon's afterlife through other memoirs, but it is likely that they were broadly able to understand Napoleon's consumed character from reviews in *Blackwood's*. The review of *Rapp's Memoirs* (1823), for example, reveals that Napoleon fixated on the battle of Waterloo, repeatedly running through every minute detail, studying Wellington's arrangement of his forces and arguing that the battle was not in the interests of the British nation: it argues that Napoleon could not come to terms with his unmanned, conquered state.[58] In a *Blackwood's* review of another St. Helena memoir, *La Campagne de 1815* (1818), written by Napoleon's *maréchal de camp*, Gaspard Gourgaud, Napoleon exclaims of Wellington, '*Great* let me call him—for he conquered *me*'.[59] Although much of the true nature of Wellington and Napoleon's obsession was revealed long after the Brontës completed their juvenilia, it is clear that each sibling picked up and expanded upon the tensions radiating from the periodicals they read. Returning to pugalism, *Boxiana* again acts as metaphorical exposition to illustrate contemporary attitudes: this time it succeeds in highlighting the tensions between the two 'equal adversaries' and transforms their military and media rivalry into a primal punch-up. An extract published in an 1819 edition uses pugilist language to allude to their military prowess:

While, in spite of the battle of Waterloo, the milling qualities of Bonaparte and Wellington are thought to be so equally balanced, that in the event of another trial it would, among the cognoscenti, be only guineas to pounds, or the Irishman for choice.[60]

Like Charlotte and Branwell, the media found it easy to imagine a physical meeting of the two, facilitating the public's sensationalist desire to repeat their mortal combat. In a similar hyper-masculine vein, Zamorna and Percy are equally introduced as physical as well as political rivals. Each demonstrates muscular, military skill yet represents opposing ideologies. Although physicality is a significant contributor to Charlotte and Branwell's shared idea of heroism, displaying the correct 'patriotic' character is also vital. Charlotte and Branwell evidently agreed on this character model, Charlotte's protagonist Zamorna allowed to exercise this trait, whilst Branwell's Percy constructed to consistently act as his foil, demonstrating his overall 'bad' character against Zamorna's 'good'. Despite Percy being both handsome and militant, it is his demonic, unpatriotic personality that disqualifies him from idealised models of manhood. Whereas Zamorna has the 'goodness' of Wellington within his blood, Percy is purely Napoleon-like in his disposition, showing potential for greatness but always resorting to cowardice and cruelty.

An 1852 article in *Bell's Life in London* corroborates the lasting legacy of Wellington and Napoleon as worthy adversaries with fundamentally different principles:

> Napoleon and Wellington were not merely individual characters: they were types of the powers which they respectively headed in the contest [...] but it was in the prevailing moral principles by which they were regulated that the distinctive character of the minds was most striking and important. Singleness of heart was the characteristic of the British heroism – a sense of duty his ruling principle. Ambition pervaded the French conqueror; a thirst for glory was his invariable incentive.[61]

This passage might well have been discussing the opposing instincts of Zamorna and Alexander Percy, Zamorna championing duty and Percy overthrowing duty for glory. Napoleon's moral corruption that 'desolated [Europe] for 15 years' correlates to Percy's constant impulse to provoke civil war[62]: his character is a fictitious model that allows evil to be unleashed

to its full, uncensored potential. The siblings evidently used Percy to further interrogate, dissect and explore Napoleon's troubled psychology, a task
that occupied them since the very beginning of their early writing career.
Written by Charlotte, in *Postscript Adressed to the Earl of Northangerland*
[*sic*] (1835), Zamorna exclaims that he has always viewed Percy:

> as a deadly dangerous man whose gigantic genius, if united with virtue might
> have made him the benefactor of his kind, but which, being unhappily asso-
> ciated with fiend–like vice, transformed him into a scourge so deadly, that
> had Sodom or Gomorrah owned such an inhabitant they would have needed
> no fire from heaven to punish their iniquity.[63]

Despite this passage's heightened melodrama, its inquisitional tone is comparable to *Blackwood's* evaluations of Napoleon. Contributors even went
so far as to analyse Napoleon's physical features, with the science of cran-
iology used as a means of understanding and justifying psychological and
physical differences. In 'The Craniologist's Review', published in *Blackwood's* in 1818, phrenologist Ulrick Sternstare attempts to rationalise
Napoleon's character through a physical examination. Like Percy, who lacks
virtue, Napoleon's forehead suggests that he 'never had the graciousness
nor urbane good-nature', and, like Percy's 'fiend–like genius', Napoleon's
organs have ferocity, but 'his nervous system is of the best quality, and
his sensations, volitions and intellectual movements, all of them intense'.[64]
Percy resembles Napoleon in his embodiment of intense light and dark
characteristics. In Charlotte's *High Life in Verdopolis*, Zamorna expresses
his complex and violent feelings for his father-in-law, describing him as:

> that great, vile, splendid, hateful, fiendish, angelic, black, bright, abominable,
> blessed scoundrel, that Northangerland [Percy], that illustriously infamous
> relative of mine, whom I abhor and yet admire, detest and yet love, that
> bundle of contradictions and yet that horribly consistent whole.[65]

Percy's Napoleon-like character traits remove all possibility of being
branded conventionally heroic. Repeatedly described as villainous, old,
tired and ill, Percy merely displays a surface level of chivalry whilst
instead plotting full-scale revolution with the assistance of Glass Town
and Angria's underworld. In contrast, Branwell in *The Wool is Rising*
describes Zamorna's character as the complete opposite of his alter ego
(Fig. 3.2):

Fig. 3.2   Brontë, Charlotte (1833–1834). *Alexander Percy* (Image used courtesy of the Brontë Parsonage Museum)

[Zamorna has] A splendid exterior of appearance. and. kingly loftiness of character and. mind formed on the model. of a conqueror. a life of brilliant performances. have all crowned the fate. of. the man destined as Africas cherished and darling hero.[66]

Zamorna's regal character is compared to Percy's in Charlotte's *The Foundling* (1833). Although Zamorna is complimentary about him, stating that he is handsome, Marian Hume, Zamorna's current wife, has different views:

> 'He is not so [handsome] in mine, though,' replied she. 'His very look frightened me so far from my propriety that I could not muster sufficient sense to frame [an] answer to his question.' 'Why you carping critic, what particular feature in his face do you find fault with?' 'His eyes, I think, though I can't say with exactness, where all are so ugly [...] They are totally unlike yours, not so large, not so bright, not so smiling, and therefore I hate them'.[67]

Additionally, in her *Characters of Celebrated Men* (1829), Charlotte touches upon Percy's heroic facade, revealing his attempts to imitate the persona of Wellington, a trait that Zamorna naturally embodies. Percy instead fails to achieve this, purely down to his unhinged, wicked mind:

> His manner is rather polished and gentlemanly, but his mind is deceitful, bloody and cruel. His walk (in which he much prides himself) is stately and soldier-like, and he fancies that it greatly resembles that of the Duke of Wellington.[68]

These juxtapositions of character truly separate Zamorna and Percy. It is from the greatness of his 'Wellington-like' mind that Zamorna is able to achieve the optimum model of soldierly heroism, despite his minor defects. He is able to radiate an essence of warmth and patriotism that securely establishes his kingly position. It is interesting, however, to consider that Percy [Napoleon], despite his innate flaws, wishes to be like Wellington: although this may be an attempt by Charlotte to frustrate her brother by impressing her ideals on to his character, it is a uniting feature that strengthens a homosocial potentiality between the two rivals. This hope, however, appears too unrealistic. Unlike Zamorna, Percy's morality is unbalanced,[69] the ideal of soldierly manliness literally gone rogue. Unable to match Zamorna's military ideal, Percy is offered no source of redemption.

Branwell's character, although allowed sustained moments of success, is never permitted to triumph, Zamorna's sun-like rays re-establishing the 'Wellington' soldierly archetype as triumphant.

Despite being convoluted and fictional, Charlotte and Branwell's depictions of their juvenile heroes—first Wellington and Napoleon, and then Zamorna and Alexander Percy—showcase contemporary reactions to Wellington and Napoleon's eminent personalities. Responding to the post-Waterloo popular commentary, the siblings acknowledged, interpreted and incorporated the personality traits and military antagonisms of the two illustrious titans whilst imagining a powerful, binding relationship based on that antagonism, where admiration for one another's military prowess, mental brilliance and lust for power secured an eternal bond of mutual respect and hero worship. Growing up in a post-war age, the unpublished narratives of these siblings demonstrate the impact celebrity culture had on contemporary society, when late Georgian Britain was still caught up in the excitement and scandal of Waterloo well over a decade after Napoleon was defeated. This chapter has shown that Charlotte and Branwell's writings are inextricably bound up in post-war conversation; the siblings took on a role as social commentators and reworked their understandings into an alternative, playful history. The various subsections of this chapter have penetrated through a number of layers of Wellington and Napoleon's representations—public perceptions, fictional reconstructions, fictional reinventions—leaving this chapter firmly within the complex world of the Brontë juvenilia.

NOTES

1. *Tales*: 257.
2. Andrew Roberts, *Napoleon and Wellington* (London: Phoenix, 2010): xxxvii.
3. Walter Scott, *The Life of Napoleon Buonaparte in Nine Volumes* (Edinburgh: William Blackwood, 1827): 73.
4. Ibid., 331.
5. George Gleig, *Life of Arthur, First Duke of Wellington* (London: Longman, 1862): 579.
6. Roberts, *Napoleon and Wellington*, 291.
7. Scott, *Life of Napoleon*, 500.
8. "The Military Sketch Book," *Blackwood's Edinburgh Magazine*, June 1827, 840.
9. "Foreign Policy," *John Bull*, 22 February 1830, 60.
10. Lieutenant Spencer Moggridge, "Letters from the Peninsula No. 2 The Battle of Vittoria," *Blackwood's Edinburgh Magazine*, June 1828, 190.

11. Morgan Odoherty, a *Blackwood's* contributor, wrote a scathing article attacking the Duke's military skills titled, 'On the Military Errors of the Duke of Wellington' (1819).
12. "American Writers No. II," *Blackwood's Edinburgh Magazine*, October 1824, 422.
13. Charlotte Brontë, *Jane Eyre*, ed. Margaret Smith and Sally Shuttleworth (Oxford: Oxford University Press, 2008): 99.
14. David Snowdon, *Writing the Prizefight* (Bern: Peter Lang, 2013): 120.
15. Ibid., 149.
16. "Russia," *Blackwood's Edinburgh Magazine*, April 1826, 456.
17. *Tales*: 11.
18. *WPB I*: 166.
19. *Tales*: 14.
20. *WPB I*: 169.
21. *Tales*: 15.
22. "Wellington in Cadiz; Or the Conqueror and the Cortes," *Blackwood's Edinburgh Magazine*, December 1829, 248.
23. "Sketch of the Battle of Salamanca," *The United Service Journal and Naval Military Magazine*, March 1829, 96.
24. Morgan Odoherty, "Military Errors of the Duke of Wellington," *Blackwood's Edinburgh Magazine*, December 1819, 291.
25. Z, "Nugæ Literariæ No. I: The Duke of Wellington," *Blackwood's Edinburgh Magazine*, February 1826, 133.
26. *EEW I*: 104.
27. *WPB I*: 408.
28. Simon Bainbridge, *Napoleon and English Romanticism* (Cambridge: Cambridge University Press, 1995): 135.
29. *Lord Byron—The Major Works*, ed. Jerome McGann (Oxford: Oxford University Press, 2008): 253.
30. *WPB I*: 33.
31. Scott, *Life of Napoleon*, 335, 337.
32. Byron, *The Major Works*, 257.
33. *WPB I*: 60.
34. Scott, *Life of Napoleon*, 328.
35. "Napoleon's Address to the Statue of His Son," *Blackwood's Edinburgh Magazine*, December 1822, 760.
36. *EEW I*: 36.
37. "Las Cases Journal," *Blackwood's Edinburgh Magazine*, August 1823, 169.
38. "Rapp's Memoirs," *Blackwood's Edinburgh Magazine*, July 1823, 39.
39. *WPB I*: 59.
40. Ibid., 60.
41. "Las Cases Journal," *Blackwood's*, 170.
42. Ibid., 171.

43. *EEW I*: 222.
44. Ibid., 223.
45. Drew Lamonica, *We Are Three Sisters—Self and Family in the Writing of the Brontës* (Missouri: Missouri University Press, 2003): 42.
46. *WPB II*: 32.
47. *Tales*: 15.
48. Z, *Blackwood's Edinburgh Magazine*, February 1827, 227.
49. George Elliot, *The Life of the Most Noble Arthur Duke of Wellington* (London: Sherwood, Neely and Jones, 1816): iv.
50. *EEW III*: 292.
51. *WPB II*: 602.
52. *PCB*: 194.
53. This is comparable to Napoleon's banishment to the Isle of Elba in April 1814, sanctioned by the Treaty of Fontainebleau. He escaped in February 1815 and triumphantly returned to Paris in March, resuming his role as Emperor.
54. *Tales*: 113.
55. *WPB III*: 270.
56. *EEW III*: 33.
57. Roberts, *Napoleon and Wellington*, 251.
58. "Rapp's Memoirs," *Blackwood's* , 40.
59. "Remarks on General Gourgaud's Account of the Campaign of 1815," *Blackwood's Edinburgh Magazine*, November 1819, 222.
60. "Boxiana—Civil Wars," *Blackwood's Edinburgh Magazine*, September 1819, 664.
61. "A Comparison Between Wellington and Napoleon," in *Bell's Life in London and Sporting Chronicle*, 21 November 1852, 8.
62. Ibid.
63. *EEW III*: 310.
64. "The Craniologist's Review," *Blackwood's Edinburgh Magazine*, May 1818, 146–148.
65. *EEW III*: 33.
66. *WPB II*: 23.
67. *EEW II*: 78–9.
68. *EEW I*: 128.
69. This is made explicit in Branwell's series *Life of Alexander Percy* (1834–1835), which documents Percy's disturbing Bildungsroman. As well as suffering an intensely traumatic childhood he plots with his first wife, Augusta de Segovia, to kill his own father.

CHAPTER 4

The Napoleonic Wars

This chapter explores the broader impact of the Napoleonic Wars on Charlotte and Branwell's early writings. Whereas the previous chapter discussed the role of military hero worship—especially in relation to Wellington and Napoleon—as a primary theme in Charlotte and Branwell's military kingdoms, this chapter moves on to explore the siblings' immersion in the everyday narratives circulating in post-war Britain. In particular, it looks at the siblings' interest in Napoleonic storytelling through their reading and reimagining of military memoirs and oral ballads. It is through their engagement with raw, revelatory life writing, written by the 'everyday' soldier, that Charlotte and Branwell were able to grasp the day-to-day life of a soldier and understand and replicate the more personal experiences of life in the army, be that positive and negative. This chapter consists of three sections. The first introduces Charlotte and Branwell's engagement with these memoirs; the second demonstrates their use of memoirs and oral ballads to foster military spectacle and patriotism in their saga; and the third—and arguably most revelatory—shows how they used soldiers' biographies to gain a sophisticated, highly intuitive understanding of war trauma and alcoholism. It is through these multifaceted understandings of military life writing that readers can comprehend how invested the Brontë siblings were in reworking authentic war sources in their play.

© The Author(s) 2019
E. Butcher, *The Brontës and War*,
https://doi.org/10.1007/978-3-319-95636-7_4

The Rise of the Military Memoir

In the years following the Napoleonic Wars, a war-orientated literary move-ment began to surface within British culture. More and more, soldiers were publishing their experiences of war and releasing them either as stand-alone books, or through features in the periodical press. The nation was hooked, reading tales of militarism and adventure. This movement inspired the Brontë siblings to participate, their juvenilia imitating and adopting this phenomenon. Whereas the previous chapter highlighted the role of the periodical press in the Brontës' recognition and reinvention of military celebrity culture, the media also facilitated their interest in and engage-ment with the 'everyday' soldier: their juvenilia are an extension of these memoirs, reimagining soldiers' states of being in a fantastical, exotic saga, yet still vicariously responding and contributing to a poignant moment in history.

On a superficial level, military features published in the periodical press served to reignite the spirit of war as various commentators reflected on an exciting bygone era. Surprisingly, Britain's reaction to the end of the Napoleonic Wars was relatively mournful: many saw the recent conflicts as a stimulating period that brought life and sensationalism to the nation. In 1827, a contributor to *Blackwood's* declared, 'the golden days of the army are gone; the sword rusts in its scabbard and literature and half pay are now the order of the day'.[1] With melancholic nostalgia in the air, the soldier author sought to cash in on this monotony, providing a literary service to a nation that needed their appetites whetted.

The mass publication and widespread distribution of war biographies meant that members of the late-Georgian British public were able to vicar-iously experience the landscape of war from the safety of their homes. Neil Ramsey provides a definitive account of this war literature 'boom':

> A considerable body of soldiers' writing emerged during the 1820s and 1830s [...] Reviewers increasingly remarked, typically with some surprise, that they were witnessing an outpouring of personal accounts of the Napoleonic Wars [...] The military author assumed a prominent position in British literature, with the soldier's personal narrative, his 'military memoir', forming a recog-nisable and commercially successful genre.[2]

Ramsey continues to propose that these accounts established a sense of 'knowing' in the nationwide experience of war. The Napoleonic memoir proved that the common man could teach a disengaged nation to under-stand and sympathise with the duty of an everyday soldier.[3]

It will become clear throughout this chapter that Charlotte and Branwell were part of this literary military movement: their contemporary reading of memoirs allowed them not only to connect with the nation's recent mili-tary history but also provided the necessary contextual background to build their imaginary kingdom. In essence, these biographical texts were funda-mental to the geography and characterisation of Glass Town and Angria. Through this influx of life writing, Charlotte and Branwell were able to transmogrify their reality of the Napoleonic Wars into fantasy literature. Military memoirs acted as a springboard through which the siblings could identify with highly humanised accounts of wartime topography and, with them, forge a world that addressed the darker—even mundane—elements of war, beyond the superficial glamour and macho-militarism.

Christine Alexander's discovery of missing pages to Charlotte's early manuscript '*Anecdotes of the Duke of Wellington*' (1829) gives an important insight into the specific military memoirs the Brontë family read and, more generally, the types of memoir that impacted Charlotte's consciousness and fed into her writing. Although clearly seeking particular facts about the Duke, Charlotte's 'Anecdotes' also provides evidence of a young woman engaging with military memoirs.[4] Extract II is directly transcribed from John Malcolm's biography, *Malcolm's Tales of Field and Flood: With Sketches of Life at Home* (1829):

> no one who has once seen, can ever forget that [face] of the Duke of Welling-ton; it is, moreover, but little changed, and yet wears the same still smile and calm dignity which never for a moment forsook it, even in the mortal struggle and earthquake shock of battle.[5]

Other anecdotes are recollected from memory. Extract III recalls a dinner party scene, with Wellington as the life and soul of the party: 'his sparkling wit & playful humour were making the hours dance pleasantly along'.[6] As Alexander notes, Charlotte's imagined scene is similar to an account given by Major Stothert in July's edition of the 1829 *The United Service Journal*, which the Brontë family owned. As quoted in 'The Editor's Port-folio', Stothert exclaims that Wellington joined a large dinner party 'with his accustomed vivacity, in the conversation of his guests'.[7] *The United Service Journal* a completely military-based magazine that included war memoirs such as 'Battle of Salamanca', seen in this July issue, and 'Advance from Salamanca' included in part II of the same issue, would have been a useful source of military reading for the siblings. Finally, excluding a paragraph transcribed from Walter Scott's *Life of Napoleon* (1827), Extract VI is a close transcription from an anonymous military memoir published in *The New British Novelist: Comprising Works of the Most Popular and Fashionable Writers of the Present Day, Vol. XXII* (1830). It details a doctor's engagements at home and out in the Peninsular, including vivid descriptions of battle: 'the hottest of the battle raged around him the belching cannons roared almost incessantly'.[8] This memoir joins an eclectic range of Charlotte's military reading, creating a substantial portfolio of military sources that she could draw from and rework. This evidence is integral to supporting the argument within this book: that the juvenilia were shaped within a historical framework of war, written by youthful war writers.

Although there is no such manuscript to support Branwell's interest in reading military memoirs, it can be deduced from his writings that he actively engaged with the genre and shared Charlotte's enthusiasm for the 'red-coated author'. Instead, he demonstrates his knowledge of the genre through his choice of narrator. Throughout Angria's ferocious war-torn years (especially 1831–1837), Branwell introduces ordinary soldier figures that record their experiences of war through biography: this technique attests to Branwell's direct mimicry of narration styles from contemporary military memoirs. In Branwell's early tales, *Letters from an Englishman* (1830–1832), J. Bellingham—a Glass Town banker thrust into the midst of battle—describes Alexander Percy's insurrection of Glass Town throughout the years 1830–1832. Spanning the years 1833–1834, the Wars of Encroachment and Aggression see Branwell's pseudonym, the historian John Flower, describe his experiences of battle as a military leader. Similarly, in the Angrian and Glass Town Civil Wars of 1835–1837, Branwell's later pseudonym, the Angrian poet Henry Hastings, provides a dramatic and violent account of the battles fought between the Angrian nation and the enemies bonded together by Ardrah's Reform Party. Through Hastings' narratives, starting from *Angria and the Angrians I(d)* (1834) and ending with *Angria and the Angrians III(a)* (1836), Branwell provides a heroic, poetic, yet nightmarish vision of the 'real' soldier, reanimated from the mouths of everyday military men that directly spoke to the Brontës' imaginations through the memoirs they read throughout their adolescent years. The siblings, together, acted as historians and commentators in a nation trying to process war, inventing new, fictional military voices that would regurgitate, reprocess and reinvent the post-war feelings of the present age.

READING AND REIMAGINING MILITARY MEMOIRS

In the second chapter of this book, the section 'Walter Scott' highlights the importance of Scott's literary technique 'fog of war' in relation to Branwell's battle writings and briefly alludes to its presence in contemporary military memoirs. Whilst maintaining that Scott's literature was the main literary source behind Branwell's technique, it is crucial to highlight that Branwell's memoir-style 'fog of war' narratives were part of a national movement. Whereas Scott pioneered this device in a canonical context, the late-Georgian explosion of military biography meant that soldiers turned to writing 'in the moment' in a cathartic bid to relive their experiences of combat and relate it to the British public. A number of the military memoirs that were available to the Brontës contained convincing, highly emotive scenes of battle. In *The Subaltern*, serialised in *Blackwood's* throughout 1825, George Gleig recounts the Siege of St Sebastian (1813), conjuring confused 'fog of war' imagery in the thick of battle:

> Shouts and groans were now mingled with the roar of cannons and the rattle of musketry [...] A shell from one of our mortars had exploded [...] sweeping the storming party into eternity [...] It was a spectacle as appalling and grand as the imagination can conceive, the sight of that explosion. The noise was more awful than any which I have ever heard before or since; whilst a bright flash, instantly succeeded by a smoke so dense, as to obscure all vision, produced an effect upon those who witnessed it, such as no powers of language are adequate to describe.[9]

In keeping with the chaotic descriptions of 'fog of war', Gleig's final statement highlights the need to evoke intense, sensational imagery to demonstrate the horrors of a situation where words ultimately fail. Similar language is used in Lieutenant Spencer Moggridge's 'Letters from the Peninsula No. 1', published in *Blackwood's* in 1827. At a climactic point in the battle, Moggridge describes a confused assault upon the enemy:

> There was little order in our proceedings; by the difficulties and inequalities of the ground, the battalion had become clubbed; and when we crowned the hill, and opened fire on our antagonists, we found ourselves certainly not in the same place we formerly occupied in the line. The firing was continued for a minute or two, and then we charged with the bayonet; while advancing with this view, I remember stumbling over the stump of a tree, and immediately afterwards I felt myself to be wounded.[10]

Like Gleig, Moggridge seeks to convey the true experience of war through, rather than poetic verse, a collation of bewildered statements. From these brief examples, it is clear that 'fog of war' was a staple technique of wartime biography. It is therefore unsurprising that the impressionable young Branwell adopted this style, repeatedly reconstructing and applying these dramatic portrayals of war onto his own imaginary battles. Branwell's descriptions of conflict in his and Charlotte's saga are crucial for understanding the changing nature of mass warfare, emulating a new, more personal response to military mentality and encouraging a dramatic response to soldierly combat (Fig. 4.1).

Letters from an Englishman, Vol. VI (1832) is an explicit example of how Branwell imitates the language of 'fog of war'; the narrative mimics the phrasing of the two extracts above. At the end of the tale, Alexander Percy is sentenced to death by firing squad. As the gunshot is fired, Branwell's pseudonym narrator, J. Bellingham, describes a similar 'bright flash' experienced by Gleig in *The Subaltern*: 'My head grew dizzy. The soldieirs [*sic*]

Fig. 4.1   Brontë, Branwell (1829). *Grotesque Figures and Soldiers* (Image used courtesy of the Brontë Parsonage Museum)

fired. I saw a bright flash and loud crash. He fell dead'.[11] Furthermore, like Moggridge's clumsy account of charging, stumbling and wounding in his memoir, Bellingham describes how earlier, in the fictitious Siege of Marchtown, 'showers of balls whizzed constantly through the air a spent bullet struck me I fell amid the feet of a crowd. A torrent of people rushed over me and I fainted'.[12] To add further credence to these 'fog of war' parallels, Branwell pointedly explains his switch in narrative style at the tale's climactic finale, directly addressing his use of the literary technique: 'Here my *historic* relation of this rebellion terminates herefter [*sic*] I can only relate a *narrative* of things in which I was immediatly [*sic*] concerned. to go on'.[13] In other words, Branwell justifies that his war writing must remain in the moment, evoking feelings of immediacy rather than reflection.

'Fog of war' is also used in *A Historical Narrative of the War of Encroachment* (1833–1834). In one section, detailing the disastrous retreat of the Federation against the French, Branwell writes in one quick, energetic paragraph how there was 'the wildest and inextricable confusion', 'a tremendous tempest of rain and wind', and 'tumult and darkness'.[14] These compact examples of 'fog of war' are indicative of Branwell's wider adoption of this literary technique. He consistently emulates the language of military life writing over the course of his Glass Town and Angrian tales until it becomes second nature. The endurance of this writing style is indicative of its consistent popularity throughout the late-Georgian period.

Charlotte uses military memoirs differently from her brother. Rather than applying this literary technique to descriptions of the battlefield, Charlotte reimagines and transposes these intimate, interior monologues onto a domestic setting: she successfully and harmoniously brings warfare into the home. In her Islander series, Charlotte introduces the reader to domestic military life. *Tales of the Islanders, Vol. III* (1830) depicts the siblings' imaginary visit to a 'baking day' at the Horse Guards. Within the Palladian building in Whitehall, they reach a scene where '2 or 3 hundred soldiers were standing busily employed in the manufacture of coarse loaves and cakes',[15] and, later in the story, they find 'the public apartment of the officers [...] A billiard table stood in the middle about which a number [of] uniform officers sat playing or talking'.[16] The soldiers are, ultimately, both masculine and domestic. Charlotte's conflation of militarism and domesticity is propelled to new heights in her later tale 'The Post Office' in *Arthuriana or Odds & Ends* (1833). The story is set completely within a domestic setting, transposing the battlefield from its typical outdoors location into the home. The tale climaxes with a party hosted by Bellingham, which is suddenly gatecrashed by rare lads who immediately throw the gathering into debauched chaos. Charlotte takes this opportunity to satirise military memoirs. Like Branwell, Charlotte uses 'fog of war' to convey the horror of the boisterous scene. When the rare lads 'rush in', the narrator, Samuel Smith, states, 'At this climax of horror I fainted [...] How long I continued in a state of torpor I know not, but when I recovered my sense it was only to behold a scene of unexampled barbarity'.[17] The scene is one of drunken depravity, with Smith at last crawling out from his hiding place at the end of the party. He describes the carnage much like a battle scene; one that strikes vivid parallels to 'fog of war':

> Shattered glass and porcelain, spilt wine, crushed and trampled sweetmeats, broken furniture and torn tapestry met the eye on every side. But that which affected me most and struck a cold chill to my heart were the seven corpse–like and breathless bodies which, huddled each in the blanket that had been made the instrument of murdering them, lay strewed around as if on a field of battle.[18]

In response to this scene, Zamorna looks on whilst Smith states: 'My lord [...] they are not drunk but slain'.[19] Zamorna answers: 'Ah, true [...] slain by Bacchus, chicken–headed fools. They've had a battle with the bottle and wine has worsted them. Thou only, Smith, art escaped alone to tell me'.[20] Although a parody, this sketch allows the reader to recognise Charlotte's intimate knowledge of the language used in military biography and foreshadows the permeation of future wars into the everyday lives of her Angrian characters. Indeed, the military memoirs published in *Blackwood's* were not wholly battlefield orientated. A number included long, vivid descriptions of home, before or after battle. In *The Last Words of Charles Edwards Esq* (1823), the narrator of the same title combines his war tales with reflections on his life as a whole: 'confinement, monotony, coarse society, and personal privation; – the simple fact is worth all the argument'.[21] Moreover, adding to this domestic narrative, 'Letters from the Peninsula No. 3' (1828) describes life at a 'Depot on the Isle of Wight' before soldiers are shipped to the Peninsula. Finally, *Passages in the Life of Francis Flagstaffe, Esq* (1828) opens in a 'well-furnished drawing-room' where numerous guests are discussing youth, education and the rise of the military memoir, inspiring Flagstaffe to write an account of his life.[22]

With so many military personnel within the siblings' Glass Town and Angria, it is unsurprising that Charlotte creates vivid descriptions of the 'domestic soldier'. Whilst Branwell occupied the action of battle, Charlotte manned the household fort, consolidating the new humanisation of the soldier in the late-Georgian public mindset. It is through Branwell's descriptions of vulnerable soldiers in battle and Charlotte's reintegration of soldierly men into their respective societies that demonstrate the significance of the military memoir in both siblings' creativity. Both Charlotte and Branwell act as testimony to the impact of the rise of military life writing, proving that the genre was successful in reorienting the public to imagine the soldier as a human being, capable of relating experiences of war (in regard to both the self and the domestic landscape) to a much greater effect than historical descriptions of the army *en masse*.

Patriotism and the Military Spectacle

> Smart jaunty personages, attired in military costumes, passed [...] with the dashing step and bearing peculiar to their profession. Now and then a superior-looking cavalry officer galloped by on horseback.[23]

The military personnel in Glass Town's capital city, Verdopolis, are highly visible and impressive. As the above extract from Charlotte's *The Foundling* (1833) suggests, the military is, against the backdrop of the metropolis, a glamorous profession. The extract is almost Jane Austen-esque, similar to Lydia Bennet's description of the 'glories of the [Brighton] camp' in *Pride and Prejudice* (1813), which was 'crowded with the young and the gay, and dazzling in scarlet'.[24] This sexualisation of soldiers, as Catriona Kennedy and Gillian Russell have noted, was not an unusual characteristic of late-Georgian Britain.[25] Although Charlotte would not have read Austen at this early stage in her writing life, the alluring pull of military masculinity as a source of patriotism was ingrained in the public imagination: as the previous chapter explored, the birth of military celebrity and its sensationalism in the periodical press was one factor that contributed to a conflation of sexualisation and spectacle. Moreover, artwork emphasised the soldier's sexual allure. James Gillray's *Fatigues of the Campaign in Flanders* (1793)—which depicts women gazing in infatuated awe at a bawdy soldiers' gathering—introduces the soldier as a symbol of sexual worship. As late as 1839, Charlotte was still using this trope: her novella, *Henry Hastings* (1839), depicts her strong female protagonist, Elizabeth Hastings, the precursor to her later famed Jane Eyre, imagining her soldier brother, Henry, as a sexually active soldier figure:

> She realised him in a hundred situations – on the verge of battle, in the long weary march, in the halt by the wild river banks. She seemed to watch him slumber under the desert moon, with large–leaved jungle plants spreading their rank shade above him. Doubtless, she thought, the young Hussar would then dream of some one that he loved; some beautiful face would seem to bend over his pillow such as had charmed him in the saloons of the capital.[26]

Although this is far from an incestuous imagining and more a translation of Charlotte's—and by proxy, the nation's—sexual desires, it is an important indication of the contemporary idealisation of the military body as a romantic fighting body: the average citizen, it appeared, considered soldierhood as a profession of feeling where the spirit of patriotism, mingled with seductiveness, defined the Napoleonic military man.

As well as engaging with the sexual military body, it is clear that the siblings were fixated on the body *en masse* as a broader military spectacle. Although common soldiers are given voices as pseudonyms, the 'common' military archetype is represented as a collective military identity: it is mainly through military display that the full glory of patriotism and military manliness is exercised. Throughout the saga, Charlotte and Branwell repeatedly seize the opportunity to write gushing, highly sensationalised patriotic scenes. From the early Glass Town saga, in which the Genii—representing the four siblings—reign over their colonial army, to the creation of Angria, in which Zamorna is crowned in a lavish ceremony, patriotism is associated with royalty. In 1829, Charlotte exclaims in her *Blackwood's Young Men's Magazine*: 'O may they [the Genii] reign eternally, / In the glory of their might;/ May their armies be victorious, / While they like stars light'.[27] Branwell echoes this patriotic zeal in his 'Anthem of the Coronation' (1834), where the Genii's religious sovereignty has been replaced by what appears to be a more recognisably Christian form of God: 'But God save our King / Joy to him we sing […] Swear while thou her sword shall weild / It shall not be overthrown'.[28] These poems coincide with the rising significance of Britain's national anthem, which rose to prominence in the early nineteenth century.[29] Imitating the imperialist tones of the well-known verse, 'God save the King, / Send him victorious, happy and glorious' along with the now neglected militaristic verse 'O Lord our God arise, / Scatter her enemies, / And make them fall',[30] Charlotte and Branwell write in celebration of the bonds of nation and patriotism at a time when wars were increasingly fought overseas and dissociated from the motherland.

Charlotte and Branwell's poetry become further intertwined with nationhood through their recognition of contemporary military songs. 'God Save the King' is just one melodic example that Mark Philps recognises as 'linked to an unprecedented level of national mobilisation in which music and song played a major role'.[31] Philps argues that the Napoleonic Wars prompted highly politicised, poignant and patriotic oral expression that resonated in concert halls, taverns, streets and other public spaces. Militaristic songs were common, the recent wars generating melodies that covered topics such as heroism, death and the role of women in wartime: one that Paula Guimarās notes Charlotte recognised and responded to.[32] Over the course of the juvenilia, both siblings—although mostly Branwell—composed a number of warmongering anthems at appropriate climactic moments. Branwell's 'Sound the Loud Trumpet', 'Welcome Heroes to the War' and 'History stood by her Pillar of Fame' alongside Charlotte's 'Hurrah for the Gemini', all composed in 1834, are written by Branwell's pseudonym Henry Hastings, the national soldier poet of Angria. To highlight his importance within the Angrian regime, Hastings' 'An Angrian Battle Song' (1836) was sung by 'Our Noble band of Royal Guards' during the final Angrian wars. Each song is deeply patriotic and powerful in its rhetoric. 'Hurrah for the Gemini' attests that through battle's 'blasts we may defy, / Still our flag aloft shall fly'.[33] Furthermore, stirring phrases such as 'Rise Man and Monarch and City and Nation' and 'Shake the shackles from your feet / WELCOME TO THE WAR' in 'Sound the Loud Trumpet' and 'Welcome Heroes to the War', respectively, emphasise the carnivalesque display of overt patriotism.[34] Hastings' channelling of the siblings' militarism not only heightens the fun of the saga, but also conveys important reflections on contemporary feeling. Julie Donovan's reflections on Branwell's poetry and prose touch upon the importance of music in Branwell's conceptions of war and patriotism:

The cohesive, emblematic quality of music to establish feelings of nationhood emerges in the exhortations characterizing Branwell's Angria, some of which are accompanied by Angria's Band of Royal Guards [...] [Branwell's poetry] links the polite and popular genres [...] reinforcing the legitimacy of the Angrian state and justifying the wars in which it takes part.[35]

Within Angria, song is the most explicit form of nationalism. Both Charlotte and Branwell recognised that in order to unify a country, it must be done through the unity of spectacle. Despite living in a post-war period, the siblings were still able to imagine and imitate a wartime spirit within their saga. It is clear that the excitement generated by a romantic age of war had passed the parameters of peace in 1815 and was continuing to resonate well into the late 1820s and 1830s.

Interestingly, the majority of post-war musical spirit andspectacle was revived by the publication of poetry and songs in the contemporary media as complementary material to soldiers' biographical reflections: periodicals sought to document and record the oral culture of the recent past, reflecting on the brotherhood that war offered and reviving the sentimentality of wartime feeling through common soldier culture. In regard to the Brontë family, their recognition and lyrical imitation of a cultural consciousness of military patriotism came from these retrospective verses. A number were published in *The United Service Journal,* giving the young Brontës early exposure to military music and oral culture: between 1827 and 1830, many traditional and Napoleonic military songs were printed alongside other militant material written by soldiers: 'The British Sailor's Song' (1827), 'Les Dragons' (1827), 'The Regiment first coming into a Country Town' (1828) and 'The Soldier's Camp–Song on the Eve to Battle' (1829) are just a few examples that appear between 1827 and 1829. More specifically, poems such as 'The Soldier's Song' (1827), which laments, 'Lo! th'adverse Cheiftains take their stand [...] The sons of Mars, in frequent shock / Oppos'd meet hand to hand [...] O Britain! how sublime thy course, / Brilliant in arms and lore' encompass the themes seen throughout this study: classical influence, Scott-like chivalric warriors and patriotic warmongering.[36] Moreover, the poem 'Spanish National Song' (1829) is echoed in the title of Branwell's poem 'Sound the Loud Trumpet': 'Then sound the loud trumpets, / The standards advance– / Down, down with the tyrant, / And vengeance on France!'[37] Finally, 'Song of Mina's Soldiers' (1830) evokes imagery of Charlotte's character Mina Laury, Zamorna's pre-eminent mistress, who takes on the role of safe-houser and entertainer for Angria's soldiers. In Charlotte's *Passing Events* (1836), Mina is shown entertaining the military elite, many of whom, such as Warner and later General Thornton, become infatuated with her. 'Song of Mina's Soldiers', a ditty sung by the troops during the Peninsular War, is a likely inspiration for Mina's soldierly love triangles: 'We heard thy name, O Mina! [...] Thy name our trumpet, Mina! – The mountain bands are thine'.[38] Overall, as this list has clarified, the siblings had easy access to lyrical war rhetoric: the similarities in language between the juvenilia and published verse indicate that these contemporary publications had a likely role in the saga's imitation of contemporary wartime spectacle.

Branwell regularly ties in the oral tradition of militaristic patriotism with parading, an explicit act of military spectacle. In *A Historical Narrative of the War of Encroachment*, he refers to 'Military Music swelling and. bursting along the lines Accompanied the compact Regiments as they shoaled away out of the square own the great sweeping street and. out of sight mingling in the crowds and darkness'.[39] Again, in *Angria and the Angrians I(a)* (1834), a large military recruitment parade is described: 'All the City of Adrianopolis rose in a wild ferment of excitement and that the spirit which reigned through it was instantaneously dispersed through the whole kingdom'.[40] The parade consists of soldiers in 'their new scarlet uniforms and gilded bells and the caps with their Sun starred from the swagger of the plumed head'.[41] This display of nationalism and sun-soaked symbolism overwhelms the narrator:

> struck by the blaze the perfect flash of gold and scarlet which met my eye [...] The air was filled with one vast flutter of the Angrian banners huge sheets of silken scarlet flung themselves abroad in the breeze. and blazed out in their rustling folds the broad bright sun rising in burnished. gold I felt <instantly> the effect this show produced on me and I well knew the transient enthusiasm which roused me as I beheld. the wind and the marching unroll to the sight on scarlet after scarlet the one single word 'ARISE'.[42]

Branwell's breathtakingspectacle was born from the periodical press. Alongside poetry and song, the spirit of parading was kept alive by military memoirs. For example, Gleig's *The Subaltern* makes reference to numerous parade grounds throughout.[43]

As illustrated by Branwell's showstopper procession, recruitment parades were the most popular and effective form of nationalistic posturing.[44] Numerous stand-alone memoirs published during the Brontës' childhood mention these types of parade, such as *Memoirs of a Sergeant Late in the Forty-Third Light Infantry Regiment* (1835). Although the siblings may not have read these stand-alone accounts, it is likely that they would have been aware of these recruitment methods due to their pervasive nature in British society. The military spectacle was a consistently popular way to recruit impressionable young men. Kennedy explains:

> Recruiting parties put a great deal of effort into creating military spectacles that would convince young men to enlist. Regimental posters in the style of theatrical playbills were pasted up in towns and villages […] This would be followed by a lavish and colourful parade of the regiment's finest recruits decked out in their best uniforms and accompanied by the regimental band. Several soldiers' memoirs cite the allure of these martial displays in prompting them to enlist.[45]

Whereas Branwell was attracted to the extravaganza of this superficial, idealised portrayal of army life, Charlotte's writings shatter this military paragon, often acknowledging the attractive elements of military display yet equally emphasising war's more sinister undertones. In *My Angria and the Angrians* (1834), Charlotte combines violent language with glorified representations of the military spectacle. Focusing on a militaristic country parade, she narrates that the country hall contained 'gilded banners red as blood, so brilliantly vermilion in the lights', yet they were equally 'so gory in the shadows'.[46] Although Charlotte is evidently exhilarated by the imagery of warlike splendour, she also reminds the reader of the horrors that lay dormant and disguised underneath military grandeur. A similar sinister undertone re-emerges in *Passing Events* where Charlotte conjures an atmospheric image of eerie pre-war calm. In the early dawn of the saga's final wars, Charlotte describes a romantic image of a parade at sunset; yet this is overshadowed by the looming toll of minster bells, which are, in turn, overpowered by the firing of guns:

> Night closed on the holy city of Angria! the ecclesiastical city! now alas the depot of war. Former[ly] that ancient town rested quietly among the moors under the shade of the minster, now it seemed but one great barracks. The evening drum, the twilight bugle, sounded from the band of many a regiment. Soldiers & plumed officers were parading the streets where staid civilians formerly walked, the peal of the minster–bells was drownded [*sic*] in the deep boom of the sunset gun.[47]

Passing Events' poignant scene presents, on the one hand, a united, com-
forting vision of the army in the hush of twilight, yet Charlotte's narrative is
punctuated within realistic imagery of war; symbolically, the monotonous
sound of the guns blocks out the sound of the church. This image of
'the calm before the storm' almost parallels Gleig's description of a parade
ground in *The Subaltern*:

> At the first blast I sprang from my bed, and, drawing aside the curtain of my
> window, looked out. The day was just beginning to break; the parade ground,
> into which I gazed was as yet empty, only two or three figures, those of the
> trumpeters, who were puffing away with all their might, being discernible
> upon it; and not a sound could be distinguished except that which their
> puffing produced. The moon was shining brightly overhead; not a breath of
> air was astir; in short, it was just half-past three o'clock and the time of the
> parade was four.[48]

Like Charlotte, Gleig lingers on the pre-war calm the parade symbolised.
Although Charlotte's parade is already in full swing, the tone of Gleig's
extract evokes the same melancholic foreboding of loss mingled with the
beauty of spectacle.

In one instance, Branwell also becomes disenchanted with the collective
military ideal. Towards the end of Angria's war with Frenchysland (1834),
the military turn vigilante, staging a coup in an attempt to save their nation
from the continuous onslaught of the French troops. Whilst overpowering the Verdopolitan government in *A Historical Narrative of the War of
Aggression* (1834), Branwell states that 'the area was choked with plumes
and bayonets'.[49] The military spectacle has become stifling. Branwell ends
his observations with: 'Rumours of the french were thickning [*sic*] and
darkning [*sic*] round us. and it was the Army alone this terrible Army which
could save us'.[50] This brief epiphanic moment shatters the illusion of the
mass military ideal. Branwell's great body of men is depicted as frightening
and undisciplined rather than sun-blazed heroes in well-disciplined parading formations. Branwell's sudden anxiety directed at the army may have
been generated from the more unflattering contemporary commentaries
regarding Napoleonic soldierhood that had, in themselves, borne a legacy.
As Gavin Daly notes:

Wellington characterized British plunder as the product of a soldiery composed of the 'scum of the earth'; a phrase that influenced later military historians in portraying British plunder as the word of a 'criminal' or 'semi–criminal'
class within the army.[51]

Wellington's stereotype filtered through the national media. A pertinent
example lies in an 1807 edition of the *Oxford Review*, which the Brontës
may have read at Ponden Hall. At one point, a contributor brands soldiers
mean; another observes how a soldier has 'peculiar animal qualifications'.[52]
With the murmur of primal soldierly criminality within the British cultural
fabric, Branwell would most likely have been aware of this lower-class make-
up of the British Army, possibly using it as inspiration for this unidealised
scene. Once again, despite showing moments of promise, the full collective
military ideal cannot be achieved. The soldierly mass becomes less glorified
the more war is thrust upon them; it is only through military display that
the army *en masse* can truly be idealised and glorified.

Trauma and Alcoholism

In contrast to the previous section's focus on Charlotte and Branwell's
adoption of patriotic values, this section explores how the siblings' reading
of military memoirs also exposed them to the sinister elements of warfare.
As Ramsey emphasises, the military memoir opened up a 'spectator's reaction to the suffering body'.[53] In other words, trauma emerged as a collective, vicarious experience through the medium of storytelling: although life
writing is not quite the same as fiction, the memoirs promote creativity as a
medium for traumatic expression. Despite belonging to a post-war gener-
ation with no direct links to the military, the siblings' vicarious response to
the media's treatment of damaged psychology, and the harmful substance
abuse used to curb and relieve war's adverse impact, enlightens present-
day readers of the post-Napoleonic suffering that was embedded in social
consciousness and considered a national problem. This final section shows
the ways in which the Brontë siblings became aware of war trauma in a
culture where it was not sufficiently recognised and how they embedded
their acute understanding of this phenomenon within their writings.

TRAUMA

He could not sleep!, his temples prest [*sic*]
To the hard pillow throbbed with pain
The belt around his noble breast
His heart's wild pulse could scarce restrain.
And stretched in feverish unrest
Awake the Great Commander lay [...]
The sods of batle [*sic*] round him welter
In noble blood that morning shed.
And gorged with prey & now declining
From all the fire of glory won
watchful & fierce he lies repining
O'er what may never be undone[54]

Charlotte's insightful poem, 'He could not sleep!' (1837), depicts an anxious Zamorna lamenting over the battle of Evesham, the final battle of the Angrian and Glass Town Civil Wars (1835–1837). Its rhetoric combines both traumatic knowledge and figurative language to close, what Geoffrey Hartman explains as, 'the disjunction between experiencing (phenomenal or empirical) and understanding'[55]; the poem constructs a dialogue of (non)experience to artistically convey knowledge of an experience where literal retellings are not adequate. The traumatic implications of the verse are evident through an initial reading: the uncontrollable, contorted body at war with mundane reality—his belt, a supposed symbolic object of heroism, loops round him in a restrictive circle that intensifies the conflict between objective military performativity and true bodily and spiritual suffering—the sensational language, the confusing nature of recalling the battle 'welter' and the painful poignancy of reflection. The cyclical nature of the poem emphasises Zamorna's disquiet: the rhyming pattern brings tight closure whilst the content runs on in a form of traumatic enjambment as the wounds are reopened anew. Charlotte also uses single words that create a paradoxical tension within themselves. The present participle verb, 'repining', indicates a form of physical stillness and contradicts his active, fraught mind, which is, in itself, a form of battlefield. The final line that laments 'O'er what may never be undone' consolidates the Freudian nature of traumatic repetition; the need to repeat becomes compulsive and involuntary.

Although Freud's *Beyond the Pleasure Principle* (1920) is usually considered within the context of the First World War, which aligned twentieth-century understandings of trauma alongside mechanised, modern warfare, a Freudian reading can be convincingly applied to Zamorna's plight. As Freud recognises the pressure towards death categorically named as the death drive,[56] so too does Charlotte's protagonist, fixating on instances of military violence and finality in the face of mortality. This Freudian reading is strengthened by the frequency of its patterns within the juvenilia. Like his sister Charlotte, Branwell also recognised the same compulsive, cyclical motions through his anti-hero, Alexander Percy. In *The Wool is Rising* (1834), the tale begins with Percy locking himself away 'harassed' by the late war and poetically lamenting his reflection of:

> Man dashed on man. in trampled blood. [...]
> Where am I. dashed into the hold upon a strangling foe
> All men and smokes and shouts above
> a writhing wretch below.[57]

Again, this description depicts a soldier focusing on a moment of mortality as he replays the incident through a similar repetitive psychological framework.

In the context of the early nineteenth century, the siblings' comprehension of war trauma appears remarkable. In a broad sense, Jill Matus's research on pre-Freudian, emerging understandings of trauma throughout the mid-late nineteenth century emphasises the importance of literature as a tool for understanding how psychological suffering embedded itself in the social fabric of Victorian Britain. Although Matus's research concentrates on a much later period than the focus of this book (1850–1886), her assertion that trauma is, in fact, 'dependent less on scientific discoveries than it is on cultural attitudes and ideology' complements this book's focus on the vicarious psychological impact of war on the Brontës and, more broadly, the British nation.[58] Moreover, Matus' assertion that 'literary narratives helped to shape and influence the cultural practises and narratives out of which the concept of trauma developed' can also be applied to this earlier period.[59] The importance of literature as a cultural outlet for trauma has been repeatedly applied to history: notably, critics such as E. Ann Kaplan, Ron Eyerman, Christopher Herbert and Jeffrey E. Alexander have considered the role of cultural trauma in reaction to notorious historic movements and moments ranging from slavery to war crime.[60] As will become clear, the Brontës' comprehension of an unmedicalised condition was indicative of how 'shock' encoded itself artistically into post-Napoleonic culture rather than how it evolved into a scientific taxonomy.

There is a lack of scholarly engagement with the presence of cultural trauma in post-Napoleonic Britain. As summarised by Roger Luckhurst, it was not until the later nineteenth century when trauma drifted from the 'physical to the mental realm'.[61] This justifies the rationale for Matus' study of mid-late nineteenth-century trauma narratives. Although Matus acknowledges the legacy of suffering subjects in the history of literature, her focus on the 'extensive traffic between literary and psychological discussions' best suits the emerging published studies in psychology and memory science in the latter half of the century.[62] Alongside the rising awareness of trauma as a psychological condition, Matus uses literature as a primary cultural document in order to posit nineteenth-century ideas of shock and trauma within their contemporary moment, using them as a precursor but not directly leading to the evolution of Freudian psychology. The Brontë siblings' juvenilia was written in the 1820s and 1830s, before any convincing medical engagement with war trauma. As Chris Cantor states, at the beginning of the century the phenomenon was open to 'a bewildering array of labels and concepts'.[63] Although there is an established legacy of literature that stresses the connection between war and Romantic suffering throughout the late eighteenth and early nineteenth centuries,[64] individual medical trauma and collective cultural trauma are still underresearched and ambiguous avenues of research.

A number of historians and psychologists have traced the etymology of war trauma through medical accounts and memoirs.[65] It is only recently that there has been a trend in psychological journals to retrace and rediagnose battle disorders. For example, Edgar Jones and Simon Wessely have published their retrospective case studies of nineteenth-century war trauma and chronic fatigue syndrome in the *British Medical Journal* and *Journal of Psychiatry*.[66] These re-evaluations, however, seem alien when situated within the contextual discourse of the period. Laurent Tatu and Julien Bogousslavsky note how several conditions during the Napoleonic Wars were associated with *le vent du boulet*, literately meaning 'wind of a cannonball'.[67] Similarly, Philip Shaw's research on Robert Hamilton's *The Duties of a Regimental Soldier* (1787) exposes a new line of enquiry into the history of sensibility and emotions. Hamilton's observations of lower-ranking soldiers suffering from 'nostalgia' are, according to Shaw, symptomatic of a desire to be released from all forms of regimentation in late eighteenth-century society.[68] From a purely medical standpoint, Shaw recognises the frequent application of nostalgia—*nóstos*, meaning 'home-coming', and *álgos*, meaning 'pain' or 'ache'—as a medical term to diag-nose soldiers' mental maladies when their spirits weakened and they became 'gripped by fantasies of return [to the home]'.[69] These abstract concepts of war trauma indicate an absence of formal categorisation within medi-cal terminology, yet an underlying recognition of its effects within medical spheres.

By proxy, it is likely that the British public would have been aware of the Napoleonic War's detrimental effect on their male population as more soldiers returned to Britain. Charlotte—the eldest surviving Brontë sibling, born in 1816—would have grown up in a nation recovering from wide-scale conflict, the Battle of Waterloo ending decades of overseas conflict just one year previously. Moreover, it is evident that Haworth housed some of the returning veterans, although there is no evidence to suggest that the children ever came into contact with them. As Simon Bainbridge notes, 'The returning soldier was a troubling figure, socially, psychologically and politically'.[70] Aside from highlighting poetry by writers such as Robert Burns and William Wordsworth that sentimentalises the unsettling image, Bainbridge uses James Gillray's print *John Bull's Progress* (3 June 1793) as a representative portrayal of the damaged soldier and his disturbing presence in Britain's post-war landscape: in the final image, a redcoat returns to his domestic realm as 'an emaciated cripple with only one eye and one leg' as his family cower from him.[71] Although this is a physically traumatic portrait, more reminiscent of the disturbing impact of war on a nation more generally, it is indicative of a wider theme of suffering that permeated the arts of the late eighteenth and early nineteenth centuries. As the second chapter of this book shows, leading canonical authors that the Brontës enjoyed, such as Byron and Scott, focused on war within their literature and touched upon soldiers' suffering and the tragic aftermath of conflict: Byron's *Childe Harold's Pilgrimage* (1812–1818) was a direct response to the carnage of Waterloo, and Scott successfully displaced the horrors of contemporary warfare on to the past in his *Waverley Novels*. As Chad May summarises, Scott's novels present the 'traumatic repetition of the past [...] as blood that cannot wash away'.[72] Although the Brontës may not have come into contact with any examples of war first-hand, the seeds of suffering had been implanted in popular consciousness and, as is now explained, continued to reverberate in the literary currents of the post-war era through the media material the siblings were reading and emulating.

Both Charlotte and Branwell construct a convincing pathology of trauma in their early writings with a number of their military characters undergoing life-changing psychological alterations as a result of their battlefield experiences. In Charlotte's *Lily Hart* (1833), the Duke of Fidena's post-battle manner is described as 'cold and distant',[73] and in *A Leaf from an Unopened Volume* (1834) Alexander Percy's son, William Percy, explains: 'When the battle was o'er and the victory was won I have frequently felt much depressed in spirits'.[74] In Branwell's *A Historical Narrative of the War of Encroachment*, his pseudonymous soldier-historian, John Flower, repeatedly comments on the traumatic imprint the current war with the French is having upon the minds of the Verdopolitan soldiers: the troops were 'harassed' and 'exhausted'.[75] Elaborating further, he narrates that Alexander Percy's 'fatigue combined with Bodily and mental irritation and weakness reduced him to temporary delusion'.[76] Additionally, Flower himself is shown to undergo mental disturbances in the space separating battles:

> between cold and excitement I could not close my eyes to sleep. but lay listning to the dying sounds of encampment and the troops. all. marching to their resting ground [...] a wild and delightful feeling came over me [...] About Midnight when I had almost composed myself to sleep with. rousing and depressing thoughts I heard some one speak. not far off the voice was soft. and solemn. and recited. with repressed feeling the following lines. [...] 'Why does my spirit chilled and drear, In this dark vision linger here.'[77]

Many keywords in this section—cold, excitement, wild and depressing—are indicative of Flower's psychological upheaval. Branwell's recognition of 'repressed feeling' and a need for composure is also significant, exposing that Flower's struggles are specifically psychological. Collectively, the quoted passages all engage with explicit rhetoric of mental suffering ranging from depression and irritation, to delusion and exhaustion. Although the concept of war trauma was still abstract, the juvenilias' repeated, compulsive discourse of trauma exemplifies the anxious mood of post-Napoleonic Britain. With the social and cultural landscape of Britain conveying the visible effects of war on male soldiers' psychology, it is understandable that the Brontës—and the broader nation—had the potential to understand early conceptions of war trauma whilst lacking first-hand engagement in battle.

Another source for understanding early nineteenth-century conceptions of war trauma lies in the rise of the military memoir. Charlotte and Branwell read and engaged with particularly traumatic memoirs in their early writing lives, such as Gleig's *The Subaltern* and Malcolm's *Tales of Field and Flood*. Each tale provides graphic descriptions of male suffering and mortal delusions. Conjuring similar imagery to Flower's haunting lament, 'Why does my spirit chilled and drear, In this dark vision linger here',[78] in *Tales of Field and Flood*, Malcolm laments over his psychological wounds: he can 'find no respite from the pains of memory but in slumbers of the night, when, in the land of shadows and of dreams, they meet with the distant and the dead![79] In an earlier section of the memoir, Malcolm recalls sitting by a campfire, listening to the story of his friend, Captain Douglas, who experiences vivid hallucinations in the catacombs of Paris whilst passing through the capital on his way to England after a short peace in 1814:

> a cold perspiration broke over my whole body; I stood fixed to the spot in a trance of horror and despair. A thousand hideous forms of darkness seemed to flit past me, – the skulls with their eyeless sockets, seemed to scowl upon me, – my head became dizzy, – the vaults, with their skeleton pillars spun me in the dance of death, – my brain reeled, and I fell against a crashing pile of mortality, where I swooned away.[80]

Gleig also recounts a similarly horrifying experience in *The Subaltern*. After discovering a watchman in a swoon, the narrator takes him back to a safe house where he recounts how he saw a 'troop of devils dancing beside the water's edge and a creature in white [...] groaning heavily'.[81] He then swears that a 'dead man sat up, and stared at him in the face'.[82] This is not the only time Gleig summons imagery of trauma in his writings. Three years later, his tale, *The Brothers*, was published in the 1829 edition of the annual *Friendship's Offering*, which the Brontë family owned. The story tells the tale of two brothers, Allan and Donald, who go to fight in the Peninsular War. Allan eventually dies in the Siege of St Sebastian, leaving his brother devastated:

> Donald Cameron has never been himself from that moment. When first discovered [after the battle] he was in a state of pitiable idiocy; and he has continued ever since a melancholy maniac. Whether he will ever recover his senses, God alone can tell; but I confess that I entertain but slender hopes of any such desirable communication [...] Donald Cameron was soon afterwards sent home as incurable; and the probability is, that he still continues the

victim of a calamity, by far the most distressing of all to which frail humanity is liable.[83]

Such an explicit traumatic ending to a story is likely to have affected the siblings.[84] Use of language such as idiocy, melancholy maniac and recognition of incurability provides a convincing portrait of war trauma, adhering to ambiguous understandings of 'nostalgia' as associated with both fatality and severe melancholia. With the nation's new focus on the individual soldier, it is clear how memoirs such as these contributed to a national, cultural trauma that the siblings responded to. Although the extent of memoirs published after Waterloo is suggestive of a form of cathartic process that soldiers embarked upon to come to terms with the recent wars, the disturbing nature of passages such as these would have served only to heighten the anxiety, sensations and, in part, understandings, of Britain's reading public. The Brontës, as part of this shared experience, would also have been absorbed into this widespread fixation with soldiers' mentality.

In addition to these biographical recollections further highlighting Charlotte and Branwell's exposure and subsequent reaction to traumatic military literature, the memoirs' conflation of trauma and the supernatural gives further insight into a particular tale of Charlotte's, *The Green Dwarf* (1833). Charlotte's tale recounts Napoleon's nightmarish dream of death and repentance, where he is led by his French General, Jean-Charles Pichegru, around the streets of Paris in an effort to mitigate his unjust war ethics.[85] On their travels, Napoleon is confronted with terrible visions, seeing 'fine female figures' who 'wore on their heads garlands of the most beautiful flowers, but their faces were concealed by ghastly masks representing death's heads'.[86] Like Douglas' experiences in the catacombs, this shocking encounter with death imagery causes Napoleon psychological upheaval: he fell 'into a fit of catalepsy, in which he continued for the whole of that night and the greater part of the next day'.[87] Catalepsy is often described as a nineteenth-century symptom of trauma. Martin Willis recognises its presence in Charlotte Brontë's later work, *Villette*—'In catalepsy and dead trance I studiously held the quick of my nature'—[88] and in George Eliot's *Silas Marner* (1861), where it is representative of alienation and suffering.[89] In the case of Charlotte's Napoleon, the alarming experience of witnessing the wider repercussions of mass civilian murder dictated by his own hands causes his psychological state to malfunction as he attempts to process his own actions.

Although Napoleon's traumatic state is dramatised, and the tale is a highly moralistic, metaphorically encoded work, Charlotte's early prose consolidates the siblings' preoccupation with descriptive—occasionally hyperbolic—literary material that contributed to a cultural trauma. The multitude of soldiers introduced within this section demonstrates that trauma, despite being an underdeveloped line of medical enquiry, was viewed by the siblings as a national problem. The intensity of the post-war moment, prompting an explosion of national anxiety, life writing and predisposition for sentimentalism, fed into the siblings' psychology and writings. Their Glass Town and Angrian saga encapsulated the contemporary spirit of suffering and prefigured modern, progressive understandings of medicalised, traumatic discourse. The following section remains grounded within an early nineteenth-century contextual framework, building on notions of trauma and suffering as a national problem by focusing on its destructive counteragent, alcohol. It will become clear that, although trauma itself remained an abstract concept in the social and literary imagination, alcoholism was considered a sister-disease to this undisclosed psychological anguish, intoxicants used as a coping mechanism that numbed and comforted. Although trauma, in a modern sense, is difficult to visualise in an early nineteenth-century historical context, the next section demonstrates how its presence latently manifests through the pervasive image of the soldierly drunkard, a figure caught between the stereotyped labels of comedic reveller and degenerative traitor.

Alcoholism

Entwined with Charlotte and Branwell's highly developed, intuitive understanding of military trauma was an equal awareness of the coping mechanisms that accompanied it. Embedded in the saga, alcoholism manifests alongside trauma, contributing to the downward trajectory of the military characters, with a vice-like lure that promised comfort and release. It is unsurprising that the characters in Charlotte and Branwell's kingdom turn to alcohol, the expression of trauma through conversational, emotional means strictly prohibited. In *A Leaf from an Unopened Volume*, Alexander Wellesley, the elder twin son of Zamorna and Mary Percy, is scorned for potentially harbouring a traumatic response to war:

> Once, I remember Ravenswood […] in the Emperor's presence asked me if my nerves were shocked and my courage shaken by the terrors of war.

> I scorned to answer him, but the Archduke curled his lip contemptuously, and Stanley smiled like a fiend and Seymor laughed and, by heaven, my father frowned not on them but on me.[90]

In this passage, Charlotte brings to the fore the tensions that resided between contemporary binaries of hero worship and personal experience. Current scholarship has engaged with these tensions, debating the consensus that an ideology of militant masculinity was foundational to an overarching national character. Whereas Linda Colley describes the Napoleonic period as an age of 'heroic endeavour and aggressive maleness',[91] Kennedy contests this, claiming that the image of the 'diminished figure of the war-weary subaltern officer' problematises this generalised statement.[92] These opposing images are further consolidated with, on the one hand, the contemporary championing of patriotic, masculine titans such as Wellington and, on the other, the rise of the sentimental military memoir, which, as Tom Mole states, confirmed the 'disjunction between the sublime heroism of military glory and [...] forms of virtuous suffering'.[93] Indeed, one must only look at the military memoirs published in *Blackwood's* to see expositional statements of fear and shock, identical to what is being chastised above. In *The Last Words of Charles Edwards Esq*—which records the autobiography of a sailor before he commits suicide—the narrator remarks:

> There are limits to the capacity of human endurance. We are none of us so far from insanity as we believe ourselves. My temper had suffered in the course of these conflicts, a shock from which, I think, it never afterwards recovered.[94]

Charlotte, in her wide spectrum of reading, evidently picked up on the pressures and unstable expectations of militant masculine conduct and national honour. Wellesley's display of homosocial bravado and paternal disappointment is indicative of a moment of change: there is a collective recognition of trauma, yet an anxiety that a newer honest attitude is substituting traditional notions of heroism.

The most prominent character caught between these ideologies is Branwell's protagonist, Henry Hastings. After initially holding the title of 'Angria's National Poet'—writing highly patriotic, Royalist verse seen in the previous section—Hastings joins Zamorna's army in the Angrian and Glass Town Civil Wars (1835–1837). After Zamorna's subsequent defeat, however, and losing his Royalist ideologies, he deserts for the Republican enemy, kills his superior officer and becomes a gambler and alcoholic. When Zamorna finally returns to power, Hastings has degenerated into a 'penniless and proscribed debauchee' on the run from the law.[95] He is described in *Angria and the Angrians V(b)* (1838) as 'miserably sick in both body and mind' usually found drinking in a 'sordid inn' whilst revelling in his own shame.[96] This traumatic image is strikingly different from the Hastings initially introduced in *Angria and the Angrians I(d)* who was formerly an enthusiastic and determined young soldier and patriotic poet: 'I was Now a SOLDIER. and I was going to WAR. war had always [given] to me a glorious and mighty feeling'.[97] Despite his promising start, the wars of 1835–1837 had reduced him to a severe state of suffering: 'indeed his shattered nerves were horrified by the fears of soldiers or police [...] he was utterly sick and every limb shook with tremor'.[98] In *Angria and the Angrians IV(e)* (1837), his new-found dependence on alcohol to combat war trauma is revealed to its full extent; Hastings is shown to be reliant on intoxicants in the midst of the Battle of Evesham, the last battle of the civil wars:

> Brandy in plenty [...] I was so weak and in such a fever that I could hardly sit on my horse so to mend the matter I filled the canteen with liquor and swigged till I forsook the beast for the ground and then vomiting violently I gained relief enough to mount once more beholding my comrades giving way to Intoxication and leaving their ranks to plunder.[99]

Hastings is not, however, the only soldier that falls into irredeemable intoxication. Alexander Percy, Branwell's other protagonist and alter ego, is a conflation of violent instinct, alcoholism and trauma. Percy's history is described in Branwell's *The Life of Alexander Percy* (1834–1835), which recounts a series of traumatic events he endured as a child and young adult. Unpopular with his adult associates, he is described to be excited, delirious and cruel, whilst his mother finds him 'passionate revengeful and headstrong'.[100] Throughout the saga, his repeated, almost obsessive need for rebellion, spurred by his love of violence and radical political views, shapes him into a demonic figure who becomes weaker and more unstable through each passing war-torn year of the siblings' saga. In Branwell's post-war *Angria and the Angrians IV(j)* (1837), after he loses power for the final time to Zamorna, he recalls how he lay:

> day and night for a month after month companionless in the voiceless and burning forests of Stumphasland [*sic*] stupefied by the effects of my own wanton insanity and tormented by the agonys of a breaking constitution.[101]

Dejection and frustration are characteristic responses from Percy, whose plans of rebellion are frequently thwarted by the hero of the saga, Zamorna. Regularly, his involvement in personal as well as national war is shown to stimulate high levels of trauma. Indeed, in Branwell's *Real Life in Verdopolis, Vol. II* (1833), after losing in a physical fight with Zamorna, he orders himself to a pothouse to 'forget' the day's events, drinking himself into 'a state of bestial intoxication'.[102] In the same tale, after brawling, he leaps 'headlong into the blazing fire'.[103] Fuelled by alcohol, he terrorises Angria and his closest circle. In Charlotte's *The Foundling*, he even holds his wife at knifepoint:

> Rogue [Percy] arrived – He entered the room with a firm step, but Zenobia shuddered to see the savage light of intoxication glancing in his at all times fiery eye —— threatens Zenobia 'you shall not die the easy death of having your brains blown out. No! I'll thrust this sharp blade slowly through you, that you may feel and enjoy the torture.[104]

This brutality and thirst for alcohol-fuelled violence are unleashed through the relentless wars that rage through Angria. Repeatedly changing sides, Percy's mental cycle of instability and self-abuse makes him a highly dangerous and merciless military figure. His physical and mental state exemplifies trauma and its ramifications, his character an embodiment of Glass Town and Angria's sinister vices and repetitive mental upheaval caused by uprising and war.

As their depictions of Percy and Hastings suggest, the Brontë siblings appeared to recognise that alcoholism was commonplace in the military. Drinking in the army was a symbol of conviviality. This alliance was consolidated in the songs that emerged in the late-Georgian period and were published in the military journals the siblings read. For example, in keeping with this section's previous focus on Napoleonic oral culture—a song, 'The Soldier's Camp-Song on the Eve of Battle', appeared in *The United Service Journal* in 1829. The poem explicitly highlights how alcohol was an antidote in the face of mortality:

> Comrades! take a last farewell,
> To–morrow comes the fight,
> And ere it end shall toll the knell
> Of many a living wight!
> Then drain the glass,

> Ere pleasure pass –
> And then! – strike home for England's right![105]

Scott Myerly notes that 'For most soldiers, alcohol was the only escape; it was customary in many regiments to pay the men once a month, and most would then drink until their money was gone […] it was the army's greatest discipline problem.'[106] Unremittingly, the soldier characters in the Brontë juvenilia are drawn to drink. In *Angria and the Angrians I(d)*, Hastings is shown to smile 'to see a troop of Bloodhounds who stood by […] all tossing off their horns of Brandy without a hair'.[107] In Charlotte's later tale, *Henry Hastings*, an anonymous lady in a tavern declares to Charles Townsend that 'they [the Angrian soldiers] do their duty drunk better than most men do sober'.[108] Alcoholism, although treated humorously in these latter excerpts, is flagged as a customary habit for military personnel. The shocking yet casual and necessary role it plays throughout the saga is indicative of how deeply embedded the problem was in the contemporary Georgian army.

As Myerly suggests, the emergence of the military memoir exposed a more sinister and disturbing justification for alcoholism during the Napoleonic Wars. Although the role of alcohol was multifaceted, many soldiers turned to it to escape the mundane elements of army life; the memoirs the Brontës read provide evidence that drinking was used as a coping mechanism for traumatic experience. In *The New British Novelist* (1830), the narrator describes how:

> the road smelt most offensively of *gin*, from the staving casks, and the evacuation of their contents. Coupled with the sight of here and there, a corpse (some of them females) which had been trampled to death, the influence was sickening.[109]

In another section, detailing a medical station within a farm in St Jean, the narrator conflates both the bawdy legacy of drink with the contemporary threat to national masculinity. The memoir remarks how all five hundred patients had managed to succumb to intoxication: 'Five hundred men drunk!! Quite ridiculous […] besides, it was a *physical* as well as a *moral* impossibility that so many helpless beings […] should join in one general scheme of disorder and hilarity'.[110] It is clear from this extract that alcohol and masculine morality are incompatible; the men are reduced to a primal, vulnerable state of being. Gleig's *The Subaltern* also indicates that alcohol is a cause of chaos and impropriety. In one instance, after the fighting has calmed, the troops break into civilian houses: 'The houses were every where ransacked [...] wine and spirit cellars were broken open, and the troops, heated already with angry passions, became absolutely mad by intoxication. All order and discipline were abandoned'.[111] Later, the narrator describes how several casks of brandy had to be 'poured out into the street, as the only means of hindering our men from getting drunk, and saving ourselves from a defeat'.[112] This lack of self-control in military men positions the siblings' soldiers in the midst of this contemporary social problem. The memoirs generate a confusing image of alcoholism, one that was, on the whole, critiqued and denounced by the narrators—who, significantly, do not take part in the revelry—but was also spoken of in a humorous, bawdy fashion. Its damage to masculinity, physically, professionally and morally, is emphasised, yet, it appears to have been an essential antidote to trauma, numerous men participating in a shared method of coping that guarantees memory loss and a collective rebellion against disciplined murder. Although the siblings allow their armies to indulge in this bawdiness *en masse*, Hastings, unlike these multitudes of men, becomes the symbolic image of its dangerous undercurrent, his painful deterioration representative of contemporary life writing's subtle, traumatic connotations.

In line with military memoirs' depictions of alcohol as a coping strategy, post-war Angria conveys an astonishing insight into post-battle mentality and substance abuse. Two characters are of particular significance, General Hartfield, ex-commander in Zamorna's army, and Macara Lofty, ex-ally of both Ardrah and Alexander Percy. Firstly, Hartfield, after suffering the hardships of war, is dealt another blow when he is rejected and demoted from Zamorna's inner circle for attempting to court Zamorna's mistress, Mina Laury. Whereas once held in high esteem by the Angrian gentry, he is shown in Charlotte's *Mina Laury* (1838) to be a dishonoured alcoholic: 'most people thought the noble General's brains had suffered some slight injury amid the hardships of the late campaign'.[113] Furthermore, he also uses drink to 'drown' the feeling 'about his heart'.[114] In a similar manner, Lofty, once Verdopolitan Chancellor of the Exchequer under Ardrah's brief reign in 1837, is presented as a decadent opium addict in Charlotte's *Stancliffe's Hotel* (1838). It is supposed the substance quickly transforms his emotions from misery to happiness, elevating the seemingly unjustifiable 'gloom' and 'despair' whose 'power I could no longer withstand'.[115] Although the latter does not concern alcohol specifically, these presentations of post-war military men follow the same pattern of using

mind-altering substances to disguise the trauma wrought by the previous war-stricken years. Indeed, this complementary dependence and abuse
would have been common knowledge to the British public, returning soldiers still under its influence. It may be possible that the young Brontës
were exposed to these returning addicts, their father having initiated the
founding of Haworth's temperance society.

Despite the obvious plight of the alcoholic soldier, little sympathy
appears to extend to damaged military men both in the saga and in reality. Articles and tales about military punishment used as a warning against
alcoholism in the army appeared in periodicals and memoirs the Brontës
read. For example, in 1824, a *Blackwood's* article titled 'Punishments in the
Army' (1824) expressed a contributor's view of the various punishments
executed by European armies.[116] Additionally, in *The New British Novelist*,
the narrator describes a graphic scene of corporal punishment:

> several men had come drunk to duty [...] He stood close to the culprits,
> refused all solicitations on the part of their captains [...] and seemed as anx-
> ious that every lash should be well laid on, as if the whole safety and credit
> of the British army depended upon it.[117]

Charlotte and Branwell emulated this unsympathetic attitude demonstrated
in contemporary accounts and commentaries. Charlotte's early tale, 'Military Conversations' (1829), demonstrates her early understanding that
alcohol abuse was a negative feature of the military and deserved punishment. In her story, Wellington orders the drunken Alexander Hume
Badey to be taken to the 'triangle', a frame to which a soldier was bound
in order to be flogged.[118] Furthermore, Branwell carries out a form of
alcohol-based punishment in his early tale *Letters from an Englishman, Vol.
V* (1832). A passage depicts the military trial of Alexander Percy's associate,
O'Connor, accused of drinking on duty and causing victory to be delayed.
Although his sentence is to be sent to the guillotine he refuses: '"Wretch!
Villain! I will never suffer such a death I will die like a soldier". So saying
he snatched a pistol from the table and directing it to his heart fired and
fell'.[119] O'Connor, like so many real-life Napoleonic soldiers, appears in a
tragic bind, caught between a requirement to exhibit natural strength and
the temptation to use alcoholism as a method of coping.

It is clear that the Brontë siblings understood and related to war trauma and the harmful coping mechanisms that were used to ease its damaging effects. Their raw, unedited narratives, written nearly a century before war trauma was recognised in present-day medical vocabulary, can be used as tools for understanding nineteenth-century responses to the impact of total war upon a nation. Like Britain, the inhabitants of their fictitious kingdoms attempt to cope and rebuild from the devastating effects of conflict. The siblings recognised that alongside persistent Angrian conflict, there would be recurring psychological instability, many of their eminent military characters carrying with them profound mental scars through the majority of the saga. Despite their age and surroundings, the siblings were capable of producing recognisable and important portrayals of trauma and alcoholism.

The Brontë juvenilia act as one example of just how deeply the rhetoric and feeling of war were embedded in the cultural fabric of Britain. War was still on the tip of the media's tongue, and the siblings were engrossed in and inspired by the excitement of war stories at a time when there was relative peace and uneventfulness. The Brontë siblings' replication of both the patriotic and traumatic elements of the previous war establishes them as important voices in an alternative history of war. Despite their unusual position as exceptional child writers, their sensitivity to a wide range of discussions about abstract and underresearched mental maladies of the period give present-day readers an intuitive insight into the kind of material that the British reading public were exposed to and the potential for that public to understand and respond to the complex and highly traumatic experiences soldiers had been subjected to.

NOTES

1. "The Military Sketch Book," *Blackwood's Edinburgh Magazine*, June 1827, 838.
2. Neil Ramsey, *The Military Memoir and Romantic Literary Culture 1780–1835* (Farnham: Ashgate, 2011): 51.
3. There are instances of other military memoirs published before this boom. They did not, however, achieve the same popularity as those relating to the Napoleonic Wars. Ponden Hall housed a number of these early examples, including, William Thomson's *Military Memoirs Relating to Campaigns, Battles and Stratagems of War Ancient and Modern* (1803) and Robert Beatson's *Naval and Military Memoirs of Great Britain, from 1727 to 1783* (1804).

4. In *The Military Memoir and Romantic Literary Culture 1780–1835*, Ramsey notes that a large portion of nationwide readers interested in military memoirs were women. In Moggridge's "Letters from the Peninsula No. 1 The Battle of Barrosa," published in *Blackwood's*, the author directly addresses the gruesome tastes held by women.

5. John Malcolm, *Malcolm's Tales of Field: With Sketches of Life at Home* (Edinburgh: Oliver & Boyd, 1829): 89. Transcribed by Charlotte Brontë and reprinted by Christine Alexander in Charlotte Brontë, "Anecdotes of the Duke of Wellington," *Brontë Studies*, 35.3 (2010): 211.

6. Ibid.

7. B., "The Editor's Portfolio," *The United Service Journal and Naval Military Magazine*, July 1829, 110.

8. Brontë and Alexander, "Anecdotes of the Duke of Wellington," 213.

9. George Gleig, "The Subaltern," *Blackwood's Edinburgh Magazine*, March 1825, 294.

10. Moggridge, "Letters from the Peninsula No. 1. The Battle of Barrosa," *Blackwood's Edinburgh Magazine*, June 1827, 702.

11. *WPB I*: 238.

12. Ibid., 236.

13. Ibid.

14. Ibid., 390–391.

15. *EEW I*: 149.

16. Ibid., 150.

17. *EEW II*: 214–215.

18. Ibid., 215.

19. Ibid.

20. Ibid.

21. Charles Edwards, "The Last Words of Charles Edwards Esq.," *Blackwood's Edinburgh Magazine*, October 1823, 397.

22. Francis Flagstaffe, "Passages in the Life of Colonel Flagstaffe," *Blackwood's Edinburgh Magazine*, March 1828, 273.

23. *EEW II*: 53.

24. Jane Austen, *Pride and Prejudice*, ed. Vivien Jones (London: Penguin, 1996): 224.

25. See Gillian Russell's chapter "The Army, the Navy and the Napoleonic Wars," in *Blackwell's Companion to Austen*, ed. Claudia L. Johnson and Clara Tuite (Malden: Blackwell, 2009): 261–271. See also Catriona Kennedy, *Narratives of the Revolutionary and Napoleonic Wars* (London: Palgrave, 2013).

26. *Angria*: 289.

27. *EEW I*: 63.

28. *WPB II*: 206.

29. See Jeffrey Richards, *Imperialism and Music: Britain, 1876–1953* (New York: Palgrave, 2001).
30. See transcriptions in Richards, *Imperialism and Music*, 91.
31. Mark Philps, *The British Response to the Threat of Invasion* (Aldershot: Ashgate, 2006): 173.
32. See Paula Guimarãs, "Dramatizing the Conflicts of Nation and the Body: Displacement in Charlotte and Emily Brontë's Poetry of Home and Exile Dualities," *A Journal of English and American Studies*, 38 (2008): 63–77.
33. *EEW III*: 289.
34. *WPB I*: 204, 252.
35. Julie Donovan, "The Poetry and Verse Drama of Branwell Brontë," in *A Companion to the Brontës*, ed. Diane Long Hoeveler and Deborah Denenholz Morse (Oxford: Wiley Blackwell, 2016): 217.
36. Lieut–General Dirom, "The Soldier's Song," in *The United Service Journal*, December 1827, 438.
37. "Spanish National Song," *The United Service Journal*, December 1829, 696.
38. "Song of Mina's Soldiers," *The United Service Journal*, March 1830, 414.
39. *WPB I*: 374.
40. *WPB II*: 253.
41. Ibid., 201.
42. Ibid. Elaborate uniforms were popular during the Napoleonic Wars. Scott Myerly notes the officers' uniforms were 'trimmed with gold or silver button lace'. Scott Myerly, *British Military Spectacle: From the Napoleonic Wars Through the Crimea* (Cambridge: Harvard University Press, 1996): 19.
43. Parades are mentioned eleven times in the extracts published in *Blackwood's* throughout 1825.
44. Another popular time to parade was in the event of a military funeral. Branwell describes a military funeral in his *A Historical Narrative of the War of Aggression*. Hodding Carter writes, 'No doubt the Napoleonic Wars and victories enhanced the appeal of military funerals. By the 1830's frequent notices of funeral parades appeared in the newspapers'. See Hodding Carter, *The Past as Prelude: New Orleans, 1718–1968* (Gretna: Tulane University, 1968): 227.
45. Kennedy, *Narratives of the Revolutionary and Napoleonic Wars*, 38.
46. *EEW III*: 256.
47. Charlotte Brontë, "Passing Events," in *Five Novelettes*, ed. Winifred Gérin (London: The Folio Press, 1971): 60.
48. Gleig, *Blackwood's*, 279–298.
49. *WPB I*: 426.
50. Ibid., 434.
51. Gavin Daly, *The British Soldier in the Peninsular War* (London: Palgrave, 2013): 14.

52. *The Oxford Review or Literary Censor, Vol. I*, January–June 1807, 295, 582.
53. Ramsey, *The Military Memoir and Romantic Literary Culture 1780–1835*, 13.
54. *PCB*: 234.
55. Geoffrey H. Hartman, "On Traumatic Knowledge and Literary Studies," *New Literary History*, 26.3 (1995): 540.
56. See Sigmund Freud, *Beyond the Pleasure Principle* (London: Penguin, 2003).
57. *WPB II*: 29.
58. Jill Matus, *Shock, Memory and the Unconscious in Victorian Fiction* (Cambridge: Cambridge University Press, 2009): 185.
59. Ibid., 12.
60. See Ann E. Kaplan, *Trauma Culture: The Politics of Terror and Loss in Media and Literature* (New Brunswick: Rutgers University Press, 2005), Jeffrey C. Alexander, Ron Eyerman, Bernard Giesen (eds.), *Cultural Trauma and Collective Identity* (Berkeley: University of California Press, 2004), and Christopher Herbert, *War of No Pity: The Indian Mutiny and Victorian Trauma* (Princeton: Princeton University Press, 2008).
61. Roger Luckhurst, *The Trauma Question* (Abingdon: Routledge, 2008): 3.
62. Matus, *Shock, Memory and the Unconscious in Victorian Fiction*, 9–10.
63. Chris Cantor, *Evolution and Posttraumatic Stress: Disorders of Vigilance and Defence* (London: Routledge, 2005): 9.
64. See Philip Shaw, *Suffering and Sentiment in Romantic Military Art* (Farnham: Ashgate, 2013).
65. For an interdisciplinary study of trauma and cultural memory, see Nigel Hunt, *Memory, War and Trauma* (Cambridge: Cambridge University Press, 2012).
66. See Edgar Jones and Simon Wessely, "Case of Chronic Fatigue Syndrome after Crimean War and Indian Mutiny," *British Medical Journal*, 319 (1999): 1645–1647. Also see Edgar Jones and Simon Wessely "Psychiatric Battle Casualties: An Intra- and Interwar Comparison," *The British Journal of Psychiatry*, 178 (2001): 242–247.
67. J. Bogousslavsky and Laurent Tatu, *Hysteria: The Rise of an Enigma* (Basel: Karger, 2014): 157.
68. Philip Shaw, "Longing for Home: Robert Hamilton, Nostalgia, and the Emotional Life of the Eighteenth–Century Soldier," *Journal for Eighteenth–Century Studies*, 39.1 (2014): 25–40.
69. Ibid.
70. Simon Bainbridge, *British Poetry and the Revolutionary and Napoleonic Wars* (Oxford: Oxford University Press, 2003): 43.
71. Ibid.
72. Chad May, "The Horrors of my Tale: Trauma, the Historical Imagination, and Sir Walter Scott," *Pacific Coast Philology*, 20.1 (2005): 98–116.

73. *EEW II*: 303.
74. *EEW II*: 331.
75. *WPB I*: 381, 391.
76. Ibid., 392.
77. Ibid., 393–394.
78. Ibid.
79. Malcolm, *Malcolm's Tales of Field: With Sketches of Life at Home*, 160.
80. Ibid., 50.
81. Gleig, *Blackwood's*, 197.
82. Ibid.
83. George Gleig, "The Brothers," in *Friendship's Offering: And Winter's Wreath—A Christmas and New Year's Present* (London: Smith, Elder & Co., 1829): 58.
84. Erin Nyborg argues in her PhD thesis that this memoir influenced Anne Brontë's war poem, 'Z – a's Dream', written in 1846. See Erin Nyborg, *The Brontës and Masculinity*, PhD thesis, University of Oxford (2016): 88.
85. The tale is structured in a similar format to Charles Dickens' *A Christmas Carol* (1843), predating Dickens' story by eleven years.
86. *EEW II*: 142.
87. Ibid.
88. Charlotte Brontë, *Villette*, ed. Margaret Smith (Oxford: Oxford University Press, 2008): 109.
89. See Martin Willis, "*Silas Marner*, Catalepsy, and Mid-Victorian Medicine: George Eliot's Ethics of Care," *Journal of Victorian Culture*, 20.3 (2015): 326–340.
90. *EEW II*: 331. Alexander Wellesley, also known as Victor Frederick Percy Wellesley is the heir apparent of Angria and Wellingtonsland. He is the elder twin son of Zamorna and Mary Percy described in the *My Angria and the Angrians* coronation.
91. Linda Colley, *Britons: Forging the Nation, 1707–1837* (New Haven: Yale University Press, 2005): 303.
92. Kennedy, *Narratives of the Revolutionary and Napoleonic Wars*, 128.
93. Tom Mole, *Romanticism and Celebrity Culture, 1750–1850* (Cambridge: Cambridge University Press, 2009): 13.
94. Edwards, *Blackwood's*, 409.
95. *WPB III*: 216.
96. Ibid., 215.
97. *WPB II*: 280.
98. *WPB III*: 216.
99. Ibid., 111.
100. *WPB II*: 107.
101. *WPB III*: 165. The island's secluded location and overwhelming population of 'retired' Verdopolitans make it a popular destination for Percy to reflect upon his actions and, more ominously, plot his evil schemes.

102. *WPB I*: 301.
103. Ibid., 311.
104. *EEW II*: 87–88.
105. G. O. G., "The Soldier's Camp Song on the Eve of Battle," *The United Service Journal*, November 1829, 593.
106. Myerly, *British Military Spectacle*, 73.
107. *WPB II*: 323.
108. *Angria*: 204.
109. *The New British Novelist; Comprising Works of the most Popular and Fashionable Writers of the Present Day, Vol. XXII* (London: Colburn and Bentley, 1830): 136. For Charlotte's citation see *EEW I*: 89.
110. Ibid., 174–175.
111. Gleig, *Blackwood's*, 295.
112. Ibid., 458.
113. *Angria*: 23.
114. Ibid.
115. Ibid., 73.
116. "Punishments in the Army," *Blackwood's Edinburgh Magazine*, April 1824, 399–406.
117. *The New British Novelist*, 174–175.
118. *EEW I*: 148.
119. *WPB I*: 216.

CHAPTER 5

Colonial Warfare

In 1823, the First Anglo-Ashanti War broke out in the Akan interior of the Gold Coast between the native Ashanti tribe and the British colonisers. Despite this being a relatively low-key war compared to the recent Napoleonic Wars, the exotic location of these conflicts captured the attention of the British public and tapped into contemporary British attitudes towards race. Building upon the siblings' fascination with the documentation of, and response to, transnational warfare, this chapter demonstrates how Charlotte and Branwell engaged with this early nineteenth-century fascination with racially aggravated war and chose to adopt the racist discourse of the period: this, in turn, would feed into their violent representations of race in their later works. Their engagement with colonial warfare emphasises their interest in war in a generalised sense: they did not just focus on one (primarily white) war, but instead recognised the diversity of wars being fought in their contemporary period and sought to evaluate, understand and replicate different types of battles and soldiers within their early writings.

Much scholarly criticism has been devoted to the Brontës and race. Notably, Heathcliff in Emily Brontë's *Wuthering Heights* and Bertha Mason in Charlotte Brontë's *Jane Eyre* (1847) have been the focal point of postcolonial scholarship: throughout the late-twentieth and early twenty-first centuries scholars have read for colour clues in the texts and have applied it to a range of criticism from historicism, to orientalism and feminist theory. This is not to say that the juvenilia have not been acknowledged in this theoretical trajectory. Christine Alexander explores

© The Author(s) 2019

E. Butcher, *The Brontës and War*,

https://doi.org/10.1007/978-3-319-95636-7_5

the role of the Brontës' exotic African setting in her chapter in *The Child Writer* (2005), where she states that 'Angria becomes a place for the libido'.[1] Susan Meyer in *Imperialism at Home* (1996) offers a more detailed analysis of the siblings' Ashanti chief, Quashia Quamina, noting that their (especially Charlotte's) representation 'reflects her participation in conventional nineteenth-century British conceptions of African inferiority'.[2] She achieves this by presenting Quamina as lustful, lascivious and a drunkard, and by using etymology to immediately convey her racism: Quashia, which derives from the epithet 'Quashee', is a nineteenth-century racist slur equivalent to 'nigger'. Meyer also asserts that the 'King of the Blacks', as Charlotte defines him, becomes a symbolic figure for Charlotte's own rage at the hands of society's gendered oppression.[3] In short, race became a way in which Charlotte dealt with her own social standing, a theme that carries through to her later texts, such as *Jane Eyre*.[4]

Mary Jean Corbett contributes to this argument of inequality and otherness by summing up the role of blackness in the juvenilia: 'colonized adoptees have little or no access to narrative voice or agency'.[5] Prefiguring the later Brontë writings that grapple with problematic marginalised figures, Quamina has been classified as an early outsider, his racial and hyper-masculine otherness often compared to Emily's later male protagonist, Heathcliff.[6] What if, however, this racial analysis extended to a wider backdrop of colonial warfare? If the lens is shifted so that racial discourse can be tied into the siblings' broader interest in warfare, it may become clear how their racial prejudices formed against a broader canvas of Anglo-African racial conflict, which they sought to understand and reconstruct.

This chapter is divided into four sections. The first two present the historical context that inspired this colonial military strand of the juvenilia. As well as engaging with the exotic, military material the siblings read from a young age, these sections prevent scholarly discussion from focusing on purely racial representation (in a broad sense) and seek to contextualise Charlotte and Branwell's attitudes towards race through canonical/media-based accounts of war and the contemporary, conflicting construction of the romantic/violent warrior myth. These two sections also argue that the Brontës were part of a rhetoric of racism; their interest in war is taken to a new extreme that aligns them with a sensational racially-militant moment. Bearing this in mind, the following section builds a necessary discussion of the Brontës' engagement with race and Christianity, addressing their lack of engagement with the nineteenth-century missionary movement alongside their problematic social status as parson's children. Finally, the chapter ends with a redemptive discussion of military fatherhood, tying together ideals of war and masculinity by exploring the role of Wellington and Zamorna as both domestic fathers and public fathers of their nations. Through militaristic tensions between white and black, this section's varying perspectives reaffirm Charlotte and Branwell's interest in war and violent masculinity but also add a colonial context to this book: light is shed on how the siblings' struggled to justify the ethics of war and come to terms with its disastrous consequences.

BUILDING THE WARRIOR SAVAGE

In her introduction to *Tales* (2010), Alexander mentions that the siblings' African prejudices originated from a conflation of fiction, geographical books and periodicals.[7] Their broad representations of exoticism derived from a childhood love of *Arabian Nights* (1706) and James Ridley's *Tales of the Genii* (1764), which would have introduced the young siblings to tropical locations in faraway places that were riddled with the myths, romances and stereotypes imprinted upon the Orient. Additionally, it is also likely that they would have read non-Asiatic tales, such as Daniel Defoe's popular adventure novel, *Robinson Crusoe* (1719), which was saturated with contemporary nineteenth-century prejudices: Defoe's narrative is permeated by racial intolerance and bigotry, a colonial discourse that is mimicked in the Brontës' juvenile descriptions.

The siblings' representation of Africa is constantly in flux. It is well acknowledged that their early romantic descriptions of the African landscape owe much to *Nights*. Charlotte and Branwell's Glass Town poetry contains orientalist imagery: in her poem 'The Glass Town' (1829), Charlotte writes that the 'crimson light / above the horizon glows / tinting all nature with the bright / gay colours of the rose / and over all the eastern sky / the robe of twilight gray / is heaving up the heavens nigh'.[8] Like *Nights*, however, tension between beauty and danger is evident throughout the siblings' early juvenilia. War between good and evil shatters illusions of the landscape's beauty and exposes the true evil of the Orient: this image of evil comes in the form of the desert. The Brontës would likely have read of the enchantress who transformed 'a populous and flourishing city' into a desert in *Nights*'s 'The Story of the Three Calendars'.[9] In 'The Story of the Young King of the Black Isles', an old man asks a traveller: 'what brought you to this desert place [...] to see these beautiful trees one would imagine it was inhabited, but it is a dangerous place to stop long in'.[10] These stories mark the desert as a cursed place. It is unsurprising, then, that the Brontës designated the Ashantis' settlement as one of danger and destruction. Whereas Charlotte describes the Ashanti dwellings in *Two Romantic Tales* (1829) as a 'wild, barren land, the evil desert',[11] Branwell writes in 'Ode on the Celebration of the Great African Games' (1832) how the beauty of summer is projected on 'the deset [*sic*] drear and grim' where 'famine and war foretell and mortal misery / All these the blighters of the varied year / All these and more than these before my eyes appear / Yes more far more a horrid train'.[12] Thus, before the siblings even considered their present-day influences, a link between exotic topography and evil in the form of otherness had already been engrained into their imaginations.

Tales in *Nights* were a vital source that taught Charlotte and Branwell how to blend war with the fantastical. As Robert Irwin writes, 'Centuries and wars were confounded in tales which tended to stray into fairyland and their topographical edges'.[13] War became incorporated into *Nights* through the ages (most notably in the later Egyptian revisions). For example, 'The Tale of Omar bin al–Nu'uman' and 'History of Gharib and his brother Ajib' are derived from independent epics circulated in the medieval Arab world that were, in turn based on a conflation of the Arab-Byzantine Wars and the twelfth-to-thirteenth-century jihad against the Crusaders. It is clear then how an ancient legacy of war, orientalism and the fantastical entered Haworth parsonage and acted as a canonical template upon which the Brontë siblings could build. Like these exotic tales that drew from the colonial warscape around them, the Brontës subsequently drew from the commentary of current affairs, recorded by correspondents from othered lands.

Aside from these likely canonical influences, the Brontës' reading of their local newspapers kept them up-to-date with the 'skirmishes' occurring in the Anglo-Ashanti colonial narrative. The family read about the British defeat at the hands of the Ashanti in 1824, which was reported in the *Leeds Mercury* and *Intelligencer*.[14] Snippets of information recurred throughout the 1820s but waned towards the end of the decade before peace was temporarily reached in 1831. By then, however, racially aggravated discourse had been firmly engrained in the siblings' imaginary landscape and characterisation. Although most pieces of information published in the papers were small updates on the conflicts, a number of articles contained emotive bias that may have contributed to the siblings' perceptions of the tribes. For example, on 16 November 1826, *the Leeds Intelligencer* ran an article that not only alluded to an engagement that involved 25,000 Ashantis but described the warriors as 'imposing and determined'.[15] Previous articles drew from the contemporary shock that the Ashantis contradicted previous preconceptions of African savagery. On 13 May 1824, a commentator noted that Ashanti was 'at present the powerful and civilized nation in Africa'.[16] Instead of this being a compliment, however, the remainder of the article is filled with prejudice; their leaders are 'despotic' and the army had an 'overbearing spirit which is the characteristic of victorious barbarians'.[17] Bearing in mind these rumblings of resentment, it is clear why the Brontës aligned themselves with the general public's opinion. Like chapter three of this book, which discusses the contemporary respect for, yet dislike of, Napoleon, the same can be said for the population of Ashanti. Although they did, in fact, impress and intrigue the British population with their civilised structure, their otherness and violent temperament made them appear both threatening and detestable.

More than newspapers, however, this book returns again to contemporary memoirs published in periodicals as a key source for the siblings' engagement with colonialism and warfare. Much like the previous chapter's discussion of Napoleonic memoirs—which were, in themselves, rich in their illustrative insights regarding overseas military climates—travel memoirs of Africa published in periodicals such as *Blackwood's* and *Fraser's Magazine* inspired the young siblings. Like the military memoir, the colonial memoir allowed the British reading public to visualise foreign terrains yet also distance themselves from menacing and unfamiliar representations of the 'dark continent'. It is well known that the foundations of the siblings' African kingdom can be traced back to a copy of *Blackwood's*, published in June 1826, which contained an article by James McQueen, a geographer and manager of a sugar plantation,[18] and a map of Dixon Denham and Hugh Clapperton's explorations of 'darkest Africa'. What has not previously been discussed, however, are the latter's military connections. Both Denham and Clapperton had successful military backgrounds. Denham was a Royal Welsh Fusilier and close companion of the Duke of Wellington, and Clapperton was an experienced naval officer who saw much active service during the Napoleonic Wars. In a *Blackwood's* article titled 'Geography of Central Africa' (1826), reviewing their *Narrative of Travels and Discoveries in Northern and Central Africa* (1822–1824), the military focus of Denham and Clapperton's narrative is unavoidable. Despite their intention for the memoir to act as a comprehensive geographical study of an underresearched continent, the travelogue is laced with conflict and military conquest. After leaving Clapperton at Kouka, Denham writes how he marched southwards with Barch Gana, a 'negro general', on a 'slave-catching' expedition.[19] Moreover, when Denham reaches Mora, the capital of Mandara, a description of a mountain range is interrupted by a local conflict: 'At this point the combined forces of the Arabs, Bornou, and Mandara, were defeated and driven back'.[20] As these examples demonstrate, although the purpose of this text may have been to educate readers about African geography, it is clear that soldierly eyes are devouring the landscape of Africa and their words are delivered in a militant discourse.

It is within these periodicals that the Brontës' racist attitudes were consolidated. In 'Geography of Central Africa' once again the negative topography of the desert is used to accentuate the otherness of its inhabitants. The *Blackwood's* reviewer of Denham and Clapperton's journals highlights a section that skilfully posits the broad population of indigenous African peoples amongst 'barrennes and sterility', branding them 'miserable, rude, ignorant, barbarous'.[21] This was not an uncommon assertion. In another *Blackwood's* article titled 'British Settlements in Western Africa' (1829), a contributor echoes the mixed respect and warlike threat voiced in the local media about Ashanti: 'it is a powerful and barbarous country'.[22] Even the annuals that were housed in the parsonage use casual racial stereotyping that allude to the violent potential of the foreign other. In the 1829 edition of *Friendship's Offering*, which the family owned, Richard Howitt's poem 'The Truant' references the 'savage beasts, and men as wild, / That herd in foreign lands'.[23] Overall, it is clear that the journalism the siblings engaged with was infiltrated with racial slurs and militant dialogue, whilst, in contrast, other publications such as *Nights* offered an idealised exotic mythology and topography. The siblings were caught in a colonial, rhetorical bind of both attraction and repulsion.

(RE)BUILDING THE ASHANTI ARMY

In the Brontë juvenilia, it is the Ashanti who commit the most shocking and brutal war crimes of all villainous parties. Branwell's *Angria and the Angrians I(b)* (1834) demonstrates the siblings' emulation of contemporary prejudices. Whilst crossing the Calabar river, Branwell's pseudonym, John

Flower, is anxious about straying into 'dangerous ground' as the Ashantis' 'savage and relentless cruelty was well known'.[24] Unlike the Brontës' reimaginings of the Napoleonic Wars, the wars between the colonisers and the Ashanti are purely two-dimensional: the wars are without consideration of humanity or feeling. The siblings project contemporary savage imagery onto their fictitious Ashanti tribe by making their war tactics as grotesque as possible. Out of the two siblings, the bulk of colonial war writing was taken up by Branwell, who—like with his Napoleonic material—commits to locating himself on the battlefield to write his epic, detailed saga.

Branwell evidently relished his chance to let the violent elements of his imagination run wild. The Ashantis' brutal methods of warfare are encapsulated in the slaughter of Dongola, the desert frontier between the Angrian and Ashanti territories. In *Angria and the Angrians I(d)* (1834), Henry Hastings, Branwell's war poet narrator, describes a scene where the Angrian army arrives and discovers the repulsive aftermath of the massacre:

> hung suspended almost over my head a raw and bloody corpse. the skin flayed off. the gore blackened over the carcase [*sic*] and the throat severed with a ghastly gash stretching from ear to ear [...] There Nailed upon close rows of wooden crosses reared up along the side of the fort and houses I beheld more than 200 Dead Bodies of men with the scalps torn from their heads and their mouths skewered up with knives and the dried gore hanging in the black lines from their livid sides In the midst of the area. a heap of several hundred carcases their heads chopped of and piled at random among them and all burnt and blacked by a fire which had been kindled round them, diffused through the air a dreadfully singed and putrid smell.[25]

This is one of the most explicit descriptions of war's brutality in Branwell's juvenilia. Although the language is hyperbolic, the imagery is powerful and visually stimulating. It is clear that Branwell *felt* and could tune into the sensations of battle: racism became a powerful expedient by which Branwell could play with the taboo elements of war to the extreme. The climactic ending of the description builds a clear picture of the rancid smell of bodies, immersing the reader in these disturbing visuals.

A description of Fort Enara in this same tale equally demonstrates the Ashantis' brutalism. When Hastings reaches the fort, he 'beheld 9 Blackened Negroes dangling on gibbets over the parapet a stern spectacle and calculated to strike due terror on the prowlers of the desert. I confess they struck terror into me too'.[26] Unlike his transmogrification of the Napoleonic Wars, which was more subtly concerned with the mechanics of 'civilised', Western military strategy and domestic/psychological impact, Branwell's writing here is pure sensation. Although his relentless battle scenes are typically a stream of consciousness that explicitly emphasise the violence of battle, Branwell's descriptions of Ashanti warfare are taken to a new level. This emotive, visual imagery of barbaric Ashanti battle tactics was, however, not uncommon in the public consciousness. British citizens would have been familiar with the highly overdramatised accounts of Ashanti warfare that were published in periodicals and stand-alone journals. In fact, the quoted battle scene above is similar to that described in a *Blackwood's* review of Thomas Edward Bowdich's *Mission from Cape Coast to Ashantee* (1819). Describing the Yam custom, a festival where slaves are sacrificed at the discretion of the chiefs, Bowdich's account explains how 'At one of these inhuman butcheries, the executioners wrangled and struggled [...] the right hand of the victim was lopped off, and the sawing of his head was most cruelly, if not wilfully prolonged'.[27] Similarly, Bowdich's follow-up text, *An Essay on the Superstitions, Customs, and Arts, Common to the Ancient Egyptians, Abyssinians, and Ashantees* (1821), declares that it was custom to throw:

> a lacerated jaw, a ghastly head or a bloody weapon of the conquered enemy before the king; and in battle, the reeking heads of the slain are hurried into the rear to be pressed by the foot of the reclining general.[28]

As this passage implies, it is perhaps the Ashantis' unrelenting methods of warfare that construct them as the most warmongering and savage of the entire saga's military groups. Cannibalism was seen as an extreme barbaric activity, contemporary writings deeming it the most repulsive of all crimes. Its presence in African warfare rituals was seen as a point of national concern: on 21 May 1823, Parliament described the act as 'perpetrated only by man in the lowest and basest form of the savage state'.[29] Cannibalism as a means of military strategy invigorated the imaginations of the siblings in their fictitious accounts of savage warfare. Two striking examples appear in Branwell's *The History of the Young Men* (1830–1831) and *Angria and the Angrians I(d)*. In the former, Branwell describes the aftermath of the initial wars after the Twelves land in the Ashanti Kingdom. After the death of Cheeky, Gravey and Cracky, the remainder of the soldiers are reported to have been taken by the natives who 'retired to a small distance from the capital and there horrid to relate roasted and made a feast of them'.[30] Following this, Crashie implores the Genii: 'to root from the earth these infamous monsters who have so horridly slain and feasted on thy favoured warriors [...] who are stretched pale and mangled round these fires'.[31] Similarly, in *Angria and the Angrians I(d)*, the carnage wrought by the massacre of Dongola is reported by Hastings to contain 'corpses flayed alive the Burnt Bodies and half eaten flesh and gnawed and scattered bones'.[32] These repeated references to cannibalism only perpetuate the Ashantis' role in the text as aliens and enemies.

Charlotte, although less graphic in her descriptions of Ashanti warfare, also makes known the Ashantis' repulsive deeds in her later work *Stancliffe's Hotel* (1838). William Percy describes a scene of cannibal butchery: 'A soldier had been missing some days from his regiment stationed at that place. His remains were at length found in a neighbouring jungle, hideously mangled, and displaying all the frightful mutilation of negro slaughter'.[33] It is through these horrifying descriptions that the siblings were able to convey the prejudices displayed in contemporary writings. By vicariously participating in the most inhumane of acts, the siblings were able to justify the repeated Ashanti massacres, attempting to liberate Africa from its primitive danger and restore civilised justice. In addition, Branwell's, and to an extent, Charlotte's interest in and imitation of exaggerated graphic descriptions of mutilation and slaughter allowed them to explore the brutal extremes of militant masculinity and, moreover, the depths of human nature. In restricting the readership merely to themselves, both siblings could disregard any need to write with propriety. Early on, their imaginations and writings were firmly grounded in the lurid language of published war reportage. Their mimicry of racism consolidates their position as recorders of their society's prejudices, creating an alternative history where the conflation of war and race is pushed to an extreme.

The subject of cannibalism was prolific in the periodicals the siblings read. In James McQueen's *Blackwood's* article 'Civilisation of Sierra Leone' (1827) the natives were said to rip people open 'across the belly, and plunging their hands in, they tore the heart from its skat [*sic*], pouring the blood on the ground'.[34] Alongside this, these 'ferocious' Africans were 'but yesterday engaged in eating human flesh'.[35] Although this article—amongst others—lingered upon these details for impact, most African-based articles the Brontës engaged with casually associate indigenous African people with this ritual. In 'Geography of Central Africa' the reviewer briefly mentions that the Yem Yem is inhabited by cannibals,[36] and in an 1826 *Blackwood's* article titled 'London' the contributor compares the massacres of Greece to Ashanti cannibalism.[37]

Real-life accounts were not, however, the only source that exposed the Brontë siblings to cannibalism. It was also present in the canonical works that initially introduced the siblings to tales of otherness. Daniel Defoe's *Robinson Crusoe* depicts the narrator, Crusoe, as shipwrecked on an unknown island inhabited by cannibals. This popular text repeatedly condemns the islanders throughout the narrative, consistently referring to them as 'savage wretches' and stressing to the reader their ignorance of and inferiority to the Christian faith. In terms of their cannibalism, which is much like Branwell's description in *The History of the Young Men*, Crusoe describes at one point how 'the savage wretches had sat down to their inhuman feastings upon the bodies of their fellow-creatures'.[38] Another example sees Crusoe observing 'nine naked savages' sitting around a fire. After they depart he inspects their camp: 'This was a dreadful sight to me, I could see the marks of horror which the dismal work they had been about had left behind it—viz. the blood, the bones, and part of the flesh of the bodies, eaten and devoured by those wretches with merriment and sport'.[39] As well as *Robinson Crusoe*, the siblings would have been acutely aware of Sinbad's voyages in *Nights*. 'The Fourth Voyage of Sinbad the Sailor' is set on a cannibal island where the natives attempt to fatten up Sinbad and his crew with the intention of eating them. After refusing to eat, Sinbad 'fell into a languishing distemper, which proved my safety; for the blacks, having killed and eat my companions, seeing me to be withered, lean, and sick, deferred my death till another time'.[40] After escaping this island, the end of the extract sees him sailing past the 'Isle of Bells' whose 'inhabitants are so barbarous, that they still eat human flesh'.[41] It is these problematic accounts of estranged, indigenous tribes that encouraged the siblings to imagine and incorporate some of their most violent battle imagery in the entire saga.

Circulating descriptions of the Ashantis' sadistic battle tactics spewed emotive, violent language that was emulated by the siblings in their writings. The levels of explicitness in these representations indicate a different type of reaction to warfare that was present in the contemporary late-Georgian public domain. Whereas the journalism surrounding the Napoleonic Wars displayed a multidimensional level of feeling towards the recent wars, and thus was explored in different ways by the Brontë siblings, the publications the Brontës read concerning the Ashanti were already conclusive: the Ashantis were evil and their interior warrior selves, expanding out to their war tactics, were rotten. Conflating racism with war—a situation where the human character emits the most intense levels of human savagery and brutality—would instil an alternative 'military spectacle' in the British reading public and left the siblings with one overpowering option: to construct their writings as a private propaganda machine, using racist rhetoric to present the rituals of colonial war as the most radical form of violence.

This is not to say, however, that Charlotte and Branwell did not find equal delight in the military spectacle of the exotic. Whilst condemning the Ashanti as a tribe, the siblings, especially Charlotte, did not entirely abandon the lure of Africa's beauty in their descriptions of the Ashanti military *en masse*. Whereas Branwell, as usual, focused mainly on battlefield combat, Charlotte, at points, chose to engage with the more romantic, cultural elements of overseas warfare and exoticism: in one instance she provides a brief yet informative account of Ashanti war costume. In *The Green Dwarf* (1833) she vividly illustrates the enemy emerging through the mountains:

> About day break they arrived at a wild mountain pass, through which might be seen a vast plain where the allied forces of the Moors, Ashantees, and Abyssinians were all drawn up in battle array. It was a gorgeous but terrific spectacle, as the first sunbeams flashed on that dusky host and lighted up to fiercer radiance their bright weapons and all the barbarous magnificence of gold and gems in which most of the warriors were attired [...] a young horseman sped suddenly to the front of the African array [...] the golden diadem glittering on his forehead had revealed the arch–rebel, Quashie.[42]

This spectacular image is most likely inspired by a description of an Ashanti war captain in *Bowdich's Mission from Cape Coast Castle to Ashantee*. A reviewer transcribes this section in *Blackwood's*:

> The dress of the captain was a warcap, with gilded rams–horns projecting in front, and the side extended by immense plumes of eagle feathers. Their vest was of red cloth, covered with fetishes, or chains in gold and silver, intermixed with small brass bells, the horns and tails of animals, shells, and knives, long leopard tails hung down their backs. They wore loose cotton trowsers [*sic*],

with immense boots of dull red leather, and fastened by small chains to their eartouch, or wait–belts. A small quiver of poisoned arrows hung from the right wrist, and they held a long iron chain between their teeth, with a scrap of Moorish writing affixed to the end of it. A small spear was in the left hand, covered with red cloth and silk tassels. Their black countenances heightened the strange effect of this attire, and completed a figure scarcely human.[43]

It is also possible, if the Brontës were able to acquire a copy of Bowdich's text, that they would have seen a coloured plate titled 'Ashantee captain in his War Drefs' (1819) depicting a figure draped in plumes, tassels and bells of various colours.

This general image of an exotic warrior appealed to Charlotte. Her description is permeated with words that emphasise the gold and grandeur of his dress. Her artistic representations problematise the violent narrative of the Ashanti and demonstrate the continued lure of exoticism on the popular imagination. The materialistic focus of the Ashanti warrior in these extracts—Charlotte's focus on gold and gems and, likewise, *Blackwood's* on cloth and silk—constructs an aesthetic, Caucasian view of the Orient: these narratives build on the mythical legacy constructed by centuries of story-telling filtered from culturally engrained stereotypes. In sum, the siblings are engaging with two separate narratives, militant fearmongering racism, and the exotic warrior myth. It appears that, as seen before with the Brontës' engagement with Napoleonic material, the siblings were transfixed by both the paradoxical glamour and violence of war; they were lured into the stereotypical rhetoric of colonialism—both violent and romantic—that reverberated through their present age.

The Problem with Christianity, Race and War

It is clear thus far that the Brontës conformed to contemporary British stereotypes that derided the Ashanti natives and—more broadly—the foreign other. It is unsurprising, then, that all wars fought between the natives and colonisers are racially orientated. The siblings would have been aware of white communities living in Africa, a contributor to *Blackwood's* expressing in 'The British Settlements of Western Africa' (1829): 'As many of your readers, doubtless, are aware, the Ashantees have at various times annoyed our different settlements on the Gold Coast'.[44] Similarly, 'Geography of Central Africa' also reported a case of 'white natives' living in Goobeer who:

were not negroes, but a different race, and fair in their complexion [...] descendants of the COPTS, the ancient inhabitants of Egypt [...] He says also, that they are all 'Free Born;' and, of all his provinces and his subjects, that they, the population of the Goobeer, are the 'most warlike;' which may readily be accounted for from the wars which they have, through so many ages, been compelled to wage in order to maintain their independence.[45]

Although not considered white in a Western, Caucasian sense, these accounts of white settlers would have opened Charlotte and Branwell's minds to alternative representations of Africa. In the latter passage, although this 'race' is warlike, the contributor's emphasis on their fair complexion and freedom of mobility implants a message that other communities affiliated with British values can thrive in this climate. In addition, the Copts' values derive from a Christian tradition: although separated from mainstream Christianity, the ethno-religious group is the largest Christian denomination in North Africa. To the British public, and by proxy the Brontës, this image would have provided a positive reinforcement of the international doctrines of Christianity and equally allowed readers to visualise a white, warlike, free empire that triumphed over the threat of Ashanti rule.

Despite the evident presence of Christianity in Africa and the Brontës' saga, what remains striking about the Brontë juvenilia are the siblings' decision to disregard Christian ideals of compassion and conversion in favour of war. Considering their social position as parson's children, the former narrative would seem a likely underlying theme in the siblings' exploration of the dynamic between the colonisers and colonised. Evidently, in the case of St. John Rivers—Jane's missionary cousin in Charlotte's *Jane Eyre*—missionary figures were not evaded in the Brontës' writings and were seen as powerful figures of respectability within the Brontë universe. Instead, the Brontë juvenilia substitutes conversion for conflict.

The traditional desire to spread the Christian message overseas—and the more specific desire to convert African natives—was overtly present in the publications the early nineteenth-century public and, specifically, the Brontës read. Although traditional Christian roots have been traced back to Africa as early as the fourth century—and, evidently religious sects such as the Copts were present in Africa—Edmund Abaka notes that it is the sustained missionary activity from the early nineteenth century that led to political and commercial expansion in Africa, and, as a consequence, attitudes towards missionaries softened.[46] Epitomising the missionary tradition, Thomas Pringle and Josiah Conder's statement in *Narrative of a*

Residence in South Africa (1835) reflects the rise of the nineteenth-century Christian mission in Africa.

> The Native Tribes, in short, are ready to throw themselves into our arms. Let us open our arms cordially to embrace them as MEN and as BROTHERS [...] Let us subdue savage Africa by JUSTICE, by KINDNESS, by the talisman of CHRISTIAN TRUTH.[47]

Some two decades previously, in *Blackwood's*, the author of 'Geography of Central Africa' acknowledges that Britain had 'spent millions in our attempts to civilise and to benefit Africa'.[48] The longevity of Britain's colonial civilising mission implies that, when the Brontës were writing, the religious partnership between the church and the colonies was firmly engrained in the public and media mindset.

Futhermore, it is clear that Christianity exists within the Glass Town and Angrian saga.[49] This book's subchapter 'Walter Scott' demonstrates the siblings' interest in and engagement with the Crusades, which helped construct an image of the religious militant warrior. Charlotte's poem 'The Red Cross Knight' (1833), penned by her young Zamorna—the Marquis of Douro—is a nod to the history of the Christian colonial message: 'To the desert sands of Palestine, / To the kingdoms of the East, / For love of the cross and the holy shrine, / For hope of heavenly rest, / In the old dark times of faintest light / Aye wandered forth each Red Cross Knight'.[50] The flamboyant language in this poem encourages the violent spread of religion: 'The cross [...] Their weapon and their shield; In vain the lance and scymitar'.[51] Charlotte's conflatory language of religion and militarism promotes an early message within the saga that divinity does not come without its links to patriotism and war. As the saga evolves into Angria, Charlotte's *My Angria and the Angrians* (1834) further promotes this message with military anthems and rallying war speeches scheduled at the christening of Zamorna's twin sons. In the concluding prayers, the militant gathering collectively declares: 'We praise Thee O God! We acknowledge Thee to be the Lord, all the Earth doth worshipp Thee'.[52] In Branwell's *Angria and the Angrians I(a)* (1834), Zamorna, after his coronation as King of Angria states:

> 'your Sky shall never be clouded your Land shall never be invaded your sun shall never set and your reign shall never end will be and shall be the determination and care of your King Arthur Wellesley [Zamorna] [...] and

by this I will abide so help me God'. The Earl of Northangerland [Alexander Percy] stepped darkly forward and stretching forth his hands he cried in the loudest and most warlike voice. God save the King.[53]

In *Angria and the Angrians I(d)*, Alexander Percy produces a similar stirring speech urging the people of Angria to go to war: 'Make yourselves the Glory of Creation I merely ask you Now. through your country attend to my bidding &. up and ARISE!'.[54] This combination of religion and militarism culminates in the image of the Christian, muscular warrior forcefully spreading his religion through the godless lands of Africa. Although the term 'muscular Christianity' was not technically coined until the mid-Victorian age, the juvenilias' pre-empting of muscular Christian ideals some twenty years earlier foreshadows the importance of this masculine—and future colonial—model throughout the mid-late Victorian period.

Despite the presence of religion in the juvenilia, Charlotte and Branwell chose to use its presence superficially rather than adopt the ideals of Christian conquest. Instead, in regard to colonisation, the siblings merely concerned themselves with merciless, mechanised brute force. Their literature even goes so far as to demonstrate a brutal wish to exterminate the Ashanti natives. In Branwell's *Angria and the Angrians I(d)*, Zamorna vents his desire to conduct a mass execution of the Ashanti people:

You must spare nothing Angrians slay them whenever wherever however you can find them slay the men slay the women slay the children give no quarter but exterminate from the earth the whole d—d race of Ashantees.[55]

Some four years later it appears that their attitudes had not changed. Charlotte's later work, *Stancliffe's Hotel*, reveals that Angrian soldiers set 'slothounds on negro-tracks' and how, after catching two Ashanti murderers, William Percy 'shot through the head where they stood, and their bodies merged in the filth which afforded them such a suitable sepulchre'.[56] With the exception of Wellington's adoption of Quamina—which is discussed in the following section—there is no evidence in the entire saga to suggest that any form of Christian kindness or acceptance is extended to the indigenous peoples. Instead, the Glass Town and Angrian inhabitants are programmed to immediately resort to war. In *Angria and the Angrians II(d)* (1836) Branwell lists the enemies of Angria as the French, Ashanti, Quacco Camingo and the Negroes, and the Bedouin Arabs who all 'hate and detest Africa'.[57] From this statement, it is clear that the word 'Africa' has now become the property of the colonisers, the continent now alienated from the native people. It is this apparent hate of the colonisers' Africa that justifies the indigenous people's slaughter.

Repeatedly, Charlotte and Branwell attack their fictitious Ashanti verbally and physically using their imaginary white soldiers. Over the course of the saga their colonisers are presented as ethereal warriors. In *Stancliffe's Hotel*, Charlotte notes how her 10th Hussars are 'all gods as they are, or god–like men'.[58] In addition, during the Twelves' first battle when they arrive on the West Coast—documented in Branwell's *The History of the Young Men*—the magic-believing indigenous peoples are convinced that the Twelves were Gods and 'immediatly [*sic*] turned back and fled down the steep to the plain'.[59] This notion of 'godly whiteness' is also reiterated in Charlotte's poetry, an example being 'A National Ode for the Angrians' (1834):

> Lift, Lift the scarlet banner up! Fling all its folds abroad / And let its bloody lustre fall on Afric's [*sic*] blasted sod [...] We'll sheath not the avenging sword till earth & sea & skies / Through all God's mighty Universe shout back 'Arise! Arise!' / Till Angria reign's Lord Paramount wherever human tongue / The slave's lament, the conqueror's hymn in woe or bliss hath sung.[60]

The tension between white (as godlike) and black (as sin) reaches a climax on the battlefield in *Angria and the Angrians I(d)*. In the midst of a series of battles, Zamorna and Quamina finally confront each other on the battlefield, each on their 'chargers snowy white and raven black'.[61] In this climactic confrontation they both 'dealt blows. upon blows as fast as lightning' and 'grappled by their necks while their eyes might have scorched with their infernal glowing'.[62] Their intense and highly brutal combat encapsulates the racial aggression that permeates the siblings' early writings, each colour attempting to violently assert authority. It is, however, white superiority that once again reigns victorious. Whilst, after the battle, Quamina is branded a 'butcher' with 'barbarian cunning',[63] it is Angria's injured 'noble monarch' who is laid out 'christ–like' 'reclined on cushions' next to a 'bright fire'.[64]

Imagery of the godlike soldier is used as a racial tool. Through transforming their military characters into saintlike idols, the siblings assert the superiority of white over black, choosing not to promote the missionary message. This is despite articles in *Blackwood's*, such as the review of *Bowdich's Mission from Cape Coast to Ashantee*, pleading that, as Christians, society must 'unite our best endeavours to extend the philanthropy and salvation of the gospel to those who "live without God, in the world"'.[65] The juvenilias' abandonment of religious conversion is most likely influenced by other *Blackwood's* articles. 'Geography of Central Africa' claimed that the immediate abolition of the slave trade would not rehabilitate 'deep-rooted evils [...] amongst an ignorant and extremely barbarised people',[66] and, similarly, James McQueen declared that the colonisers needed to 'teach her [Africa's] savage sons that white men are her superiors'.[67] The Brontës most likely adopted these violent and uncompromising opinions of the natives, constructing an imaginary world that fantasised about and encouraged the violent, militaristic destruction of other races.

There is no Christian message in the Brontë juvenilia and war is the key to realising this. As the rumblings of the nineteenth-century missionary movement—culminating later in muscular Christianity and imperialism—swept through the nation, Charlotte and Branwell remained faithful to contemporary racist discourse that used militant language to justify acts of racially aggravated warfare. Although the purpose of this chapter is not to question the religious beliefs or practices of the Brontë siblings, it seeks to highlight the integral part war played in their freedom of expression: in colonial warfare's case, it was more important for the siblings to indulge in their passion for violence than remain faithful to their social background and upbringing. War was, in part, an obsession that tapped into their vivid desires concerning savage masculinity. Whereas their transmogrification of the Napoleonic Wars acted as a process of reflection, understanding and reimagining, their alternative history of colonial warfare became a cathartic outlet where they could, in secret, promote their xenophobic, controversial—although contemporary—outlooks.

Colonial Military Fatherhood

This section moves colonial warfare into the domestic realm by analysing the role of the colonial father in the siblings' saga. In Glass Town and Angria, fatherhood combines with militarism to represent wider themes of colonialism and, within this, interracial sex and sociality. Two characters within the saga represent this conflation of father-son relationships, racism and militarism: Quamina, Wellington's adopted Ashanti child, and Finic, the love-child of Zamorna and his 'negro mistress', Sofala.

The most significant characteristic of Quamina, the Ashanti chief, is his position as both a savage and a soldier. In Charlotte's *A Leaf from an Unopened Volume* (1834) he is branded with the same rhetoric used in the contemporary periodical press: 'brave, heroic, high-minded, though ferocious and barbarous'.[68] Although possibly the most flattering description of Quamina in the entire saga, his prerogative as a soldier had been predestined from birth. Charlotte's *The African Queen's Lament* (1833) explains Quamina's romanticised adoption by the fictitious Wellington when he stumbles upon an exhausted, dying mother singing a battle song to her child[69]:

> Awake my child, lift up thine eyes / And ere our souls are sundered / Swear by the silences of those skies / Where late the war storm thundered [...] / Tyrants, a dying woman's moan, / An orphan infant's wailing cry, / Shall rise to the eternal throne, / Shall send us final victory.[70]

This song reiterates that Quamina is a child born of war, violence and bloodshed. From this 'advice', as Wellington deems it, the child is predestined for revenge. Wellington remarks how he must keep 'a vigilant eye to observe his motions; he may give our nation trouble yet'.[71] A possible influence for these verses arise in a poem published in *Blackwood's* titled 'The Negro's Lament for Mungo Park' (1819), which foreshadowed future racial tensions in the run-up to the First Anglo–Ashanti War. Dedicated to Mungo Park, a Scottish explorer who drowned whilst being attacked by natives, the short lament states:

> Where the wild Jolibs / Rolls his deep waters, / Sate at their evening toil / Afric's dark daughters. / Where the thick Mangroves / Broad shadows were flinging, / Each o'er her lone loom / Bent mournfully singing– / 'Alas! for the white man! o'er deserts a ranger, / No more shall we welcome the white–bosom'd stranger![72]

Like *The African Queen's Lament*, these verses reiterate the antipathy that existed between the colonisers and the colonised, predetermining the natives' desire for conflict.

Quamina is a typical product of this mythology. Despite Wellington's unconditional display 'of care and tenderness as if he had been that monarch's son instead of his slave',[73] as quoted from Charlotte's *The Green Dwarf*, by the time he turned seventeen: 'It now began to appear that notwithstanding the care with which he had been treated by his conquerors, he retained against them, as if by instinct, the most deeply rooted and inveterate hatred'.[74] Rather than show gratitude to his 'saintly', 'tender' captors, Quamina's anger is not attributed to his colonised slave-like position, but through his preprogrammed desire to rebel.

What becomes clear, however, is that, like previous examples within this chapter, violence prevails over compassion: Wellington abandons his supposed paternal tenderness on the immediate discovery of his adopted son's vendetta, wishing to maintain his metaphorical role as 'father of a nation' over the welfare of his child:

> When the fact of the rebellion was known […] Wellington immediately desired that the punishment of the rebels might be left to him, as the young viper who commanded them had been nourished on his own hearth and brought up by him with almost parental tenderness.[75]

Disregarding his previous paternal laments, Wellington immediately reverts to his role as coloniser and soldier rather than family protector, enthusiastic to ride into battle and personally conduct his own son's punishment or death. Quamina exposes Wellington's 'paternal weakness' and 'limitations as a father' through their colonial kinship.[76] Essentially, Quamina is a product of colonial warfare, his family homeland slaves to the hegemonic instruction of Glass Town's white invaders.

Bearing this in mind, it may be that the siblings decided to interpret James McQueen's statement that emphasised tensions between colonisers and colonised in a literal, militant sense:

> In the name of our country, are the heroes who fought and who bled under Wellington, and who chased Napoleon from the carnage-covered Waterloo, to be herded with and insulted by such stinking savages as these! […] unless we can command […] we never can reclaim Africans from their present state of barbarity and ignorance, nor succeed in raising that quarter of the world from its present extremely debased and demoralized [*sic*] state.[77]

McQueen's quintessentially 'British' opinion explicitly voices the impossibility of harmony between the oppressed and the oppressors; that taking, metaphorically, a child nation, such as Africa, and nurturing it to obey the colonisers' rule, would ultimately end in intolerance and bloodshed. From this statement we see a merging of wars: Napoleonic and Ashanti. Wellington was the emblem of Britishness; his soldierly masculinity was an ideal example of the 'correct' military form that the Ashanti natives could learn from. Overall, McQueen expresses how Western warfare—which was sensationalised and celebrated by the British public—was the answer to maintain strength and domination overseas. Inspired by statements such as this, it is evident how the Brontës adopted military narratives to explore wider colonial issues. In this instance, although the siblings offer white, military paternity as a form of reconciliation, it is soon deconstructed by the stereotypes awarded to the natives' violent temperaments.

Finally, it is Finic who truly deconstructs the impossible paternal relationship between coloniser and colonised. Like Quamina, Finic has been discussed in a number of colonial studies. Corbett argues against Firdous Azim's claim that the dwarf 'stands as a warning against the sexual transgression of racial boundaries'.[78] Instead, she proposes that Finic's deformity is not a result 'of miscegenous intercourse' but of the falsity of the 'treacherous white man'.[79] This is supported by Charlotte's narrative that describes how Finic was not born deformed, but grew deformed at the vengeful request of his dying mother to shame her lover.

Ultimately, both of these suggestions are true: Finic is the contemporary product of biological, racial inequality; a deformed dwarf. He is both the aftermath of interracial copulation and the revenge of the colonised, rejecting his father by waging a—*literal*—physical war as a means of rejection through deformity. This physical revenge, however, is little acknowledged, as his appearance demotes him to a slave of his father, who punishes him in an abusive and torturous manner. In *The Spell* (1834), Charlotte writes, 'He mouthed, gesticulated, & capered furiously. The Duke first laughed, then hit him a sound stunning blow'.[80] Rather than take pity on his 'creation', Zamorna merely mistreats his offspring, refusing his paternal duty out of racial disgust, and instead resorting to his position as a militaristic, violent figure to reassert dominance over his child. Essentially, like Quamina, Finic represents the contemporary viewpoint that an interracial relationship is unworkable and incompatible biologically, politically and socially: the forced, militant merging of the Glass Town and Ashanti nations is problematic and deformed. Fatherhood, instead of representing tenderness and care, is mutated into merely a power structure, the doctrines of paternity reinvented into an assertion of dominance. Charlotte, in this instance, portrays Wellington and Zamorna as degenerate, militant fathers of colonisation, unable to relate to their colonised and unable to act as literal fathers to their alienated offspring. Instead they retreat into the comfort of their nation; an elite, colonial safe house in which they may truly reign as sovereigns, publicly and domestically.

This chapter has shown that the siblings engaged with war as a form of playful, violent expression. Their interest in colonial warfare is sophisticated in their foresight of the Victorian imperial legacy, but it is also much more concerned with imitation rather than independent thought. In this instance, the Brontës used war as a template, which they could use to replicate contemporary racial prejudice. It is through their attitudes to race that we can learn of the nation's explicit, sensational responses to racially aggravated warfare in the early nineteenth century: it is clear that a picture of primal savagery, otherness and primitivism must be built in order to justify forceful colonisation and extreme levels of violence. Society cannot have a civilised Ashanti. Although this is the predominant picture of the Ashanti *en masse*, Charlotte and Branwell did make an attempt to give multidimensional personalities to individual black characters, such as Quamina, and introduce them to the Western world. This attempt, however, was usually futile and reverted to black characters reacting against their colonisers and consolidating their otherness. This is a crude representation of war; their alternative history became a space where they could engage with and explore their own prejudices, imitating the militant, racist rhetoric of the period and further playing with this rhetoric to expose the horrors of racial warfare in early nineteenth-century society.

NOTES

1. Christine Alexander, "Autobiography and Juvenilia: The Fractured Self in Charlotte Brontë's Early Manuscripts," in *The Child Writer from Austen to Woolf*, ed. Christine Alexander and Juliet McMaster (Cambridge: Cambridge University Press, 2005): 165.

2. Susan Meyer, *Imperialism at Home: Race and Victorian Women's Fiction* (Ithaca: Cornell University Press, 1996): 46.

3. Ibid.

4. This symbolic use of Quamina is used in Charlotte's *Roe Head Journals* (1836–1837), in which she uses oppressive racial imagery to consider her constrained situation as a governess. The use of symbolism as a means to

question women's place in society carries through to her later works. For example, in *Jane Eyre*, when Jane is oppressed and othered in the Reed household, she reveals her temperament to be that of a 'rebel slave'. See Charlotte Brontë, *Jane Eyre*, ed. Margaret Smith and Sally Shuttleworth (Oxford: Oxford University Press, 2009): 12.

5. Mary Jean Corbett, *Family Likeness: Sex, Marriage and Incest from Jane Austen to Virginia Woolf* (Ithaca: Cornell University Press, 2011): 95.

6. See Sarah Fermi, "A Question of Colour," *Brontë Studies*, 40.4 (2015): 334–342.

7. *Tales*: xvii.

8. *PCB*: 7.

9. Robert L. Mack, ed., *Arabian Nights' Entertainments* (Oxford: Oxford University Press, 2008): 67.

10. Ibid., 55.

11. *EEW I*: 7.

12. *WPB I*: 222, 225.

13. Robert Irwin, *The Arabian Nights: A Companion* (London: Tauris Parke, 2005): 88.

14. See Christine Alexander and Margaret Smith, eds., *The Oxford Companion to the Brontës* (Oxford: Oxford University Press, 2006): 23–24.

15. "Foreign Intelligence," *The Leeds Intelligencer*, 16 November 1826, 2.

16. "Leeds Thursday, May 13," *The Leeds Intelligencer*, 13 May 1824, 2.

17. Ibid.

18. McQueen would become a character within the Glass Town juvenilia, showing his influence on Charlotte and Branwell's formative imaginations.

19. "Geography of Central Africa—Denham and Clapperton's Journals," *Blackwood's Edinburgh Magazine*, June 1826, 689.

20. Ibid. Branwell adopts Denham and Clapperton's accounts of combined enemy forces: regularly, Branwell alludes to the word 'enemy' as a form of collective othered army. In *Angria and the Angrian II (f)* Branwell notes how the 'promise of Booty from the desolation of that devoted country brings in [...] the Arabs and Negroes who otherwise care for no one': *WPB II*: 529. It is clear here, along with a sense of racial generalising and stereotyping, Branwell is mimicking the rhetoric used in the periodical press.

21. "Geography of Central Africa," *Blackwood's*, 687.

22. M., "The British Settlements of Western Africa," *Blackwood's Edinburgh Magazine*, September 1829, 341.

23. Richard Howitt, "The Truant," in *Friendship's Offering: And Winter's Wreath: A Christmas and New Year's Present* (London: Smith, Elder & Co., 1829): 181.

24. *WPB II*: 250.
25. *WPB II*: 302–303.
26. Ibid., 281.
27. Edward Thomas Bowdich, *Mission from Cape Coast Castle to Ashantee, with a Statistical Account of That Kingdom, and Geographical Notices of Other Parts of the Interior of Africa* (London: John Murray, 1819): 306.
28. Edward Thomas Bowdich, *Essay on the Superstitions, Customs, and Arts Common to the Ancient Egyptians, Abyssinians, and Ashantees* (Paris: J. Smith, 1821): 29–30.
29. T. C. Hansard, ed., "Sir J Mackintosh's Motion Respecting the Rigour of Our Criminal Laws, 21 May," in *The Parliamentary Debates, Vol. IX* (London: T.C. Hansard, 1824): 417.
30. *WPB I*: 162.
31. Ibid., 163.
32. *WPB II*: 304.
33. *Angria*: 86.
34. James McQueen, "Civilisation of Africa—Sierra Leone," *Blackwood's Edinburgh Magazine*, March 1827, 326.
35. Ibid., 327.
36. "Geography of Central Africa," *Blackwood's*, 709.
37. "London," *Blackwood's Edinburgh Magazine*, August 1826, 324.
38. Daniel Defoe, *Robinson Crusoe*, ed. James Kelly (Oxford: Oxford University Press, 2008): 197.
39. Ibid., 155.
40. *Arabian Nights' Entertainments*, 158.
41. Ibid., 163.
42. *EEW II*: 188.
43. Bowdich, *Mission from Cape Coast Castle to Ashantee*, 176.
44. M., *Blackwood's*, 341.
45. "Geography of Central Africa," *Blackwood's*, 701.
46. Edmund Abaka, "Dan Fodio, Osman," in *The Oxford Encyclopedia of African Thought*, ed. Abiola F. Irele and Biodun Jeyifo (Oxford: Oxford University Press, 2010): 277.
47. Thomas Pringle and Josiah Conder, *Narrative of a Residence in South Africa* (London: Moxon, 1835): 112.
48. "Geography of Central Africa," *Blackwood's*, 708.
49. Although the saga begins with the Genii as Gods, which were based on a conflation of *Arabian Nights* and classical Greek mythology, evidence of Christianity seeps through the saga as it progresses. As the Brontës moved into Angrian territory, the Genii were confined to the recesses of the saga's Glass Town youth.
50. *EEW II*: 233.

51. Ibid.
52. *EEW III*: 291.
53. *WPB II*: 203.
54. Ibid., 271.
55. *WPB II*: 303.
56. *Angria*: 86.
57. *WPB II*: 528.
58. *Angria*: 86.
59. *WPB I*: 155.
60. *PCB:* 152–3.
61. *WPB II*: 321.
62. Ibid.
63. Ibid., 328–329.
64. Ibid., 325.
65. Bowdich, *Mission from Cape Coast Castle to Ashantee*, 310.
66. "Geography of Central Africa," *Blackwood's*, 707.
67. McQueen, *Blackwood's*, 329.
68. *EEW II*: 326.
69. This event is inspired by Wellington's real-life adoption of Salabut Khan, a four–year–old orphan rescued from the Deccan battlefield during the Second Anglo-Maratha War.
70. *EEW II*: 5–6.
71. Ibid., 3.
72. J. P. M., "The Negro's Lament for Mungo Park," *Blackwood's Edinburgh Magazine*, November 1819, 196.
73. *EEW II*: 178.
74. Ibid., 179.
75. Ibid., 180.
76. See Valerie Sanders and Emma Butcher, "'Mortal Hostility': Masculinity and Fatherly Conflict in the Glass Town and Angrian Sagas," in *Charlotte Brontë from the Beginnings*, ed. Judith E. Pike and Lucy Morrison (London: Routledge, 2017): 59–71.
77. McQueen, *Blackwood's*, 329.
78. Corbett, *Family Likeness*, 100.
79. Ibid.
80. *Tales*: 119.

CHAPTER 6

Civil War and Conflict

The final chapter of this study brings the Brontës' interest in warfare back to their immediate local surroundings. Despite the appeal of sensational, large-scale wars fought on a global platform, Charlotte and Branwell repeatedly return to civil rebellion and revolt. Although their interest in conflict cannot be classified as war in a traditional sense—between two nation states—the siblings' engagement with smaller-scale theatres of violence emphasises their interest in war in all forms. Although born into a time of relative post-war peace, rumblings of depression and discontent were ever-present throughout their childhood. The tense divide between the British government and the general public came to the fore during and following the Napoleonic Wars. Charlotte and Branwell's Glass Town and Angria were inspired by a volatile period in British history,[1] echoing the instability of contemporary society whilst equally reflecting upon other historical models of civil unrest, ranging from the American War of 1812 to the French Revolution. Their stories establish that violence within both large *and* small parameters evokes powerful emotions of betrayal and revenge; conflicts are not just fought against the other, but can also be waged against one's own.

The history of civil conflict is addressed in the second chapter of this book; the opening subchapters discuss civil war and conflict in literature ranging from classical to Romantic times. The last section on Walter Scott reflects on Britain's rebellious past, exploring the Brontës' passion for Scott's clan warfare epics, especially in relation to the Jacobite rebellions of the previous century. Moving forward to the recent past, this chapter discusses

© The Author(s) 2019   151
E. Butcher, *The Brontës and War*,
https://doi.org/10.1007/978-3-319-95636-7_6

two final global civil conflicts that captured the Brontës' imaginations: the American War of 1812 and the French Revolution, which led into the Napoleonic Wars. These sections evidence the siblings' widespread interest in the military, laying the groundwork for the salient topic of this chapter: post-Napoleonic British unrest.

It is the primary aim of this chapter to highlight that warfare, to the siblings, came in all shapes and sizes and that all manners of conflict and militarisation helped inspire their multifaceted imaginary kingdom. The previous three chapters have established and explored the foundational structures of the juvenilia: the Napoleonic Wars for the origins of characters, wartime sentimentality and strategy, and the First Anglo-Ashanti War for location, racial views and imperalist narratives. Civil warfare and local uprisings are, however, the most common type of conflict in the juvenilia. Notably, conflicts such as Rogue's insurrection of Glass Town (1830–1832) and the Angrian Civil Wars (1835–1837) between the Angrian Royalists, Republicans and Ardrah's Reform Party—acting on behalf of the Verdopolitan Union—play pivotal roles in Branwell's linear chronology. It is therefore fitting that the final chapter be dedicated to the warfare and conflict that recurs most throughout the saga, whilst weaving the contextual material back round to the siblings' local topography.

THE INITIAL INFLUENCE OF THE AMERICAN WAR OF 1812 ON THE BRONTË JUVENILIA

Branwell's firstever 'book' was based on the American War of 1812. Titled 'Battell Book' (1827), the small manuscript contains pencil drawings occasionally accompanied by an odd word or description. The prose opens with 'the Battle of Washington was fought on 12th < Sep > between the British and their Allies' and throughout the pages are childlike representations of battle scenes and military landscapes.[2] In one visually powerful page, horses are rearing, cannons are fired and a pile of dead soldiers lie abandoned on the ground. Three years later, these violent images of battle are revisited in Branwell's prose. Victor Neufeldt notes the similarities between his *The History of the Young Men* (1830–1831), the first Glass Town story, and *Campaigns of the British Army at Washington* (1821), a memoir published in *Blackwood's*. Both accounts of the battle treat violence and loss in a disconnected manner; combat is described frankly and *en masse*. Branwell writes of the Twelves' violent battle against the Dutch after they briefly land on Ascension Isle en route to the coast of Africa. He describes how 'the land party had entered the town victorious and were burning and massacring all before them'.[3] The *Blackwood's* memoir describes a similar scene. When the British Army enter Washington, they set fire to the public buildings and stores: 'Of the Senate-house, the President's palace, the barracks, the dock-yard &c. nothing could be seen except heaps of smoking ruins'.[4] Magazines are additionally burnt to the ground, just as in Branwell's tale. Like Branwell's British who 'prepared for another attempt on the Magazine and each grasping a piece of Blazing Timber they rushed forward',[5] the American memoir describes (Fig. 6.1):

> The work of destruction had also begun in the city, before they quitted their ground; and the blazing of houses, ships, and stores, the report of exploding magazines, and the crash of falling roofs, informed them as they proceeded, of what was going forward.[6]

Similarly, Branwell's massacring of inhabitants mimics the memoir's emotionless account of mass murder: 'the Americans [...] forcing their way into the battery, at length succeeded in recapturing it, with immense slaughter', and, more graphically, 'A dreadful fire was accordingly opened upon them,

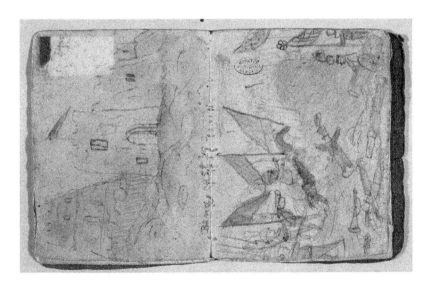

Fig. 6.1 Brontë, Branwell (1827). *Battell Book* (Image used courtesy of the Brontë Parsonage Museum)

and they were mowed down by hundreds'.[7] It is clear from these early historical accounts that Branwell was able to read and frankly replicate war in its most violent form from a very early age. Despite his ability to write poignant, reflective military narratives, Branwell's ability to sensationalise and dramatise intense battle scenes through stream-of-consciousness war epics remains his speciality throughout the majority of the juvenilia.

Although Neufeldt specifically pinpoints this particular *Blackwood's* article as a major influence on Branwell, a number of memoirs and articles regarding American warfare were published in *Blackwood's* throughout Charlotte and Branwell's childhood years. In September 1828, the periodical published 'Battle of New Orleans'—fought as part of the American War of 1812 between America and the British—which contained detailed battle plans and diagrams of the conflict. These plans evidently appealed to the young Charlotte and Branwell, their first collaborative project, *History of the Rebellion in my Fellows* (1828), a competitive written battle that focused on tactics and strategy. Additionally, American military memoirs emerged, such as George Gleig's *A Subaltern in America* (1833), serialised in *Blackwood's*, which presented themselves in a similar format to the outpourings of post-Napoleonic biographies the young siblings read and imitated. Unlike the Napoleonic memoirs, however, the American War of 1812 did not remain a primary influence on their early writings. Nevertheless, many European historians have considered the American War of 1812, as Donald Hickey states, 'a byproduct of the Napoleonic Wars and that, for the British at least, it was just another theater, and a decidedly minor one at that, in a larger more important war against France and her allies'.[8] Perhaps this is the same mentality in which Branwell saw this war. Although it was both an interesting and engaging conflict that was, in the moment, an exciting template for a ten year old, its fleeting significance to his writings evidences the strength of the Napoleonic Wars, which sidelined other wars and monopolised the siblings' attention.

After the siblings' pre-Glass Town writings, their interest in American conflict retreated into the shadows. Echoes of its appeal, however, can be traced through fleeting moments in their Glass Town and Angrian saga. In his *Life of Warner Howard Warner* (1838), Branwell briefly mentions Warner's father participating in the American campaigns under the command of General Gage, the Governor of Massachusetts and leader of the British troops at Boston.[9] For Charlotte, a reference to her juvenile interest in the American warfare can be found within her final tale, *Caroline Vernon* (1839). The daughter of Alexander Percy's mistress, Caroline, declares, 'Lord Byron & Bonaparte & the Duke of Wellington & Lord Edward Fitzgerald [...] the four best men that ever lived'.[10] Fitzgerald fought in the American War of Independence and sympathised with the revolutionary cause in France. Despite the occasional name-dropping, however, there is no sustained utilisation of American warfare. It appears that, although initially vital for their junior understandings and visualisations of conflict, American combat was not a primary source in constructing their juvenilia post-1829. Regardless of its superficial impact, it is nonetheless important to acknowledge that their first conceptualisations of war and the primitive beginnings of Glass Town were heavily grounded in the history of Anglo-American warfare. This history introduced them to soon-to-be integral avenues for understanding wars that combined both the logistics of battle and imaginative, vivid memoirs of soldiers' experiences overseas.

BRANWELL'S REIGN OF TERROR

Although the siblings lost their interest in Anglo-American warfare, one key historic conflict—which did, in turn, degenerate into civil war—continued to fascinate them. The French Revolution (1789–1799), including the Reign of Terror (1793–1794), imprinted itself onto the minds of the young Brontë siblings and provided a gruesome yet exhilarating template of violent social unrest in recent memory. The conflict was pivotal in influencing the Brontës' formation of government and sovereignty in both Glass Town and Angria. In Glass Town, Branwell's series, *Letters from an Englishman* (1830–1832), bases its entire plot on Revolutionary France: Branwell deliberately reimagines events and reconjures the feeling of 'Terror'. Most importantly, Branwell constructs his chief protagonist on the French Revolutionary blueprint: Alexander Percy is a Republican who is in favour of forming his own dictatorship. Throughout the Glass Town and Angrian saga, Percy frequently revolts against Glass Town and Angrian royalty, indulging in his passion for rioting and revolution. Charlotte acted as a witness to Percy's early revolts in her tales *The Bridal* (1832) and *Lily Hart* (1833). Meanwhile, Branwell played with and adopted this revolutionary, violent model. His *Letters from an Englishman, Vol. III–VI* (1831–1832) document Percy's insurrection of Glass Town and his attempt to execute its elite. After staging a coup, Percy successfully establishes his own 'Reign of

Terror'. The narrator of this tale, and the Englishman alluded to in the title, is J. Bellingham, a rich banker. Branwell deliberately adopts a non-militant pseudonym and promoter of capitalism to emphasise the horror, violence and instability Percy imposes on established, sovereign order. Caught in the unrest, Bellingham describes the ordeal of being led to the guillotine:

> I was conducted from the prison to a large open area which was covered with blood and dead carcases which several persons were engaged in carrying away. This area was crowded with people and at one end of it at a large table which sat Alexander Rogue and several members of the provisional Government before them was placed on a blood-covered scaffold a block and 2 executioners.[11]

The technical details of this event, depicting a primitive structure of Branwell's provisional government, are likely to have come from Walter Scott's *Life of Napoleon* (1827), which contains imagery of traitors 'dragged before the revolutionary tribunal'.[12] The blood-covered scaffold, however, was a symbolic image that was regularly discussed in the periodical press. For example, a graphic description appeared in an 1828 *Blackwood's* article titled 'An Execution in Paris'. The narrator describes a beheading: 'I saw his head slip from the body and tumble into a basket ready to receive it, which the blood spouted forth in little cataracts from the severed trunk, and dyed the scaffold with a purple tide'.[13] It is clear how an image such as this would have made an impression on the young Branwell, appealing to his appetite for gore and the macabre.

Further evidence suggests that Branwell's primary knowledge of France's Revolutionary model and its methods mainly derived from *Blackwood's* and Scott's *Life of Napoleon*. Throughout 1831—the same year as Branwell penned *Letters from an Englishman* and a few months before the Brontë family's access to *Blackwood's* ceased—a number of articles ran that focused on the French Revolution: 'On the Late French Revolution/On Parliamentary Reform and the French Revolution', 'On the Military Events of the Late French Revolution' and 'Narrative of an Imprisonment in France During the Reign of Terror'. Collectively, each contains a detailed commentary on the Revolution and its consequences. Many writers also compared the 'late' French uprising to the previous Parisian 'July Revolution' that had occurred just a year previously in 1830. Despite this saturation of the Revolution in the media, it was, however, Scott's *Life of Napoleon* that provided the siblings with a full-length narrative of the revolt, which was followed by a sizeable account of the Napoleonic Wars. It is through Scott's works that Branwell would have learned of the rationale of the Revolution, its evolution into future wars, and been exposed to the extremes of emotive, anti-Revolutionary commentary:

> Death– a grave — are sounds which awaken the strongest terrors in those whom they menace! There was never anywhere, save in France during this melancholy period, so awful a comment on the expression of scripture. 'All that a man hath he will give for his life,' Force, immediate and irresistible force, was the only logic used by the government – Death was the only appeal from their authority.[14]

It is likely that Scott's stirring descriptions inspired Branwell's construction of Percy as the epitome of anarchy, terror, force and death. Percy is relentless in his lust for violence. Finally, in Branwell's later work, *Angria and the Angrians III(a)* (1836), Percy is allowed the success of revolution, which he did not achieve during his Glass Town revolts. After an initial civil war between Zamorna's royal troops and Ardrah's Reform Party,[15] Percy breaks from Zamorna and rouses a third party, the 'country men' of Angria, with the call for 'LIBERTY'. After successfully gaining power, he exclaims:

> All Africa is Declared one great REPUBLIC. The Republic of Africa! a PROVISIONAL GOVERNMENT till such time As a regular foundation of Laws and civil polity can be laid for the people to erect a Temple of VITALITY! [...] All Titles of every rank and Degree save those military and belonging to Government Offices are to be Abolished [...] The Parliament shall be formed into one Great NATIONAL ASSEMBLY. every member of which shall be Elected by the people [...] Whoever agrees not to these fundamental Rules must DIE and his property shall be devoted to the PROVISIONAL GOVERNMENT Of this Government I for the present am constituted Head And therefore I BID YOU TO ATTEND TO ME![16]

In this one section, Branwell harnesses Scott's ultimatum: that the Revolution prompted France's people to succumb to immediate force or embrace the release of death. It even goes as far to act as a potted history of the Revolution. The tale adopts not only the facts but emphasises the feeling of force exacted by the provisional government. Percy's 1836 government continues until 1837 when Zamorna returns to Angria and reclaims his throne at the battle of Evesham. After this, Percy's revolutionary ideal topples for good.

It is, in fact, Percy's forceful bid to enact violence and death that imprints a deep psychological scar on to Angria. As chapter four of this book explores, Glass Town and Angria's soldierly inhabitants are psychologically damaged from the relentless wars that are, primarily, orchestrated by Percy. Embodying the hostility, violence and bloodshed that accompany disorder and anarchy, Percy represents the detrimental ramifications of national division and struggle, the revolutionary struggle for reform equally opening an opportunity for both butchery and bloodshed. The French Revolutionary model remained an ideal that Branwell's protagonist continued to strive for throughout the siblings' collaborative decade, demonstrating its importance in constructing both events and personalities throughout the saga. Its combination of values, ranging from Romantic notions of liberty to the sanctioning of violent, unorthodox modes of execution, ensured its persistence in Branwell's battle tactics. The Revolution's solid presence within the juvenilia demonstrates that the siblings' interest in war came in all shapes and sizes: civil conflict was as interesting, impactful and sensational as the larger-scale wars. In fact, it was Branwell's preferred war game.

THE RUMBLINGS OF CIVIL CONFLICT: POST-NAPOLEONIC BRITAIN IN THE BRONTË IMAGINATION

> Has life no variety now? [...] Does Love fold his wings when Victory lowers her pennons? Surely not![17]

Charlotte's preface to her last Angrian tale *Caroline Vernon* begins with a forthright commentary concerning her post-war kingdom. In recent memory, she had watched despairingly as her imaginative world was torn apart by a highly complex, bloodthirsty series of civil war campaigns masterminded by Branwell during the years 1835–1837. In this passage, she questions the worth and momentum of life without war. In a similar vein to post-Napoleonic Britain, Charlotte reflects on the stagnation of the period, but decides to gather herself and move on. Jibing at her brother's lust for war, she exclaims:

Reader, these things don't happen every day. It's well they don't, for a constant recurrence of such stimulus would soon wear out the public stomach & bring on indigestion. But surely one can find something to talk about, though miracles are no longer wrought in the world.[18]

Despite her humorous urge for the reader to 'solace ourselves with a chastened view of mellowed morality',[19] Charlotte's preface exudes a tone of loss. Her poetic verses such as 'there's not always an Angrian campaign going on in the rain [...] Nor a Duke & a lord drawing the sword',[20] along with her forlorn imagery of battlefields growing corn are satirical, but there is a glimmer of fondness in her tone as she pauses to reflect on her long collaboration with Branwell.

After the Napoleonic Wars, Britain's reaction was mournful and nostalgic. Despite the arrival of peace after years of global unrest, many saw the Napoleonic Wars as a stimulating period that somehow brought life to a sensation-hungry nation. As Benjamin Disraeli notes in *Vivian Grey* (1826), 'if it wasn't for the general election, we really must have a war for variety's sake. Peace gets quite a bore'.[21] Judging by this general deflated atmosphere within early nineteenth-century Britain, it is clear how Charlotte could mimic society's grief surrounding this seemingly uneventful lull in military action and heroism.

Nevertheless, all was not as it seemed. Despite a comparatively peaceful period in the history of war, post-war Britain was presented with new challenges. As well as continuing with its imperial exploits, the country turned in on itself, struggling to cope with its own minor conflicts and economic recovery.[22] Britain's stagnant, uncertain post-war condition is regularly transmogrified within Charlotte and Branwell's imaginary kingdom. Alluding to the country's social condition, Branwell's post-war narrative, *The Wool Is Rising* (1834), focuses on Angria's struggling economy after the recent war between Frenchysland and the Verdopolian nations. This is achieved through Branwell's introduction of Edward and William Percy—Alexander Percy's sons and precursors to the Crimsworth brothers in Charlotte's later work *The Professor* (1857)—who have become successful partners in their own manufacturing mill business. In this tale of industry, Branwell is shown to take note of the contemporary social conditions of the 'Frenchy' prisoners of war, a real-life presence in the British manufacturing landscape. Branwell writes, 'thousands of French prisoners. whom the Government distributed among the Manufactory are now out of employ. wandering about in a state of. perfect idiotism'.[23] In reality, an 1821 edition of *The Quarterly Review*, a publication with which the Brontë family was familiar, documents a similar reference to French prisoners of war. It declares that, due to the knock-on redundancy of local cottagers, 'prisoners were prohibited from making for sale, woolen gloves and straw hats – it would have injured, in these petty branches, the commerce of the subjects of His Britannic Majesty!'.[24] In turn, however, the prisoners were left with 'neither rent, nor taxes, nor lodging, firing, food, or clothing to find'.[25] It is clear that Branwell's tale accurately reflects the literal dilemmas ex-soldiers faced in the post-war moment. Moreover, it is clear that these dilemmas rippled through the post-war media and into public consciousness.

It is highly plausible that the siblings were writing from their own experiences. As the introduction to this book evidences, the Brontës' local parish was no stranger to the presence of soldiers; Haworth, like any other parish, had male members who served and were known in the local community. In a broad sense, the siblings would have also been familiar with the wave of returning soldiers who covered the country, many of whom lacked direction and had to adjust to normal everyday life. Haworth and the surrounding area would have welcomed home a number of ex-Napoleonic soldiers in recent years. This is in addition to the presence of French prisoners of war, of whom Britain had previously held an estimated 80,000. These returning British soldiers would have been living within the small financial parameters of half-pay. As Norman Gash notes:

> [half–pay] was not so much a pension as a species of retaining fee for hypothetical future calls on their services. Unfortunately for them, half–pay [...] was still fixed at the monetary level of 1714. An officer of thirty years service whose pay was £600 per annum received £146 on retirement.[26]

From this extract, it is clear that a soldier's life post-duty was unstable, liminal and regressive. Evidently, the lack of progression for soldiers' economic rights and their unfulfilled occupational position in society would have contributed to an already anxious post-war climate.

From this nationwide feeling, it is understandable why civil unrest generated as a consequence. The disorganisation and inequality of the military was just one example of wider problems concerned with the poor rights and injustices suffered by the working classes. National division between the British government and the people tore through the social fabric of Britain. Political and social unrest prevailed throughout the Brontës' childhood, their local community aggravated by industrial and agricultural unrest. Those in Haworth—and neighbouring towns such as Bradford and Halifax—whose livelihoods depended on the wool trade saw their employment in flux. The industrial revolution had replaced man with machine, and many working-class people found themselves out of work and in dire financial straits. Henceforth, various riots and strikes broke out across the country. In the early 1830s, the crisis had reached breaking point: many members of the population were convinced that Britain was heading for full-scale revolution. The Parisian 'July Revolution' of 1830 provoked this anxiety.[27] This event saw revolutionaries attempt to overthrow the monarchy in a bid to instigate economic reform: there was fear that this ripple of change could find its way across the channel. The Reverend Patrick Brontë expressed his concern regarding this in a letter to Mrs Franks in 1831. Speaking about temperance reform, he argued that unless this issue was addressed the 'inveterate enemies' would encourage a revolution: 'We see, what has been lately done in France – We know, that the Duke of Wellington's declaration, against reform, was the principal cause, of the removal, of him, & other Ministers, from power'.[28] Indeed, the Brontë siblings would have read warmongering articles and verse in the periodicals they subscribed to, informing their views on radicalism and reform. As late as 1834, *Fraser's Magazine* declared that the French were burning for war again 'fight or no fight'.[29] There was also a counter-reaction throughout 1830 in order to quell the fears from France. For example, a series of hurried letters were published in the high Tory paper, *John Bull*, which the Brontë family read, penned by an anonymous Englishman in Paris. It was these letters' purpose to quell fears that Europe was heading for revolution, despite the Parisian uprising occurring just a few months later. On 17 January 1830, the paper published:

Dear Bull – There are wars or *rumours of wars* from Japan to Christians, and from Washing to the Black Sea; but at present there are more rumours than wars, and by and by there are to be more wars than rumours.[30]

In this same letter, the writer even attempts to deflect the infiltration of revolutionary feeling with tongue-in-cheek humour directed at the government and the military. Taking the fear of French revolt to a new level, the author adds a new layer to Britain's anxiety by proposing that the Duke of Brunswick may invade, whose predecessor—and the Allied Army—had embarked on a failed war with France during the French Revolution. These meta-layers all contributed to the superficial status of Britain's troubled and apprehensive position: the contributor attempts to reclaim the power of reason by explicitly mocking the nation's panicked atmosphere:

> Prepare, however for the worst. Let the Martello towers be well manned – let the militia be raised – let all our forts and fortresses be put into the best possible posture of defense – for the Duke of BRUNSWICK is about the *invade England* in a brig, two corvettes and collier. The troops, mustering 500 strong, all able–bodied men, from 15 to 75, are all collected – the review has been held – the soldiers are fired with enthusiasm – and are resolved '*to conquer or die*'. The alternative of conquering they rather prefer the otherwise: and I trust that the DUKE OF WELLINGTON and our brave army will strive heart and hand to repel from our shores this new, powerful and dangerous enemy. Yet, however, as 'fortune favours the brave,' who will venture to predict that the brave Brunswick will not defeat the assembled armies of a power so pigmy and insignificant as *Old England*.[31]

Despite this attempt made by *John Bull*, a number of periodicals took the matter of Britain's perturbed landscape seriously. Like France, whose main problem rested in the class divide between the aristocracy and the people, contributors to national periodicals recognised that this similar class divide was Britain's downfall. Published in *Blackwood's*, an 1831 article titled 'On the Approaching Revolution in Great Britain' depicts the narrator, Emeritus, exclaiming: 'All is darkness. We are now in some respects in the situation of Rome at the period of the Triumvirates; we are on the brink of the same collision between our aristocracy and our people'.[32] Opposed to this looming revolution, a poem titled 'The Progression of Revolution', published in an 1832 edition of *Fraser's Magazine*, explicitly condemns the government's 1832 Reform Act,[33] legislated to appease the long campaigning reform activists:

> The change, you say, is wanted by the mass,
> And grumbling thousands choose the bill should pass!
> What! – is my country then indeed so low,
> To fear the empty, though so loud a foe! […]

See at our relics of the free,
And learn from them what England soon must be,
When strangers weep o'er London's marble gloom,
And search through ruins for a Wellesley's tomb.[34]

It was clear that, despite post-war peace ensuing after Waterloo, Britain was in flux. Its military, economic and social system was embroiled in an internal conflict that the national press could not ignore. The siblings' knowledge of national discontent did not, however, solely derive from periodicals and papers of national interest. The Brontë family was also informed of economic and social unrest around the country through their local papers, *The Leeds Mercury* and *The Leeds Intelligencer*. *The Leeds Mercury* prioritised coverage on widespread riots throughout the 1820s and 1830s, reporting cases in Norwich, Manchester, Bradford, Macclesfield, Wakefield, Sheffield and other such industrial areas. In *The Leeds Intelligencer*, as Sally Shuttleworth notes:

> The famous Bradford combers and weavers strike, for example, which involved 20,000 people and lasted for twenty–three weeks between 1825 and 1826, ending with a complete defeat for the strikers, was reported in great detail. At the same time, the economic crash, brought on by joint stock ventures and reckless financial speculation, led to widespread riots in industrial cities in the spring of 1826. On 4 May 1826, the *Leeds Intelligencer* included a chart of all the riots and disturbances which had recently taken place in the region, and Edward Baines published his 'Letter to the Unemployed Workmen of Lancashire and Yorkshire'.[35]

Expanding on Shuttleworth's observations, the commentary accompanying Baines' letter indicates the local public feeling in Yorkshire. Indeed, the extensive distribution of this letter had been by citizens who were more 'anxious to preserve the public peace by moral influence than by military coercion'.[36] This evidences that the public had reconfigured the military as the enemy—the heroes of the Napoleonic Wars were now attacking their own. Moreover, as Shuttleworth suggests, the Brontës would have also had access to visual material that showed them they were right in the centre of the industrial and social conflicts. They would have witnessed different types of conflict: the rebellious violence of the militant everyday man taking up arms, and the retaliation of the official military. It is unsurprising then, that civil conflict was a constant backdrop for the siblings' collaborative kingdom. Like Haworth, Glass Town and Angria are realms of anxiety, unrest and discontent. Despite larger-scale wars raging through their stories, the relentless disputes and squabbles amongst their saga's own inhabitants add a new layer to understandings of conflict: the siblings did not always need armies, battles and grand military idols to present war: sometimes war manifested itself as a nation turned in on itself, where the everyday man would pick up a weapon and shout 'no more!'

CONTEXT AND COLLABORATION: CIVIL CONFLICT IN GLASS TOWN AND ANGRIA

Charlotte and Branwell repeatedly plunged their decade-long saga into chaos. Their response is multi-layered. Rather than just recreating the post-Napoleonic condition, Charlotte and Branwell went further, interrogating this post-war dynamic by engaging with and mimicking political speeches in Britain's turbulent early nineteenth-century climate. Throughout 1834–1835, tensions between their protagonists, Zamorna and Alexander Percy, climax through a heated series of damning monologues. Christine Alexander recognises the link between British and Angrian politics, observing that 1834 was a turbulent time for politics: 'News of a government crisis [...] soon reached the Haworth parsonage [...] The previous ministry under Lord Grey had had to resign [...] The King called on Wellington to form a government: Wellington suggested Peel'.[37] By addressing the combination of political and social disruption present in their youth, the siblings were able to faithfully reflect that instability and antagonism within their politically driven world. In the saga, having just gained the kingdom of Angria, both characters, Zamorna as king and Percy as prime minister, are once again at war with one another. At this point, Zamorna accuses Percy of inciting rumours and indulging in conspiracy and betrayal against their kingdom. Collectively, Charlotte's *The Scrap Book: A Mingling of Many Things* (1834–1835) carries these speeches whilst her *My Angria and the Angrians* (1834) discusses their outcome. Branwell's are more fragmented, yet they are included within *Angria and the Angrians I(a–d)* (1834–1835). The speeches represent an important division between royalty and the people, Percy breaking sovereign allegiance to take up a role as leader of the Democratic Party in a bid to reform the Verdopolitan Constitution. As with the contemporary society the Brontës lived in, the political debate for public reform is paramount in the siblings' minds, acting as a catalyst for the final Angrian and Glass Town Civil Wars (1835–1837) that shattered their imaginary kingdom between 1835–1837.

Although interested in parliamentary input and impact on their saga, the siblings' were also concerned with contemporary feelings of social anger and discontent, reflecting on and responding to the events and voices of the everyday people embroiled in civil conflict. Focusing on Charlotte specifically, her two tales, *The Foundling* (1833) and *Stancliffe's Hotel* (1838), were influenced by recent riots in Britain. *The Foundling* presents startling similarities to the recent 1831 Bristol riots: both show working-class people struggling for political reformation. In the tale, 'Naughty Ned Laury' leads the working-class people of Glass Town into a violent rebellion after the disappearance of the kingdom's wise man and justice giver, Crashie:

> An immense crowd assembled [...] which, at the word of command, formed itself in squares, files, battalions, etc., etc., with the accuracy of a well-disciplined army. Through these armed and ferocious-looking ranks, Naughty passed to and fro, exhorting them, with that rude eloquence [...] They answered with loud shouts, crying out that they would tear every redcoat in Verdopolis to atoms.[38]

It is important to note that, despite expressing a hatred of the military, the crowd structure themselves into a military formation. Very early on in her writing career, Charlotte realised that it was not just the official military redcoat that could be classed as a military man, but the everyday working-class man could be a threat and execute violence with determination, precision and order.

The Brontës would have read about the Bristol riots through numerous publications. Both their local newspapers, the *Leeds Mercury* and *Leeds Intelligencer*, ran articles on the incident.[39] Additionally, an 1831 contemporary report titled *A Full Report of the Trials of the Bristol Rioters* (1832) contained a detailed account of the violent clash between military personnel and the people. These, amongst other similar titles, were distributed widely and circulated in libraries in the north.[40] Each text relayed the spectacular violence and fear present at the event:

> orders were immediately given to the troops to charge, and the scene instantly become one of the greatest confusion. The people, who ran in all directions, were pursued to the limits of the city, the rioters engaged at the Council-House taking refuge in the numerous courts and alleys in Broad–street and Wine–street, from whence they assailed the troops with stones.[41]

Although this is just one example, it is clear that the siblings were able to emulate the sensational language of the incident that was disseminated to the British public, aggravating a national reaction. In *The Foundling*, Charlotte describes in a similar style how 'a horrible struggle' occurred between the military and the people, the military with their 'superior discipline' overpowering the mob: 'By degrees the living mass melted. Thousands sought safety in flight, and the few who remained were quickly cut to pieces'.[42] Charlotte's words, in all their poetic bluntness, may well have been a realistic commentary, her tale imitating the same dramatic language used in these emotional reports, which were intended to tap into contemporary sentimentality and spur people to act.

In a similar fashion, evidence of Charlotte's imitative response to military violence directed towards rioters is found in *Stancliffe's Hotel*. Although reflective of numerous contemporary rioting and unrest, her violent narrative mostly imitates the Peterloo Massacre of 1819. A crowd, aggravated by Zamorna's relationship with Percy, starts to protest outside Stancliffe's Hotel in central Angria. After they have confronted their king and rushed at the royal carriage with a 'hideous roar', Zamorna declares:

> 'Men of Zamorna, three hundred horsemen are upon you. I see them; they are here; you will be ridden down in five minutes if you do not bear back instantly from the carriage.' There was not time: with horse–hair waving and broad sabres glancing, with loud huzza and dint of thunder, the cavalry charged on the mob [...] Causeway and carriage were cleared; the wide street lay bare in the fierce sun behind them. A few wounded men alone were left with shattered limbs, lying on the pavement. These were soon taken off to the infirmary, their blood was washed from the stones, and no sign remained of what had happened.[43]

The use of military force is reminiscent of the violence witnessed at Peterloo: panicking magistrates set yeomanry cavalry on the 50,000 peaceful protesters that assembled on St. Peter's Fields, Manchester. The massacre was discussed in newspapers and journals around the country and prompted a number of new two-penny weekly publications such as *London Alfred or People's Register* and the *Democratic Recorder and Reformer's Guide*.[44] Although uprisings such as the Peterloo Massacre and Bristol Riots are alluded to in just a few examples of Charlotte's work, each illustrates the impact of Britain's social and political instability upon the country, the

Brontë family, and more specifically, young Charlotte. Despite not exuding the same sensational modes of war as discussed in this study's previous three chapters, civil unrest in Britain was a localised threat. The reorientation of the military as the enemy and the substitution of the people as the real 'heroes' embodied the anxieties and social fears of a growing industrial nation that failed to identify with its people.

Another riotous group that resonated with the Brontë imagination was the Luddites. This group, who operated in the north between 1811 and 1816, was comprised of skilled workers who violently rebelled against the introduction of stocking frames, spinning frames and power looms in the manufacturing industry. It is likely that the siblings were aware that a number of Luddites were ex-servicemen,[45] most likely through listening to accounts from their father who dealt with the hardship in his parish. As Gash comments:

> The Luddites – or some of them – drilled and went about in military formation. Many of them had served in the militia and others... enlisted in the army to avoid detection and arrest. There were unemployed soldiers and sailors in the Spa Fields riots in 1816 and ex-soldiers were involved in the Pentridge 'rising' in 1817. The abortive affair dignified by the name of the Huddersfield 'rising' in 1820 was led by a Barnsley weaver named Comstive who had been a sergeant in the 29th Foot and fought at Waterloo.[46]

The violent methods of these textile artisans captured the siblings' imaginations, allowing them to engage with and rewrite their own local history. Charlotte's interest in the Luddites sustained, her later novel, *Shirley* (1849), is set during the riots. Although informed by her opinion of the Chartist movement, the novel provides a backdrop of industrial depression resulting from the ongoing Napoleonic Wars. *Shirley* evidences Charlotte's considerable understanding of the Luddites' actions and the moral dilemma they instigated amongst the tradespeople. In one instance, Charlotte's protagonist, Caroline, is shown to look on as her love interest's, Robert Moore's, mill is subjected to a fierce attack:

> Shots were discharged by the rioters [...] The hitherto inert and passive mill woke: fire flashed from its empty window-frame [...] the mill–yard, the mill itself was full of battle-movement: there was scarcely any cessation now of the discharge of firearms; and there was struggling, rushing, trampling, and shouting between them.[47]

Despite this narrative's intensely violent imagery, Caroline remains a passive observer of the manufacturing plight. This combination of surveillance and reflection is repeated throughout the novel. Charlotte offers a mature moral response to the Luddite cause, acknowledging the plight of the poor whilst condemning the Luddites' illegal, violent actions, ultimately aligning herself with, as Lucasta Miller notes, the 'middlerank and aristocracy'.[48] This is, however, not the case in her earlier industrial writings; *Something About Arthur* (1833) is far from the sophisticated response demonstrated here.[49] Although both stories are a revised account of the infamous attack on Rawfolds Mill at Liversedge in Yorkshire, *Something About Arthur* is a juvenile response to a sensitive local topic. In the tale, Charlotte's young Zamorna [the Marquis of Douro] helps orchestrate a group of Luddite-like rioters who burn down a 'prisoner filled' mill belonging to the 'villainous' jockey and gambler Lord Caversham. This revenge attack, spurred by Caversham's duping him into a rigged horse race, is told with childish joviality. Zamorna declares: 'if I am victorious in this undertaking I will call it my first essay in the art of war, but mind what I say, Ned, it shall not be my last'.[50] Rather than acting as a spectator, like Charlotte's later heroine, Caroline, her youthful protagonist is at the centre of the riot. The party rushes in 'ferociously', releasing the prisoners and setting the mill alight:

> In less than a quarter of an hour wreaths of dun smoke, mingled with darting tongues of fire, were seen issuing from some of the lower windows. A dull roaring noise was also heard, and, after the lapse of another fifteen minutes, the wished-for conflagration broke forth at once in a column of clear, red flame which rose suddenly with a rushing sound into the air.[51]

It is evident from this early work that Charlotte remained ignorant of the moral issues present in her later industrial novel, her young self disconnecting from recent troubles and instead using Luddism as merely an exciting, danger-infused plot development. Both texts give an insightful perspective on Charlotte's progression into maturity. Although demonstrating a deep understanding of Luddism in her childhood years, it is only later that she identified with the movement in both an adult and emotive way.

Although no reference to a Luddite attack is made explicitly, Branwell's *The Wool Is Rising* is influenced by the trading conditions during and after the Napoleonic Wars. Throughout this study, it is Branwell who is often deemed the sensationalist war writer of the pair. In regard to Luddism, however, it is Branwell who appears to respond with a maturity lacked by his youthful sister whilst retaining language that suggests the Luddites to be dangerous and somewhat animalistic in their ferocity. In tune with the British economic depression, which was prolonged by the passing of the Corn Laws (1815–1846), *The Wool Is Rising* depicts two brothers, Edward and William Percy, struggling to make their business in the wool trade. Despite their overall success, they are nevertheless both aware of the economic climate, referencing the consequential poverty that accompanied Britain's post-war trade slump. Sending his work partner Timothy to gain employees, William takes advantage of their predicament whilst warning him to steer clear of rare lads, the siblings' Luddite-influenced rogues:

> I mean to send thee instantly among the most destitute of these. workers. mind keep clear of the rare lads they are fending for themselves – but pick out the most miserable of the others – offer them but with thy native tenacity. first the sum of 1s per week for little load is better than no meat.[52]

Here, Branwell's narrative tone is concerned and sentimental, yet still manages to dress Luddism in sensational language: 'they are fending for themselves' conjures animalistic imagery. It is likely that Branwell would have been aware first-hand of the Luddite plight. Juliet Barker speculates that Branwell was part of an 'Anti-Plug Dragoon Regiment', which captured workers 'who sabotaged their employers' machinery by removing the plugs from the boilers which powered the looms'.[53] These workers were imprisoned in Haworth's pub, The Black Bull. Barker goes on to note that Branwell had once 'offered to go in during a mill riot and thrash a dozen fellows'.[54] Through his own personal experiences, Branwell would have been able to both empathise with the workers he spoke to, yet equally understand the problems and dangers of their rebellions. With this knowledge of local and nationwide recession, Branwell, along with his sister, furnished their fictitious kingdoms with a sophisticated backdrop of economically driven social feeling. Their tales, despite their playful origins, offer an important account of localised violence and what it was like to grow up in an unstable socio-economic climate.

In conclusion, Charlotte and Branwell's Glass Town and Angria reflect and reconstruct significant components of, and feelings evoked by, civil war. By taking inspiration from Britain's present condition whilst simultaneously reanimating historical uprisings of the past, each sibling was able to provide a social commentary of civil conflict. It is through this fantastical reimagining of social anarchy and civil unrest that contemporary scholars may digest an unedited insight into contemporary British revolutionary fears and also a youthful perspective of factually inspired, if somewhat exaggerated, violence. Overall, the siblings' collective understandings of civil war and conflict provide an imaginative, alternative history regarding the divide between sovereignty/governmental systems and the everyday 'common man'. Through their kingdoms, the siblings were able to indulge their passion for danger and excitement whilst equally providing an innovative and honest response to the real-life damage civil war and conflict bring to a nation. In short, this final chapter has confirmed that Charlotte and Branwell are important all-round historians of and commentators on war in early nineteenth-century Britain. Their responses to war and conflict do not always require a canvas awash with iconic military figures or overseas campaigns. This chapter has shown that some of the most influential conflicts in the siblings' saga are instigated and carried out by the common man, demonstrating the potential that anyone could be a soldier. As Charlotte muses:

Is all crime the child of war?[55]

Perhaps the Brontës thought that it was. War did not necessarily stop when the troops returned home, or international peace had been restored. Rather than be limited to a certain place, war could follow the troops back and establish itself in a domestic setting: discontented people could readily and unofficially mutate into the military itself.

Notes

1. For the purpose of this chapter, it must be clarified that the various Glass Town (Verdopolitan) and Angrian provinces act as a federation of nations. Despite Wellington assuming leadership of the Glass Town Federation as a whole, each nation has a separate king and a character of its own.
2. *WPB I*: 1.
3. Ibid., 145.
4. "Campaigns of the British Army at Washington," *Blackwood's Edinburgh Magazine*, May 1821, 182.
5. *WPB I*: 146.
6. "Campaigns of the British Army at Washington," *Blackwood's*, 182.
7. Ibid.

8. Donald R. Hickey and Connie D. Clark (eds.), *The Routledge Handbook of the War of 1812* (New York: Routledge, 2015): 272.
9. *WPB III*: 210.
10. *Tales*: 256.
11. *WPB I*: 187.
12. Walter Scott, *The Life of Napoleon Buonaparte in Nine Volumes* (Edinburgh: William Blackwood, 1827): 292.
13. A Modern Pythagoreon, "An Execution in Paris," *Blackwood's Edinburgh Magazine*, December 1828, 788.
14. Scott, *Life of Napoleon*, 275.
15. Ardrah's Reform Party attempt to destroy the newly formed kingdom of Angria from its conception in 1834 by expelling the country from the Verdopolitan Union.
16. *WPB II*: 576–577.
17. *Tales*: 223.
18. Ibid., 222.
19. Ibid., 223.
20. Ibid., 222.
21. Benjamin Disraeli, *Vivian Gray* (London: Henry Colburn, 1826): 156.
22. See Lucy Hanson, *The Story of the People of Great Britain, Vol. IV* (Cambridge: Cambridge University Press, 1923).
23. *WPB II*: 47.
24. "Dupin—The Navy of England and France," *The Quarterly Review*, October 1821, 9.
25. Ibid.
26. N. Gash, "After Waterloo: British Society and the Legacy of the Napoleonic Wars," *Transactions of the Royal Historical Society*, 28 (1975): 147.
27. Charlotte's later academic tutor and idol, Constantin Heger, would be part of the ripple of European conflicts generated by the 'July Revolution'. He relayed to Charlotte, during her time as a student and teacher in Brussels, that from the 23–27 September 1830 he had fought for Belgian liberty at the barricades. His wife's younger brother was killed in his presence during the fighting.
28. Reverend Patrick Brontë, *The Letters of the Reverend Patrick Brontë*, ed. Dudley Green (London: Nonsuch, 2005): 77. The Brontës' hero, Wellington, lost a vote of no confidence on 15 November 1830 after upholding his stance on no reform and no extension of suffrage. For more information on the public's perception of Wellington, see this study's third chapter.
29. "Stanza in a Churchyard—War or No War," *Fraser's Magazine*, February 1834, 250.

30. "An Englishman in Paris," *John Bull*, 17 January 1830, 22.
31. Ibid.
32. Emeritus, "On the Approaching Revolution in Great Britain," *Blackwood's Edinburgh Magazine*, August 1831, 328.
33. The Representation of the People Act introduced much-needed parliamentary reform, but it was limited. Despite creating new constituencies and extending the vote to all householders who paid a yearly rental of £10 or more, a majority of working-class men still could not vote.
34. "The Progression of Revolution," *Fraser's Magazine*, July 1832, 684.
35. Sally Shuttleworth, *Charlotte Brontë and Victorian Psychology* (Cambridge: Cambridge University Press, 1996): 20.
36. Ibid.
37. Christine Alexander, *The Early Writings of Charlotte Brontë* (Buffalo, New York: Prometheus Books, 1983): 134.
38. *EEW II*: 99.
39. For example, the *Leeds Intelligencer* ran 'Dreadful Riots at Bristol on the 3 November 1831' and 'The Late Riots in Bristol' on 10 November 1831. The *Leeds Mercury* also ran an article with a title of the same name, 'Dreadful Riots at Bristol', on 5 November 1831 and reported the executions of the convicted rioters on 4 February 1832.
40. Other titles that were distributed include John Eagles' *The Bristol Riots: Their Causes, Progress and Consequences* (1832) and *Trials of the Persons Concerned in the Late Riots* (1832) printed by P. Rose.
41. W. H. Somerton, *A Full Report of the Trials of the Bristol Rioters* (Bristol: W. H. Somerton, 1832): 17.
42. *EEW II*: 100.
43. *Tales*: 115.
44. See Stanley Harrison, *Poor Men's Guardians: A Survey of the Struggles for a Democratic Newspaper Press, 1763–1973* (London: Lawrence and Wishart, 1974).
45. Evidence of military men becoming revolutionaries is also seen in Branwell's *Letters from an Englishman, Vol. III* (1831): 'They had all being military men come to town for the purpose of gaining Glory in the approaching revolution'. *WPB I*: 182.
46. Gash, "After Waterloo," 51.
47. Charlotte Brontë, *Shirley*, ed. Jessica Cox (London: Penguin, 2006): 326.
48. Lucasta Miller, *The Bronte Myth* (London: Vintage, 2006): xxi.
49. Although, at this point, most of the saga's attention is on Alexander Percy's 1832 uprising, Charlotte describes how, alongside this: 'Unequivocal symptoms of dissatisfaction began to appear at the same time among the lower orders in Verdopolis. The workmen at the principal mills and furnaces struck

for an advance of wages, and, the masters refusing to comply with their exorbitant demands, they all turned out simultaneously'. *EEW I*: 344–345. Although brief, this tale demonstrates a preface to her extended interest in Luddism, exhibited in her later text, *Shirley*.

50. *EEW II*: 26.
51. Ibid., 28.
52. *WPB II*: 47.
53. Juliet Barker, *The Brontës* (London: Weidenfeld and Nicolson, 1994): 402.
54. Ibid.
55. *Tales*: 223.

CHAPTER 7

Conclusion: After Angria

If life be a war, it seemed my destiny to conduct it single–handed[1]

Charlotte and Branwell's collaborative partnership ended in 1839. In her *Farewell to Angria* (1839), Charlotte bid farewell to her characters, scenes and subjects and ventured into her publishing career: 'I feel almost as I stood on the threshold of a home and were bidding farewell to its inmates'.[2] Meanwhile, Branwell did not break from Angria, continuing to write stories relating to his kingdom up until his death. In 1845, he even made an attempt to rework the saga into a stand-alone tale titled *And the weary are at rest*, which recast his soldierly characters in an English setting. The tale, however, mutates into a ranting, bawdy fragment that describes Alexander Percy's attempts to seduce a married woman. It is not known how much of this piece survives—it begins mid-sentence—and it lacks structure and coherence.

Branwell continued to be interested in war. His later poetry draws on a number of themes that have been discussed within this book. For example, in line with his interest in classicism, Branwell challenged himself to translate Horace's militant odes throughout the 1840s. Horace was a leading Roman lyric poet, who drew from a range of subject matters—including civil war and military masculinity. Branwell also maintained an interest in key figures and literature relating to the Napoleonic Wars: he wrote a poem

© The Author(s) 2019
E. Butcher, *The Brontës and War*,
https://doi.org/10.1007/978-3-319-95636-7_7

dedicated to and titled *Lord Nelson* in 1842. Victor Neufeldt notes that
Branwell read Southey's *Life of Nelson* (1830) before composing this. Like
the majority of his Angrian poetry, Branwell conflates patriotism with suffering: 'No words of mine have power to rouse the brain / Distressed with
grief. The body bowed with pain'.[3] Although separate from the Angrian
saga, Branwell still used his position as a commentator and historian to emulate contemporary post-war feeling. This feeling extends to Branwell's new
branch of war poetry. In 1840–1842, Branwell composed two poems entitled 'The Affgan War' [*sic*] (1842) and 'Sir Henry Tunstall' (1840–1842):
the latter considered by Winifred Gérin to be Branwell's finest achievement.[4] 'The Affgan War' recounts the British Army withdrawing from
Kabul in January 1842 during the First Anglo-Afghan War (1839–1842):
the funeral bell tolls and 'no returning / Fate allows to such farewell'.[5] Julie
Donovan argues that the poem 'conveys the power of stillness and quiet-
ness',[6] an attribute of Branwell's poetry that, as this book attests, can be
traced back to his poignant and careful use of verse within his Angrian battles. The melancholic themes of this poem feed into Branwell's final draft
of 'Sir Henry Tunstall' (1842), which focuses on a soldier who returns
to Britain after sixteen years of military service in India. Throughout, the
poem laments a man who has changed both physically and mentally, who
cannot adjust to his old domestic realm. It is clear, from the similar name of
the protagonist of this poem, that Branwell has not forgotten his old protagonist Henry Hastings, whose degeneration into alcoholism as a result of
trauma is discussed in chapter four of this book. Similarly, Branwell lingers
on the plight of the returning soldier, recalling his reworking of the post-
Napoleonic social climate within the Angrian saga and transmogrifying it
in the context of this new war and character. The trauma embedded within
the verse is evident:

> They did not think how oft my eyesight turned
> Toward the skies where Indian Sunshine burned,
> That I had perhaps left an associate band,
> That I had farewells even for that wild Land;
> They did not think my head and heart were older,
> My strength more broken and my feelings colder,
> That spring was hastening into autumn sere -
> And leafless trees make loveliest prospects drear -
> That sixteen years the same ground travel oer
> Till each wears out the mark which each has left before.[7]

This extract parallels Branwell and Charlotte's earlier treatment of trauma in their Angrian verse and poetry. Like Percy, whose eyes 'wander towards the skies' in 'Misery Part II' (1836), or Hastings, who withdraws ever further from his sister Elizabeth Hastings as he descends into alcoholism, Tunstall is testimony that Branwell carried the sentimental, dysfunctional voice of the soldier into his later works: the legacy of war and its impact still affected Branwell and his characters.

'Sir Henry Tunstall' was sent to Thomas De Quincey on 15 April 1840, and the final version was sent to *Blackwood's* on 6 September 1842. Although this particular poem was not published, Branwell successfully published numerous other poems throughout the 1840s. He was, in fact, the first of the Brontë family to be published. As Neufeldt notes:

> Branwell published at least twenty-six items in his lifetime, and was in print five years before his sisters. Twenty-five of these publications appeared before his sisters published their volume of poems in 1846 [...] His last published work was a poem, fittingly titled The End of All, in the *Halifax Guardian* June 5, 1847, just four months before the publication of *Jane Eyre*.[8]

It is clear that Branwell enjoyed a wide readership of his later militant verse: for example 'The Affgan War' was published in the *Leeds Intelligencer* on 7 May 1842. Unlike his sister Charlotte, however, Branwell did not successfully channel his interest in the military into any significant published works. Despite this, his success as a poet and continued interest in war should be acknowledged. Branwell died on 24 September 1848, leaving behind a legacy of writing that, amongst other themes, provides a significant socio-historical commentary on war in a recovering nation. Critics can only speculate as to how this intuitive response to war would have taken shape had Branwell lived to develop his writing career.

Charlotte, on the other hand, went on to write published works that involve events and characters that are historically grounded in her interest in the military. Whereas *The Professor* (1845–1846, 1857), *Jane Eyre* (1847) and *Villette* (1853) contain relevant yet subtler references to the military, Charlotte's 1849 work, *Shirley*, set during the Napoleonic Wars, provides the most literal translation of war from the juvenilia to the later works. Although war in its literal sense is no longer treated as a core theme in the sister's published writing career, war and conflict are broad terms and are embedded within the fabric of her literature, from personal relationships to emotional conflict, from domestic and racial violence to warring identities. The majority of characters within the collective Brontë writings are battling inner and outer demons. There are, however, moments where military subjects are latently embedded within the subtext of her works, which demonstrate the legacy of her childhood role as a commentator and historian of war.

SILENT SOLDIERS

Mike [Hartley] was busy hedging rather late in the afternoon, but before dark, when he heard what he thought was a band at a distance—bugles, fifes, and the sound of a trumpet; it came from the forest, and he wondered that there should be music there. He looked up. All amongst the trees he saw moving objects, red, like poppies, or white, like may–blossom. The wood was full of them; they poured out and filled the park. He then perceived they were soldiers—thousands and tens of thousands; but they made no more noise than a swarm of midges on a summer evening. They formed in order, he affirmed, and marched, regiment after regiment, across the park. He followed them to Nunnely Common; the music still played soft and distant. On the common he watched them go through a number of evolutions. A man clothed in scarlet stood in the centre and directed them. They extended, he declared, over fifty acres. They were in sight half an hour; then they marched away quite silently. The whole time he heard neither voice nor tread—nothing but the faint music playing a solemn march.[9]

This poetic passage, taken from Charlotte's later novel *Shirley*, renders soldiers silent. Strangely, the achievement of Charlotte and Branwell's juvenilia to recognise and give voice to the everyday soldier is lost a decade later: the soldier is back to being a large bodily mass.[10] Despite the number of soldiers, between thousands and tens of thousands, Mike does not hear them. They move silently across the landscape as if they were part of nature. Perhaps, here, Charlotte is alluding to the relationship between soldierhood and nature she had learned through her reading of military memoirs. Although warfare blights the natural landscape, Napoleonic soldierly campaigns allowed some soldiers to reconfigure their journey as a travelogue.[11] Another explanation for Charlotte's comparison is that the presence of soldiers had become such a part of northern England's topography, that a mass of soldiers was now but everyday wildlife in the Haworthian habitat and, in an abstract sense, a staple part of the Brontë imagination. As the sixth chapter of this book demonstrates, the Brontë children grew up in a landscape that was home to returning soldiers. In addition, the juvenilias' focus on song and military spectacle is adopted and replayed in a poignant fashion. By this point, Charlotte had lost Branwell who was her fellow collaborator and songwriter—in this section the bugles, fifes and trumpets are distant and unceremonious.

Silent soldiers linger in the background throughout *Shirley*. In another instance within the text, a 'red speck' on the horizon interrupts Shirley and Caroline's conversation: 'a line of red. They are soldiers – cavalry soldiers [...] They ride fast. There are six of them. They will pass us. No; they have turned off to the right. They saw our procession, and avoid it by making a circuit [...] We see them no more now'.[12] Later, a similar interruption occurs, this time whilst Shirley and Caroline are lost in thought:

> They listened, and heard the tramp of horses. They looked, and saw a glitter through the trees. They caught through the foliage glimpses of martial scarlet; helm shone, plume waved. Silent and orderly, six soldiers rode softly by. "The same we saw this afternoon," whispered Shirley. "They have been halting somewhere till now. They wish to be as little noticed as possible, and are seeking their rendezvous at this quiet hour, while the people are at church. Did I not say we should see unusual things ere long?" Scarcely were sight and sound of the soldiers lost, when another and somewhat different disturbance broke the night–hush—a child's impatient scream.[13]

Glimpses of the juvenilia are seen here. References to glitter and 'martial scarlet; helm shone, plume waved' evoke imagery of military parades in Glass Town and Angria, or portraits of Zamorna and his loyal band of elite military brothers. Despite, however, the soldiers in *Shirley* displaying an equally 'loud' colour, they softly pass in an understated 'silent and orderly' manner, weaving in and out of the foliage. The uncanny harmony between the military and nature startles the characters; Shirley notes that this was 'unusual'. Unlike Glass Town and Angria, whose streets were littered with jaunty soldiers riding by on horseback, soldiers in this landscape take on new meaning: they are mystical and symbolic; an omen that a disruption is going to occur.

The passages here enlighten readers to the soldiers' role in the narrative. Although an understated, subtle feature of Charlotte's novel, their invisibility brands them the concealed monsters of the text. Much as Edward

Rochester's estranged wife, Bertha Mason, haunts the hallways of Thornfield in *Jane Eyre*, the soldiers' persistent presence in *Shirley's* narrative reminds readers that the Yorkshire landscape is under threat: the reader sees red. Moreover, to contribute to this book's broader historical context, the soldiers are fitting mood music for the societal grievances of the time. As *Shirley* extends the discussion of the public versus the military—seen within the final chapter of this study—it is clear why Charlotte transformed military men into something more sinister.

Some years later, Charlotte again plays with soldierhood and visibility to indicate danger and disruption. In *Villette*, Lucy Snowe travels to Villette in 'thick fog and small dense rain – darkness'. She 'passed through a gate where soldiers were stationed – so much I could see by lamplight'.[14] The presence of soldiers is, as in *Shirley*, aligned with feelings of fear. Like Mike, who sees the soldiers just before dark, Lucy approaches Villette as darkness 'had settled on the city'.[15] Along with her new surroundings, new emotions come to the forefront of her mind: she is plagued with 'ceaseless consciousness of anxiety lying in wait on enjoyment, like a tiger crouched in a jungle'.[16] When her carriage stops, her first impressions of her environment are of disruption. The conductor speaks only French and 'the whole world seemed now gabbling around me'.[17] Like *Shirley's* soldiers, who are an unnatural blemish on the landscape, Lucy takes on this alien role. The Belgian soldiers, who stand silent amidst the murky light, contribute to this uncertain, threatening terrain that she must conquer. They symbolise, as do the redcoats in *Shirley*, that the landscape is under threat. This time, however, rather than the literal landscape, the soldiers act as a carefully timed omen that the landscape of the novel will soon change: only a few paragraphs later, Lucy describes how 'Fate took me in her strong hand' as she rings the doorbell of the Pensionnat.[18]

This brief recognition of soldiers' role in Charlotte's later narratives demonstrates that, despite its subtle inclusion, the military continued to impact Charlotte's creative consciousness. Her familiarity and frequent engagement with war in her youth allowed her to reconstruct the figure of the soldier into an understated yet effective symbolic plot device. The examples offered in this conclusion are but the foundations of future studies of how soldierhood is reworked and reimagined in later Brontë literature, despite its seemingly invisible or insignificant presence. It is this concluding section's aim to offer a tantalising but convincing preface to the more identifiable examples of soldierly presence in these narratives, hoping that further research will uncover more examples using this book's argument as context.

MILITARY MASCULINITY

The remnants of soldierhood can be found implicitly within Charlotte's later masculine protagonists. Broadly, characters such as Edward Rochester in *Jane Eyre* might appear militant in their bearing; numerous critical studies have addressed his sexually dominant treatment of Jane.[19] He is, however, actively described as being the antithesis of militancy. Whilst attending an elite gathering at Thornfield Hall, Charlotte notes the characters in attendance. When Rochester enters the room, she observes that he lacks the 'military distinction of Colonel Dent, contrasted with his look of native pith and genuine power'.[20] Despite this, the sentence's final words, 'genuine power', generate imagery of war and conflict. This is, however, just one instance where the legacy of militarism is attached to individual personhood. In the fifth chapter of this book, *Jane Eyre's* missionary, St. John Rivers, is briefly alluded to within the discussion of war, colonialism and religion. Unlike Charlotte's published literature, it was clear that, in the juvenilia, the siblings preferred sensational battle scenes to Christian ideals of conversion. St. John Rivers demonstrates a maturation of Charlotte's values: despite racist overtones of the Christian mission, Rivers' aim is not to kill, but to save.

Chapter 5's discussion also alludes to the juvenilias' pre-empting of muscular Christianity. Zamorna and Alexander Percy conform to ideals of the Christian colonial warrior. *Jane Eyre*, published in 1847, consolidates the relationship between Christianity and the military. At one point, St. John reveals his divine duty, likening his mission to that of a soldier:

> After a season of darkness and struggling, light broke and relief fell: my cramped existence all at once spread out to a plain without bounds—my powers heard a call from heaven to rise, gather their full strength, spread their wings, and mount beyond ken. God had an errand for me; to bear which afar, to deliver it well, skill and strength, courage and eloquence, the best qualifications of soldier, statesman, and orator, were all needed: for these all centre in the good missionary.[21]

Here, colonisation is directly associated with the characteristics of soldierhood. His intended wife, Jane, notes his military bearing, stating to
Rochester after rejecting St. John's marriage proposal: 'He prizes me as a
soldier would a good weapon; and that is all'.[22] These direct references to
the military evoke imagery from the juvenilia, and St. John, despite being
a modern Victorian gentleman, is a direct legacy of the soldiers Charlotte
imagined in her youth.[23]

The relationship between soldierhood and religion is highlighted again
in Charlotte's later text, *Shirley*. Like St. John, whose mental and physical
attributes lend a demigod exterior to Christianity, a similar description is
awarded to Caroline's uncle, the curate Reverend Helstone:

> He should have been a soldier, and circumstances had made him a priest. For
> the rest, he was a conscientious, hard–headed, hard–handed, brave, stern,
> implacable, faithful little man; a man almost without sympathy, ungentle,
> prejudiced, and rigid, but a man true to principle, honourable, sagacious,
> and sincere.[24]

Again, this passage directly links the attributes of Christianity with the
military. It is clear through these passages from *Jane Eyre* and *Shirley* that
the legacy of militarism may not lie in soldierhood itself, but in the qualities
of characters that bring a military bearing to their everyday occupations.

In short, despite the invisibility of soldiers in Charlotte's literature, subtle references and comparisons to militarism play an important hand in
constructing some of her later key masculine characters. Although these
personalities are not directly involved in the military, their dispositions bear
the remnants of the soldiers that proliferated through Charlotte and Branwell's juvenilia, and therefore are also reimagined from the soldierly profiles
constructed in the literature they read. Thus, Charlotte's hyper-masculine
characters are historically grounded in war.

WELLINGTON AND NAPOLEON

In Charlotte's later works, the legacy of Wellington and theNapoleon is
much more explicit than the legacy of the 'everyday soldier'. Alongside a
body of scholarly literature, this book's third chapter demonstrates Wellington's early impact on Charlotte's writing career, however, his authoritative
hold on her imagination lasted into adulthood. For example, in 1850, three
years before her death, Charlotte travelled to London and caught a glimpse

of the Iron Duke himself. Moreover, Charlotte maintained an interest in Napoleon, writing a devoir commemorating his death, 'On the Death of Napoleon' (1843), during her schooling in Belgium. It is not surprising, then, that legacies of these two men are apparent in her published litera-ture. In addition, numerous Brontë biographies and scholarly pieces have alluded to and quoted passages from the later novels' engagement with Wellington and Napoleon. It is interesting to note how these representa-tions imitate or differ from those in the juvenilia that were, in turn, derived from the periodical press.

There is, on the one hand, an outburst of praise for Wellington as is repeatedly expressed in the juvenilia and post-Waterloo periodical press. In *Shirley*, characters such as Shirley and Revd. Helstone embody the patri-otic virtues akin to Charlotte's own temperament. Helstone's declarations of 'Wellington is the soul of England. Wellington is the right champion of a good cause, the fit representative of a powerful, a resolute, a sensible, and an honest nation'[25] could well have been declared by a young Charlotte or a post-Waterloo commentator in *Blackwood's*. Despite the public's increas-ing disillusion with Wellington, namely for his high Tory political views, Charlotte continued to promote his name. In her writings, as is noted by Barnard and Barnard: 'every opportunity was taken to pay tribute to him, often in disputes in which the contrary view is put by one person, who is worsted by the Duke's admirer'.[26] This is certainly true of *Shirley* and *The Professor*, whose characters often engage in carefully constructed political debates. The above extract from Shirley is from a disagreement between Helstone and *Shirley's* Belgian-born protagonist, Robert Moore. Another similar situation occurs between Frances Henri and Yorke Huns-den in Charlotte's earlier novel, *The Professor*, where a personal argument is compared to Wellington and Napoleon's battle at Waterloo. In her defence, Frances asserts: 'he [Wellington] persevered in spirit of the laws of war and was victorious in defiance of military tactics – I would do as he did'.[27] These scenarios demonstrate Charlotte's unwavering heart: she gave voice to the critics of her idol before verbally bludgeoning them, reaffirming her unconditional devotion.

Considering Wellington's continued praise, it is no surprise that, just as in her juvenilia, the language used to describe Napoleon is overwhelm-ingly negative. For example, in *Shirley*, those who were 'shuddering on the verge of bankruptcy' found Napoleon's 'insolent self–felicitations […] on his continued triumphs […] tedious'.[28] They [the British people] endured a 'hopeless struggle against what their fears or their interests taught them to regard as an invincible power, most insufferable'.[29] As the analysis of Napoleon in this book has determined, this rhetoric is not unfamiliar. Charlotte was merely continuing her interaction with the menacing representations she and Branwell had built into their juvenilia, which, in turn, engaged with negative portrayals of France's Emperor in the periodical press and influential biographies, such as Walter Scott's *Life of Napoleon* (1827).

Wellington and Napoleon continued to be an important part of Charlotte's construction of fictional personalities, their individual characteristics and rivalry an imaginative, readymade plot and character device. Interestingly, despite her lifelong hero worship of Wellington, it was Napoleon's character that particularly inspired Charlotte in her later writing career. In her last novel, *Villette*, both Lucy's Belgian love interest, M. Paul, and enemy, Madame Beck, embody the French Emperor. Madame Beck is described as looking 'like a little Bonaparte in a mouse–coloured silk gown',[30] whilst 'heroically and inexorably' ordering her female pupils away from the boys' school across the yard.[31] On the other hand, her teacher, M. Paul, embodies a more Romantic, Byronic form of Napoleon. In fact, he is more reminiscent of Branwell's youthful embodiment of Napoleon, Alexander Percy. Like Percy—and in proxy Napoleon—who is both a revolutionary and threat to social order, M. Paul is described as an 'intelligent tiger' and 'tiger–Jesuit',[32] descriptions that also adhere to Voltaire's general animalisation of common countrymen. It is clear that Charlotte revised and remoulded representations of Napoleon's power and menace, applying them in a teacher/pupil context:

> I used to think, as I sat looking at M. Paul, while he was knitting his brow or protruding his lip over some exercise of mine, which had not as many faults as he wished (for he liked me to commit faults: a knot of blunders was sweet to him as a cluster of nuts), that he had points of resemblance to Napoleon Bonaparte. I think so still. In a shameless disregard of magnanimity, he resembled the great Emperor. M. Paul would have quarrelled with twenty learned women, would have unblushingly carried on a system of petty bickering and recrimination with a whole capital of coteries, never troubling himself about loss or lack of dignity. He would have exiled fifty Madame de Staëls, if, they had annoyed, offended, outrivalled, or opposed him.[33]

Although these characteristics are not in any way new or shocking, in this instance they take on new meaning. In the novel, comparisons with Napoleon are not counteracted with the virtues of Wellington, but offer stand-alone characteristics that, in their ugliness and animalism, paradoxically and explicitly ignite sexualised imagery of power. In one instance Lucy remarks of her teacher: 'He was roused, and I loved him in wrath with a passion beyond what I had yet felt'.[34] In her final years, Charlotte's celebration of Napoleon's role as Byronic hero had prevailed over his role as Wellington's foil.

As well as Wellington and Napoleon's literal legacy in Charlotte's literature, tensions seen between France and Britain in the juvenilia continue to manifest themselves in broader ways. Anne Longmuir's argues:

> The Belgian settings in *The Professor* and *Villette* are not [...] merely a product of Brontë's own personal experience on the continent. Instead, they reflect both Brontë's own concern with the clash of British and French values and a particular mid–Victorian understanding of the significance of Belgium to British national identity.[35]

Whilst recognising these anxieties, Longmuir suggests that this mutual setting where French and British values collide is, moreover, symbolic of Charlotte's wish for reconciliation and offers a space where a new racially harmonious home may emerge.[36] Despite maintaining the public binaries of Wellington and Napoleon as arch rivals, Charlotte's negotiation of French and British peace was indicative of her wish for peace amidst war: a luxury that her brother did not grant in the juvenilia with his excessive lust for battle. In fact, this harmony could be an extension of Angria's post-war years of 1838–1839, where Zamorna and Percy reconciled and the country was rebuilding. Even one of Branwell's last narratives imagined them both walking down the stairs, hand in hand as brothers.[37]

Longmuir's article is positive in its outcomes and offers a form of Franco–British atonement. The idea, however, of a 'little Britain on the continent' reanimates elements of Charlotte's interaction with imperialism. Longmuir argues that the Belgian setting of Brontë's texts provides a positive, self–conscious reaffirmation of British identity, however, in the context of the juvenilia, it is more violent. Examples are put forward to evidence a self–conscious Britishness in Belgian topography. Notably, Longmuir references Frances and William Crimsworth's union in *The Professor*, noting that their meeting place is 'English-looking': pastoral, with English plants.[38] In *Villette*, it is noted that the Brettons furnish their Belgian home with furniture bought from England.[39] Is this intention to replicate Britain abroad a nod to Charlotte's empire-building desires? Whereas once it was necessary for Wellington and his son to be the conquerors, it now takes only the humble William Crimsworth and Lucy Snowe to establish British-ness in a foreign landscape. What is clear, however, is that the need for British colonisation has merely been displaced from Africa to Belgium. In the context of Wellington and Napoleon, the discussion has extended not just to their notability as figures but also to the legacies of empire itself and how, some years later, their rivalry has broadened to define entire nation-alities. The war between Wellington and Napoleon thrives in Charlotte's later writings, both literally and in abstract forms of nationhood.

CHARLOTTE AND BRANWELL: WAR HISTORIANS AND COMMENTATORS

> My lord, you see it, you feel it yourself. In what state was Angria last year at this time? You remember it laid in ashes – plague and famine and slaughter, struggling with each other which should sway the sceptre that disastrous war had wrested from your own hand. And I ask, my lord, who had brought Angria to this state?[40]

This book has argued that Charlotte and Branwell Brontë are important his-torians of and commentators on war in the early nineteenth century. Their eclectic and wide-ranging juvenilia offer one insight into the mosaic of facts, opinions and feelings on war that were circulating in early nineteenth-century British culture. From the literature they read, the siblings are able to provide an alternative social and cultural response to contemporary atti-tudes regarding war conflict and masculinity. The juvenilia map an exciting (post)moment in history that saw the reactions and emotions of a war-torn nation explored through artistic outlets. Although this book also empha-sises that, through the very complexity of their writings, these were excep-tional siblings from an exceptional family who were exceptionally creative, their intellectual digestion of literature ranging from periodicals to soldiers' memoirs allows their writings to capture a range of responses that were expressed by a wider writing public. Although the Brontë family had no direct experience of war, their willingness to learn and engage with others' experiences of conflict, ranging from canonical reimaginings to opinionated media pieces and biographical accounts, transforms their superficial fantasy works into a multidimensional alternative history of war and militarism. The intense, multi-layered content within the juvenilia responds to many forms of new movements ranging from the birth of celebrity culture to the rise of the periodical press, and from the proliferation of the military memoir to newly published travel narratives relating to the Dark Continent. It is clear that Charlotte and Branwell Brontë's early writings offer a new lens through which present-day scholars can view and understand the post-war social and cultural climate of early nineteenth-century Britain and, more broadly, encourage us to consider their youthful writings as important literary and historical sources in the history of British warfare.

NOTES

1. Charlotte Brontë, *Villette*, ed. Margaret Smith (Oxford: Oxford University Press, 2008): 296.
2. *Tales*: 314.
3. *WPB III*: 354.
4. Julie Donovan, "The Poetry and Verse Drama of Branwell Brontë," in *A Companion to the Brontës*, ed. Diane Long Hoeveler and Deborah Denenholz Morse (Oxford: Wiley Blackwell, 2016): 219.
5. *WPB III*: 367.
6. Donovan, *A Companion to the Brontës*, 219.
7. *WPB III*: 240.
8. *WPB III*: xix–xx.
9. Charlotte Brontë, *Shirley*, ed. Jessica Cox (London: Penguin, 2006): 16. This passage replicates images of Malcolm's army moving the trees of Birnam Wood up Dunsinane Hill in Shakespeare's *Macbeth* (1606). Charlotte's merging of military men and nature stirs this same kind of invisible, mass threat.
10. See Chapter 4 of this book, which explains how, before the rise of the military memoir, the soldier was seen as a 'cog in the war machine' and not considered as an autonomous subject. Charlotte's published literature falls in line with this representation; this with the exception of Colonel Dent in *Jane Eyre*, who attends the lavish party at Thornfield. Although explicitly named, he is still a passing, invisible figure compared to the title characters in the scene.
11. As Ramsey notes in *The Military Memoir and Romantic Literary Culture*, soldiers adopted the Romantic ethos of 'nature as a more morally pure and

authentic realm than civilian life'. Neil Ramsey, *The Military Memoir and Romantic Literary Culture* (Farnham: Ashgate, 2011): 156.

12. Brontë, *Shirley*, 287. Charlotte's description of a 'red speck' on the horizon preempts Thomas Hardy's treatment of individual humans as a 'speck' in his novels, reminding the reader of the insignificance of the human race as opposed to the seismic scale of the universe. In a similar vein, this passage in *Shirley* demonstrates the insignificance of the individual soldier, reducing his presence to that *en masse*.

13. Ibid., 305.

14. Brontë, *Villette*, 61.

15. Ibid.

16. Ibid.

17. Ibid.

18. Ibid., 62.

19. See, for example, Louisa Yates, "Reader, I [Shagged/Beat/Whipped /F****d/Rewrote] Him," in *Charlotte Brontë: Legacies and Afterlives*, ed. Amber Regis and Deborah Wynne (Manchester: Manchester University Press, 2018).

20. Charlotte Brontë, *Jane Eyre*, ed. Margaret Smith (Oxford: Oxford University Press, 2008): 175.

21. Brontë, *Jane Eyre*, 361.

22. Ibid., 405.

23. For a more detailed discussion of Rivers' metaphorical relationship to war in *Jane Eyre* see Karen Turner, "Charlotte Brontë's 'Warrior Priest': St. John Rivers and the Language of War," in *Martial Masculinities: Experiencing and Imagining the Military in the Long Nineteenth Century*, ed. Michael Brown, Joanne Begiato, and Anna Maria Barry (Manchester: Manchester University Press, 2019): 199–213.

24. Brontë, *Shirley*, 36.

25. Ibid., 37.

26. Louise Barnard and Robert Barnard, *A Brontë Encyclopedia* (Hoboken: Wiley–Blackwell, 2007): 368.

27. Charlotte Brontë, *The Professor*, ed. Margaret Smith and Herbert Rosengarten (Oxford: Oxford University Press, 2008): 200.

28. Brontë, *Shirley*, 161.

29. Ibid.

30. Brontë, *Villette*, 143.

31. Ibid.

32. Brontë, *Villette*, 143, 474.

33. Ibid., 348.

34. Ibid., 481.

35. Anne Longmuir, "'Reader, Perhaps You Were Never in Belgium?': Negotiating British Identity in Charlotte Brontë's *The Professor* and *Villette*," *Nineteenth-Century Literature*, 64.2 (2009): 187.

36. Ibid., 170, 187.
37. *WPB III*: 270.
38. Brontë, *The Professor*, 186.
39. Brontë, *Villette*, 178.
40. *Tales*: 185.

Bibliography

Primary Material

Circulating Library Catalogues

A Catalogue of Widdop's Circulating Library. Oldham: R. Green, 1825.
Catalogue of Books in the Subscription and Circulating Library of Misses M & S. Laycock. Sheffield: W. Todd, 1825.
Catalogue of Andrews' New British and Foreign Circulating Library. London: B. M. M, 1825.
New Catalogue of Hookham's Circulating Library. London: T. Brettell, 1829.

Magazines

"A Comparison Between Wellington and Napoleon." *Bell's Life in London and Sporting Chronicle*, 21 November, 1852, 8.
A Modern Pythagorean. "An Execution in Paris." *Blackwood's Edinburgh Magazine*, December, 1828, 785–788.
"American Writers No. II." *Blackwood's Edinburgh Magazine*, October, 1825, 415–428.
B. "The Editor's Portfolio." *United Service Journal and Naval Military Magazine*, July, 1829, 109–111.
"Boxiana." *Blackwood's Edinburgh Magazine*, June, 1819, 439–443.
"Boxiana—Civil Wars." *Blackwood's Edinburgh Magazine*, September, 1819, 664.
"Campaigns of the British Army at Washington." *Blackwood's Edinburgh Magazine*, May, 1821, 180–187.
Citadell, Hull. "Battle of New Orleans." *Blackwood's Edinburgh Magazine*, September, 1828, 356–357.

© The Editor(s) (if applicable) and The Author(s) 2019
E. Butcher, *The Brontës and War*,
https://doi.org/10.1007/978-3-319-95636-7

191

Cunningham, Alan. "The British Sailor's Song." *United Service Journal*, December, 1827, 600.

Dirom, Lieut-General. "The Soldier's Song." *United Service Journal*, December, 1827, 438.

"Dupin—The Navy of England and France." *The Quarterly Review*, October, 1821, 1–37.

"Early Childhood of the Brontë Family." *The Ladies' Repository*, February, 1881, 65–69.

Edwards, Charles. "The Last Words of Charles Edwards Esq." *Blackwood's Edinburgh Magazine*, October, 1823, 396–419.

Emeritus. "On the Approaching Revolution in Great Britain." *Blackwood's Edinburgh Magazine*, August, 1831, 313–329.

Finlay, John. "The Soldier in Egypt." *Blackwood's Edinburgh Magazine*, February, 1818, 490.

Flagstaffe, Francis. "Passages in the Life of Colonel Flagstaffe." *Blackwood's Edinburgh Magazine*, March, 1828, 273–290.

"French Poets of the Present Day." *Blackwood's Edinburgh Magazine*, May, 1823, 507–511.

"Geography of Central Africa—Denham and Clapperton's Journals." *Blackwood's Edinburgh Magazine*, June, 1826, 686–709.

Gleig, George. "The Brothers." *Friendship's Offering: And Winter's Wreath: A Christmas and New Year's Present*. London: Smith, Elder & Co., 1829, 37–58.

———. "The Subaltern." *Blackwood's Edinburgh Magazine*, March–September, 1825, 279–298, 442–459, 563–573, 717–727, 67–82, 195–211, 269–282.

H. "Verses." *Blackwood's Edinburgh Magazine*, April, 1817, 70.

Howitt, Richard. "The Truant." *Friendship's Offering: And Winter's Wreath: A Christmas and New Year's Present*. London: Smith, Elder & Co., 1829, 181.

J. P. M. "The Negro's Lament for Mungo Park." *Blackwood's Edinburgh Magazine*, November, 1829, 196.

Jaucourt, Comte François. "Les Dragons." *United Service Journal*, December, 1829, 563.

"Las Cases Journal." *Blackwood's Edinburgh Magazine*, August, 1823, 169–172.

"London." *Blackwood's Edinburgh Magazine*, August, 1826, 324–325.

M. "The British Settlements of Western Africa." *Blackwood's Edinburgh Magazine*, September, 1829, 341–344.

McQueen, James. "Civilisation of Africa—Sierra Leone." *Blackwood's Edinburgh Magazine*, March, 1827, 315–330.

"Mission from Cape Coast Castle to Ashantee." *Blackwood's Edinburgh Magazine*, May–June, 1819, 175–183, 302–310.

Moggridge, Lieutenant Spencer. "Letters from the Peninsula No. 1 The Battle of Barrosa." *Blackwood's Edinburgh Magazine*, June, 1827, 695–794.

———. "Letters from the Peninsula No. 2 The Battle of Vittoria." *Blackwood's Edinburgh Magazine*, February, 1828, 183–191.

———. "Letters from the Peninsula No. 3 Depot at the Isle of Wight." *Blackwood's Edinburgh Magazine*, April, 1828, 431–444.

"Narrative of an Imprisonment in France During the Reign of Terror." *Blackwood's Edinburgh Magazine*, December, 1831, 920–953.

"Napoleon's Address to the Statue of His Son." *Blackwood's Edinburgh Magazine*, December, 1822, 760.

O. G. G. "The Soldier's Camp Song on the Eve of Battle." *United Service Journal*, November, 1829, 593.

Odoherty, Morgan. "Military Errors of the Duke of Wellington." *Blackwood's Edinburgh Magazine*, December, 1819, 291–296.

"On the Late French Revolution/On Parliamentary Reform and the Late French Revolution." *Blackwood's Edinburgh Magazine*. January–December, 1831, 36–45, 175–185, 431–446, 615–626, 745–761, 919–934, v. 30, 17–133, 281–295, 432–447, 600–615, 765–781, 890–912.

"On the Military Events of the Late French Revolution." *Blackwood's Edinburgh Magazine*, January, 1831, 48–60.

P. V. "Boxing Match at Wimbledon." *Blackwood's Edinburgh Magazine*, March, 1818, 669.

"Passage Through the Desert." *Blackwood's Edinburgh Magazine*, September, 1817, 624.

"Punishments in the Army." *Blackwood's Edinburgh Magazine*, April, 1824, 399–406.

"Rapp's Memoirs." *Blackwood's Edinburgh Magazine*, July, 1823, 39–42.

"Remarks on General Gourgaud's Account of the Campaign of 1815." *Blackwood's Edinburgh Magazine*, November, 1819, 220–228.

"Russia." *Blackwood's Edinburgh Magazine*, April, 1826, 447–460.

"Sketches of Savage Life." *Fraser's Magazine*, February–April, 1836, 169–176, 316–323, 499–511.

"Sketch of the Battle of Salamanca." *United Service Journal*, March, 1829, 283–295.

"Song of Mina's Soldiers." *United Service Journal*, March, 1830, 414.

"Spanish National Song." *United Service Journal*, December, 1829, 696.

"Stanza in a Churchyard—War or No War." *Fraser's Magazine*, February, 1834, 250–252.

"The Craniologist's Review." *Blackwood's Edinburgh Magazine*, May, 1818, 146–148.

"The Military Sketch Book." *Blackwood's Edinburgh Magazine*, June, 1827, 838–843.

The Oxford Review or Literary Censor. Volume I, January–June, 1807.

"The Progression of Revolution." *Fraser's Magazine*, July, 1832, 683–689.

"The Regiment First Coming into a Country Town." *United Service Journal*, July, 1828, 345.

"Wellington in Cadiz; or the Conqueror and the Cortes." *Blackwood's Edinburgh Magazine*, December, 1829, 918–934.

Z. "Nugæ Literariæ No. I: The Duke of Wellington." *Blackwood's Edinburgh Magazine*, February, 1827, 227–237.

Newspaper Articles

"Address to the Unemployed Workmen of Yorkshire and Lancashire." *The Leeds Mercury*, 20 May, 1826, 3.

"An Englishman in Paris." *John Bull*, 17 January, 1830, 22.

"Disturbances in Macclesfield." *Leeds Mercury*, 2 May, 1829, 3.

"Disturbances in Yorkshire and Lancashire." *Leeds Intelligencer*, 4 May, 1826, 3.

"Dreadful Riots at Bristol." *Leeds Intelligencer*, 3 November, 1831, 3.

"Dreadful Riots at Bristol." *Leeds Mercury*, 5 November, 1831, 3.

"Execution of the Bristol Rioters." *Leeds Mercury*, 4 February, 1832, 4.

"Foreign Intelligence." *The Leeds Intelligencer*, 16 November, 1826, 2.

"Foreign Policy." *John Bull*, 22 February, 1830, 60.

"Leeds Thursday, May 13." *The Leeds Intelligencer*, 13 May, 1824, 2.

"Riots at Bradford." *Leeds Mercury*, 6 May, 1826, 2–3.

"Riot at Manchester." *Leeds Mercury*, 16 May, 1829, 3.

"Riot at Norwich." *Leeds Mercury*, 25 February, 1826, 2.

"Sir WALTER SCOTT, the Greatest Genius and Most Popular Writer of His Nation and His Age, Expired At." *The Times*, 25 September, 1832, 2.

"The Late Riots at Bristol." *Leeds Intelligencer*, 10 November, 1831, 3.

Edited or Translated Texts:

Austen, Jane. *Pride and Prejudice.* Edited by Vivien Jones. London: Penguin, 1996.

Austen Jane, and Charlotte Brontë. *The Juvenilia of Jane Austen and Charlotte Brontë.* Edited by Frances Beer. London: Penguin, 1986.

Brontë, Branwell. *Branwell's Blackwood's Magazine.* Edited by Christine Alexander and Vanessa Benson. Edmonton: Juvenilia Press, 1995.

———. *The History of the Young Men.* Edited by William Baker. Sydney: Juvenilia Press, 2010.

———. *The Poems of Patrick Branwell Brontë: A New Text and Commentary.* Edited by Victor Neufeldt. London: Routledge, 2015.

———. *The Works of Patrick Branwell Brontë.* Volume I. Edited by Victor Neufeldt. London: Garland, 1997.

————. *The Works of Patrick Branwell Brontë*. Volume II. Edited by Victor Neufeldt. London: Garland, 1999.

————. *The Works of Patrick Branwell Brontë*. Volume III. Edited by Victor Neufeldt. London: Garland, 1999.

Brontë, Charlotte. *An Edition of the Early Writings of Charlotte Brontë, The Glass Town Saga*. Volume I. Edited by Christine Alexander. Oxford and New York: Basil Blackwell, 1987.

————. *An Edition of the Early Writings of Charlotte Brontë, The Rise of Angria*. Volume II Part I. Edited by Christine Alexander. Oxford and New York: Basil Blackwell, 1991.

————. *An Edition of the Early Writings of Charlotte Brontë, The Rise of Angria*. Volume II Part II. Edited by Christine Alexander. Oxford and New York: Basil Blackwell, 1991.

————. *Albion and Marina*. Edited by Juliet McMaster, et al. Edmonton: Juvenilia Press, 1999.

————. *Charlotte Bronte: Juvenilia 1829–1835*. Edited by Juliet Barker. London: Penguin, 1996.

————. *Five Novelettes*. Edited by Winifred Gérin. London: The Folio Press, 1971.

————. *Four Years Ago*. Transcribed by C. W. Hatfield. Brontë Parsonage Museum: Hatfield Transcription 10.

————. *Jane Eyre*. Edited by Margaret Smith and Sally Shuttleworth. Oxford: Oxford University Press, 2008.

————. *Legends of Angria: Compiled from the Early Writings of Charlotte Bronte*. Edited by Fannie Ratchford and William Clyde DeVane. New York: Kennikat Press, 1933.

————. *My Angria and the Angrians*. Edited by Juliet McMaster, et al. Sydney: Juvenilia Press, 2015.

————. *Shirley*. Edited by Herbert Rosengarten and Margaret Smith. Oxford: Oxford University Press, 1998.

————. *Shirley*. Edited by Jessica Cox. London: Penguin, 2006.

————. *Something About Arthur, by Charlotte Brontë*. Edited by Christine Alexander. Texas: University of Texas Press, 1981.

————. *Tales of Angria*. Edited by Heather Glen. London: Penguin, 2006.

————. *Tales of the Islanders*. Volumes I–IV. Edited by Christine Alexander, et al. Edmonton, Sydney: Juvenilia Press, 2004.

————. *The Brontes: A Life in Letters*. Edited by Juliet Barker. London: Viking, 1997.

————. *The Poems of Charlotte Brontë*. Edited by Victor Neufeldt. London: Garland, 1985.

————. *The Professor*. Edited by Margaret Smith and Herbert Rosengarten. Oxford: Oxford University Press, 2008.

————. *Villette*. Edited by Margaret Smith. Oxford: Oxford University Press, 2008.

Brontë, Charlotte, Emily. *The Belgian Essays*. Translated and edited by Sue Lonoff. New Haven: Yale University Press, 1997.

Brontë, Charlotte, Emily, Anne, Branwell. *Tales from Glass Town, Angria and Gondal*. Edited by Christine Alexander. Oxford: Oxford University Press, 2010.

Brontë, Emily. *Gondal's Queen: A Novel in Verse*. Edited by Fannie Ratchford. Austin: University of Texas Press, 1955.

———. *Wuthering Heights*. Edited by Ian Jack. Oxford: Oxford University Press, 2009.

Brontë, Reverend Patrick. *The Letters of the Reverend Patrick Brontë*. Edited by Dudley Green. London: Nonsuch, 2005.

Byron, George Gordon Lord. *Lord Byron—The Major Works*. Edited by Jerome J. McGann. Oxford University Press, 2008.

Coleridge, Samuel Taylor. *Samuel Taylor Coleridge—The Major Works*. Edited by H. J. Jackson. Oxford: Oxford University Press, 2008.

Defoe, Daniel. *Robinson Crusoe*. Edited by James Kelly. Oxford: Oxford University Press, 2008.

Eliot, George. *Edward Neville*. Edited by Juliet McMaster, et al. Edmonton: Juvenilia Press, 1995.

Frank, Anne. *The Diary of a Young Girl*. Edited by Otto H. Frank and Mirjam Pressler. London: Puffin, 2009.

Freud, Sigmund. *Beyond the Pleasure Principle*. Translated by John Reddick. London: Penguin, 2003.

Gaskell, Elizabeth. *The Life of Charlotte Brontë*. Edited by Angus Easson. Oxford: Oxford University Press, 2009.

Gibbon, Edward. *The History of the Decline and Fall of the Roman Empire*. Volumes I–III. Edited by David Womersley. London: Penguin, 1996.

Herodotus. *The Histories*. Edited by Carolyn Dewald. Translated by Robin Waterfield. London: Penguin, 2008.

Homer. *The Iliad*. Translated by E. V. Rieu. London: Penguin, 2003.

Jonson, Ben. "Every Man In His Humour." In *The Roaring Girl and Other City Comedies*. Edited by James Knowles. Oxford: Oxford University Press, 2008.

Mack, Robert. L, ed, trans. *Arabian Nights' Entertainments*. Oxford: Oxford University Press, 1995.

Milton, John. *Paradise Lost*. Edited by Stephen Orgel. Oxford: Oxford University Press, 2008.

Scott, Walter. *A Legend of the Wars of Montrose*. Edited by H. J. Alexander. Edinburgh: Edinburgh University Press, 1996.

———. *Ivanhoe*. Edited by Ian Duncan. Oxford: Oxford University Press, 2010.

———. "The Lay of the Last Minstrel." In *Sir Walter Scott: Selected Poems*. Edited by Thomas Crawford. Oxford: Clarendon Press, 1972.

———. *The Tale of Old Mortality*. Edited by Jane Stevenson and Peter Davidson. Oxford: Oxford University Press, 2009.

————. *Waverley.* Edited by Kathryn Sutherland. Oxford: Oxford University Press, 2015.

Shakespeare, William. *Henry IV, Part I: The Oxford Shakespeare.* Edited by David Bevington. Oxford: Oxford University Press, 2008.

————. *Henry IV, Part II: The Oxford Shakespeare.* Edited by René Weis. Oxford: Oxford University Press, 2008.

————. *Henry V: The Oxford Shakespeare.* Edited by Gary Taylor. Oxford: Oxford University Press, 2008.

————. *Othello.* Edited by Michael Neill. Oxford: Oxford University Press, 2008.

————. *The Merry Wives of Windsor: The Oxford Shakespeare.* Edited by T. W. Craik. Oxford: Oxford University Press, 2008.

————. *The Tragedy of Macbeth: The Oxford Shakespeare.* Edited by Nicholas Brooke. Oxford: Oxford University Press, 2008.

Southey, Robert. *Robert Southey: Later Poetical Works, 1811–1838.* Volume III. Edited by Lynda Pratt. London: Pickering and Chatto, 2012.

————. *Selected Shorter Poems, c. 1793–1810.* Volume V. Edited by Lynda Pratt. Pickering and Chatto, 2004.

Spenser, Edmund. *The Faerie Queene.* Edited by Thomas P. Roche Jr. and C. Patrick O'Donnell Jr. London: Penguin, 1987.

Stevenson, Robert Louis. *First Writings: Robert Louis Stevenson.* Edited by Christine Alexander and Ellie McPherson. Sydney: Juvenilia Press, 2013.

Tolstoy, Leo. *War and Peace.* Edited by Aylmer Maude Louise and Amy Mandelker. Oxford: Oxford University Press, 2010.

Vaughan, Iris. *The Diary of Iris Vaughan.* Edited by Peter Alexander and Peter Midgley. Sydney: The Juvenilia Press, 2004.

Virgil. *The Aeneid.* Edited by David West. London: Penguin, 2003.

Wordsworth, William. *William Wordsworth: The Major Works.* Edited by Stephen Gill. Oxford: Oxford University Press, 2008.

Primary Material

Beatson, Robert. *Naval and Military Memoirs of Great Britain, from 1727 to 1783.* London: Longman, 1804.

Bowdich, Thomas Edward. *Essay on the Superstitions, Customs, and Arts Common to the Ancient Egyptians, Abyssinians, and Ashantees.* Paris: J. Smith, 1821.

————. *Mission from Cape Coast Castle to Ashantee, with a Statistical Account of That Kingdom, and Geographical Notices of Other Parts of the Interior of Africa.* London: John Murray, 1819.

Clarke, Francis L., and William Dunlap. *The Life of the Most Noble Marquis and Earl of Wellington.* Hartford: Hale and Hosmer, 1814.

Disraeli, Benjamin. *Vivian Grey.* London: Henry Colburn, 1826.

Duke of Wellington. *Despatches, Correspondence and Memoranda.* London: John Murray, 1867–1880.

Dupuis, Joseph. *Journal of a Residence in Ashantee*. London: Henry Colburn, 1824.

Eagles, John. *The Bristol Riots: Their Causes, Progress, and Consequences*. Bristol: Gutch and Martin, 1832.

Egan, Pierce. *Boxiana: From the Days of the Renowned Broughton and Slack, to the Championship of Cribb*. London: Sherwood, Jones & Company, 1823.

Elliot, George. *The Life of the Most Noble Arthur Duke of Wellington*. London: Sherwood, Neely and Jones, 1816.

Gleig, George. *A Subaltern in America*. Philadelphia: Allen & Ticknor, 1833.

———. *Life of Arthur, First Duke of Wellington*. London: Longman, 1862.

Gravestone of John Bland. Haworth: St Michael and All Angels Church, 1821.

Gravestone of William Foster. Haworth: St Michael and All Angels Church, 1807.

Hansard, T. C, ed. "Sir J Mackintosh's Motion Respecting the Rigour of Our Criminal Laws, 21 May." In *The Parliamentary Debates*. Volume IX. London: T.C. Hansard, 1823.

Jacorus. "Anecdotes, Royal and Noble." *The Mirror of Literature, Amusement and Instruction*. Volume IX. London: J. Limbird, 1827.

Kitson, John. *The Diary of John Kitson of Haworth*. Keighley: Public Library, 1843.

Malcolm, John. *Malcolm's Tales of Field: With Sketches of Life at Home*. Edinburgh: Oliver & Boyd, 1829.

Mavor, William Fordyce. *Universal History, Ancient and Modern*. Volume VI. London: Richard Phillips, 1807.

Memoirs of a Sergeant Late in the Forty-Third Light Infantry Regiment. London: John Mason, 1835.

Pringle, Thomas, and Josiah Conder. *Narrative of a Residence in South Africa*. London: Moxon, 1835.

Ridley, James. *The Tales of the Genii*. Volumes I, II. London: C. Cooke, 1764.

Sarrat, Lieutenant. *Life of Buonaparte in which the Atrocious Deeds Which He Has Perpetrated in Order to Attain His Elevated Station*. London: Crosby, 1803.

Scott, Walter. *Marmion*. Edinburgh: Archibald Constable and Company, 1808.

———. *Tales of a Grandfather*. Edinburgh: Cadell & Co., 1828.

———. *The Betrothed*. Edinburgh: Archibald Constable and Company, 1825.

———. *The Lay of the Last Minstrel*. Edinburgh: Bowhill, 2013.

———. *The Life of Napoleon Buonaparte in Nine Volumes*. Edinburgh: William Blackwood, 1827.

———. *The Talisman*. Edinburgh: Archibald Constable and Company, 1825.

Somerton, W. H. *A Full Report of the Trials of the Bristol Rioters*. Bristol: W. H. Somerton, 1832.

Southey, Robert. *History of the Peninsular War*. London: John Murray, 1823.

———. *Life of Nelson*. London: John Murray, 1830.

St Michael and All Angels Baptism Records. Haworth: St Michael and All Angels Church, 1813, 1816.

Trials of the Persons Concerned in the Late Riots, Before Chief Justice Tindal, and Justices Bosanquet and Taunton. Bristol: P. Rose, 1832.

The New British Novelist; Comprising Works of the Most Popular and Fashionable Writers of the Present Day Vol. XXII. London: Colburn and Bentley, 1830.

Thomson, William. *Military Memoirs Relating to Campaigns, Battles and Stratagems of War Ancient and Modern.* London: Johnson & Co., 1803.

SECONDARY MATERIAL

Books

Alexander, Christine. *The Early Writings of Charlotte Brontë.* Buffalo, New York: Prometheus Books, 1983.

———. *The Art of the Brontës.* Cambridge: Cambridge University Press, 1995.

Alexander, Christine, and Juliet McMaster, eds. *The Child Writer from Austen to Woolf.* Cambridge: Cambridge University Press, 2005.

Alexander, Jeffrey. C, Ron Eyerman, and Bernard Giesen, eds. *Cultural Trauma and Collective Identity.* Berkeley: University of California Press, 2004.

Amerongen, J. B. van. *The Actor in Dickens: A Study of the Histrionic and Dramatic Elements in the Novelist's Life and Works.* London: Ardent Media, 1926.

Azim, Firdous. *The Colonial Rise of the Novel.* London: Routledge, 1993.

Bainbridge, Simon. *British Poetry and the Revolutionary and Napoleonic Wars.* Oxford: Oxford University Press, 2003.

———. *Napoleon and English Romanticism.* Cambridge: Cambridge University Press, 1995.

Barker, Juliet. *The Brontës.* London: Weidenfeld and Nicolson, 1994.

Bennett, Betty, ed. *British War Poetry in the Age of Romanticism.* New York: Garland, 1976.

Bock, Carol. *Charlotte Bronte and the Storyteller's Audience.* Iowa City: University of Iowa Press, 1992.

Bogousslavsky, J., and Laurent Tatu. *Hysteria: The Rise of an Enigma.* Basel: Karger, 2014.

Caesar, Adrian. *Taking It Like a Man: Suffering, Sexuality, and the War Poets.* Manchester: Manchester University Press, 1993.

Cantor, Chris. *Evolution and Posttraumatic Stress: Disorders of Vigilance and Defence.* London: Routledge, 2005.

Carter, Hodding. *The Past as Prelude: New Orleans, 1718–1968.* Gretna: Tulane University, 1968.

Colley, Linda. *Britons: Forging the Nation, 1707–1837.* New Haven: Yale University Press, 2005.

Corbett, Mary Jean. *Family Likeness: Sex, Marriage and Incest from Jane Austen to Virginia Woolf.* Ithaca: Cornell University Press, 2011.

Cox, Jeffrey N. *Romanticism in the Shadow of War*. Cambridge: Cambridge University Press, 2014.

Daly, Gavin. *The British Soldier in the Peninsular War*. London: Palgrave, 2013.

Dillon, Matthew, and Lynda Garland. *Ancient Rome: From the Early Republic to the Assassination of Julius Caesar*. Abingdon: Routledge, 2005.

Du Maurier, Daphne. *The Infernal World of Branwell Brontë*. London: Penguin, 1960.

Duncan, Ian. *Scott's Shadow: The Novel in Romantic Edinburgh*. Princeton: Princeton University Press, 2007.

Duthie, Enid. L. *The Brontës and Nature*. New York: Palgrave, 1986.

Edric, Robert. *Sanctuary*. New York: Doubleday, 2014.

Fang, Karen. *Romantic Writing and the Empire of Signs*. Virginia: University of Virginia Press, 2010.

Forrest, Alan. *Waterloo: Great Battles Series*. Oxford: Oxford University Press, 2015.

Gérin, Winifred. *Branwell Bronte*. London: Thomas Nelson and Sons, 1961.

———. *The Brontes: The Formative Years Pt. 1*. Harlow: Northcote House, 1973.

Glen, Heather, ed. *The Cambridge Companion to the Brontës*. Cambridge University Press, 2002.

Green, Dudley. *Patrick Brontë: Father of Genius*. Stroud: Nonsuch, 2008.

Hagemann, Karen, Jane Rendall, and Gisela Mettele. *Gender, War and Politics: Transatlantic Perspectives, 1775–1830*. London: Palgrave, 2010.

Hanson Lucy. *The Story of the People of Great Britain*. Volume IV. Cambridge: Cambridge University Press, 1923.

Harrison, David. *The Brontës of Haworth*. Victoria: Trafford, 2002.

Harrison, Stanley. *Poor Men's Guardians: A Record of the Struggles for a Democratic Newspaper Press, 1763–1973*. London: Lawrence and Wishart, 1974.

Herbert, Christopher. *War of No Pity: The Indian Mutiny and Victorian Trauma*. Princeton: Princeton University Press, 2008.

Hickey, Donald R., and Connie D. Clark, eds. *The Routledge Handbook of the War of 1812*. New York: Routledge, 2015.

Hunt, Nigel. *Memory, War and Trauma*. Cambridge: Cambridge University Press, 2010.

Hurl-Eamon, Jennine. *Marriage and the British Army in the Long Eighteenth Century*. Oxford: Oxford University Press, 2014.

Irwin, Robert. *The Arabian Nights: A Companion*. London: Tauris Parke, 2003.

Jenkins, Ian Dennis, and Victoria Turner. *The Greek Body*. Los Angeles: Getty Publications, 2009.

Jorgensen, Paul A. *Shakespeare's Military World*. Berkeley: University of California Press, 1956.

Kaplan, Ann. E. *Trauma Culture: The Politics of Terror and Loss in Media and Literature*. New Brunswick: Rutgers University Press, 2005.

Kennedy, Catriona. *Narratives of the Revolutionary and Napoleonic Wars*. London: Palgrave, 2013.

King, Andrew, and John Plunkett. *Popular Print Media*. Volume I. London: Routledge, 2004.

Lamonica, Drew. *We Are Three Sisters—Self and Family in the Writing of the Brontës*. Missouri: Missouri University Press, 2003.

Langbauer, Laurie. *The Juvenile Tradition: Young Writers and Prolepsis, 1750–1835*. Oxford: Oxford University Press, 2016.

Law, Alice. *Branwell Brontë*. London: A. M. Philpot, 1923.

Lefebure, Molly. *Private Lives of the Ancient Mariner: Coleridge and His Children*. Cambridge: The Lutterworth Press, 2013.

Lightfoot, Paul. *Exploring South East Cornwall*. Cornwall: Alison Hodge, 2012.

Lloyd, Alan. *The Drums of Kumasi: The Story of the Ashanti Wars*. New York: Panther, 1965.

Lowenthal, Leo. *Literature and Mass Culture*. Piscataway, New Jersey: Transaction Publishers, 2011.

Luckhurst, Roger. *The Trauma Question*. Abingdon: Routledge, 2008.

Lutz, Deborah. *The Brontë Cabinet: Three Lives in Nine Objects*. New York: W. W. Norton, 2015.

Martin, Brian Joseph. *Napoleonic Friendship: Military Fraternity, Intimacy, and Sexuality in Nineteenth-Century France*. Durham: University of New Hampshire, 2011.

Matus, Jill. *Shock, Memory and the Unconscious in Victorian Fiction*. Cambridge: Cambridge University Press, 2009.

Maurat, Charlotte. *The Brontës' Secret*. New York: Barnes & Noble, 1970.

McIntosh, Ainsley. *Walter Scott, Marmion: A Tale of Flodden Field. A Critical Edition*. PhD Thesis. University of Aberdeen, 2009.

Meyer, Susan. *Imperialism at Home: Race and Victorian Women's Fiction*. Ithaca: Cornell University Press, 1996.

Miller, Lucasta. *The Bronte Myth*. London: Vintage, 2001.

Miller, Stephen G. *Ancient Greek Athletics*. New Haven: Yale University Press, 2006.

Mitchell, Robert. *Sympathy and the State in the Romantic Era: Systems, State Finance, and the Shadows of Futurity*. London: Routledge, 2014.

Mole, Tom. *Romanticism and Celebrity Culture, 1750–1850*. Cambridge: Cambridge University Press, 2009.

Myerly, Scott Hughes. *British Military Spectacle: From the Napoleonic Wars Through the Crimea*. Cambridge: Harvard University Press, 1996.

Nyborg, Erin. *The Brontës and Masculinity*. PhD Thesis. University of Oxford, 2016.

Pettit, C. *Reading Thomas Hardy*. New York: Springer, 2016.

Philps, Mark. *The British Response to the Threat of Invasion*. Aldershot: Ashgate, 2006.

Poplawski, Paul. *English Literature in Context*. Cambridge: Cambridge University Press, 2008.

Popper, Karl. *The Poverty of Historicism*. London: Routledge, 2013.

Ramsey, Neil. *The Military Memoir and Romantic Literary Culture 1780–1835*. Farnham: Ashgate, 2011.

Ratchford, Fannie. *The Brontës' Web of Childhood*. Oxford: Oxford University Press, 1941.

Richards, Jeffrey. *Imperialism and Music: Britain, 1876–1953*. New York: Palgrave, 2001.

Roberts, Andrew. *Napoleon and Wellington*. London: Phoenix, 2010.

Rossi, Michael John. *James Herriot: A Critical Opinion*. London: Greenport, 1997.

Russell, Gillian. *The Theatres of War: Performance, Politics, and Society 1793–1815*. Oxford: Oxford University Press, 1995.

Scädler, Karl-Ferdinand, and Armand Duchâteau. *Earth and Ore: 2500 Years of African Art in Terra-Cotta and Metal*. Neutral Bay: Panterra, 1997.

Shaw, Philip. *Romantic Wars: Studies in Culture and Conflict, 1793–1822*. London: Ashgate, 2000.

———. *Suffering and Sentiment in Romantic Military Art*. Farnham: Ashgate, 2013.

Shuttleworth, Sally. *Charlotte Brontë and Victorian Psychology*. Cambridge University Press, 1996.

———. *The Mind of the Child: Child Development In Literature, Science, And Medicine 1840–1900*. Oxford: Oxford University Press, 2013.

Sleight, Simon, and Shirleene Robinson. *Children, Childhood and Youth in the British World*. Basingstoke: Palgrave, 2015.

Smith, Kevin. *Black Genesis: The History of the Black Prizefighter 1760–1870*. Bloomington: iUniverse, 2003.

Snowdon, David. *Writing the Prizefight*. Bern: Peter Lang, 2013.

Sugden, John. *Boxing and Society: An International Analysis*. Manchester: Manchester University Press, 1996.

Thomas, Brook. *Literature and the Nation*. Tübingen: Gunter Narr, 1998.

Thormählen, Marianne, ed. *The Brontës in Context*. Cambridge: Cambridge University Press, 2012.

———. *The Brontës and Religion*. Cambridge: Cambridge University Press, 1999.

Trawick, Buckner B. *Shakespeare and Alcohol*. Amsterdam: Rodopi, 1978.

Ward, William S. *Index and Finding List of Serials Published in the British Isles, 1789—1832*. Lexington: University Press of Kentucky, 2015.

Chapters in Edited Collections

Alexander, Christine. "For Fiction—Read Scott Alone': The Legacy of Sir Walter Scott on Youthful Artists and Writers." In *The Shadow of the Precursor*. Edited by Diana Glenn, Md Rezaul Haque, Ben Kooyman, and Nena Bierbaum. Cambridge: Cambridge Scholars Publishing, 2012, 106–123.

Alexander, Christine. "Autobiography and Juvenilia: Charlotte Brontë's Early Manuscripts." In *The Child Writer from Austen to Woolf*. Edited by Christine Alexander and Juliet McMaster. Cambridge: Cambridge University Press, 2005, 154–173.

Badkhen, Anna. "Afghan Civilians: Surviving Trauma in a Failed State." In *War Trauma and Its Wake: Expanding the Circle of Healing*. Edited by Raymond Monsour Scurfield and Katherine Theresa Platoni. London: Routledge, 2013, 13.

Baker, Samuel. "Scott's Worlds of War." In *The Edinburgh Companion to Walter Scott*. Edited by Fiona Robertson. Edinburgh: Edinburgh University Press, 2012, 70–82.

Chitham, Edward. "The Irish Heritage of the Brontës." In *A Companion to the Brontës*. Edited by Diane Long Hoeveler and Deborah Denenholz Morse. Oxford: Wiley-Blackwell, 2016, 403–416.

Dawson, P. M. S. "Poetry in an Age of Revolution." In *The Cambridge Companion to British Romanticism*. Edited by Stuart Curran. Cambridge University Press, 2003, 48–74.

Donovan, Julie. "The Poetry and Verse Drama of Branwell Brontë." In *A Companion to the Brontës*. Edited by Diane Long Hoeveler and Deborah Denenholz Morse. Oxford: Wiley-Blackwell, 2016, 213–228.

Guimarãs, Paula. "'Sunny Climes Beyond the Sea' Travel Imagination in Charlotte Brontë's Juvenile Poetry." In *Intertextual Dialogues: Travel and Routes*. Edited by A. G. Macedo and Isabel Ermida. Braga: Barbosa & Xavier, 2007, 307–322.

Harty, Joetta. "Playing Pirate: Real and Imaginary Angrias in Branwell Brontë's Writing." In *Pirates and Mutineers of the Nineteenth Century*. Edited by Grave Moore. Farnham: Ashgate, 2011, 41–58.

Jack, Elizabeth. "Indexes of Quotations and Literary Allusions in the Novels of Charlotte Brontë." In *The Professor*. Edited by Margaret Smith and Herbert Rosengarten. Oxford: Clarendon Press, 1987.

Lodge, Sara. "Literary Influences on the Brontës." In *The Brontës in Context*. Edited by Marianne Thormählen. Cambridge: Cambridge University Press, 2012.

———. "Masculinity, Power and Play in the Work of the Brontës." In *The Victorian Novel and Masculinity*. Edited by Phillip Mallett. London: Palgrave Macmillan, 2015.

Morse, Deborah Denenholz. "Queer Charlotte: Homoerotics from *Mina Laury* to *The Professor*." In *Charlotte Brontë from the Beginnings*. Edited by Judith E. Pike and Lucy Morrison. London: Routledge, 2017, 111–125.

Neufeldt, Victor. "The Child Is Parent to the Author: Branwell Brontë." In *The Child Writer from Austen to Woolf.* Edited by Christine Alexander and Juliet McMaster. Cambridge: Cambridge University Press, 2005, 173–187.

Nyborg, Erin. "From Angria to Thornfield: Charlotte Brontë's Cross-Period Development of the Byronic Hero." In *Charlotte Brontë from the Beginnings.* Edited by Judith E. Pike and Lucy Morrison. London: Routledge, 2017, 141–154.

Oates, Joyce Carol. "Introduction." In *Wuthering Heights.* Edited by Ian Jack. Oxford: Oxford University Press, 1998, i–xvi.

Robertson, Fiona. "Introduction." In *The Edinburgh Companion to Walter Scott.* Edited by Fiona Robertson. Edinburgh: Edinburgh University Press, 2012, 1–9.

———. "Romancing and Romanticism." In *The Edinburgh Companion to Walter Scott.* Edited by Fiona Robertson. Edinburgh: Edinburgh University Press, 2012, 93–105.

Russell, Gillian. "The Army, the Navy, and the Napoleonic Wars." In *A Companion to Jane Austen.* Edited by Claudia L. Johnson and Clara Tuite. Malden: Blackwell, 2009, 261–271.

Sanders, Valerie, and Emma Butcher. (2017) "'Mortal hostility': Masculinity and Fatherly Conflict in the Glass Town and Angrian Sagas." In *Charlotte Brontë from the Beginnings.* Edited by Judith E. Pike and Lucy Morrison. London: Routledge, 2017, 59–71.

Smith, Nigel. "Paradise Lost from Civil War to Restoration." In *The Cambridge Companion to Writing of the English Revolution.* Edited by N. H. Keeble. Cambridge: Cambridge University Press, 2001, 255–256.

Turner, Karen. "Charlotte Brontë's 'warrior priest': St John Rivers and the Language of War." In *Martial Masculinities: Experiencing and Imagining the Military in the Long Nineteenth Century.* Edited by Michael Brown, Joanne Begiato, and Anna Maria Barry. Manchester: Manchester University Press, 2019, 199–213.

Weisser, Henry. "Radicalism and Radical Politics." In *Britain in the Hanoverian Age, An Encyclopedia 1714–1837.* Edited by Gerald Newman and Leslie Ellen Brown. New York: Garland, 1997, 585–586.

Yates, Louisa. "Reader, I [shagged/beat/whipped/f****d/rewrote] him." *Charlotte Brontë: Legacies and Afterlives.* Manchester: Manchester University Press, 2019, 258–279.

Conference Papers

Barker, Juliet. "The Life of Charlotte Brontë: What Mrs Gaskell Left Out." *Annual Victorian Lecture.* University of Hull, 5 May, 2016.

Pike, Judith. "A New Legacy for Charlotte Brontë: From Miss Foxley in the Secret (1833) to Jane Eyre (1847)." *Charlotte Brontë Bicentennial Conference*. Chawton House Library, 14 May, 2016.

Encyclopedias and Companions

Abaka, Edmund. "Dan Fodio, Osman." In *The Oxford Encyclopedia of African Thought*. Edited by Abiola F. Irele and Biodun Jeyifo. Oxford: Oxford University Press, 2010.

Alexander, Christine, and Margaret Smith, eds. *The Oxford Companion to the Brontës*. Oxford: Oxford University Press, 2006.

Barnard, Louise, and Robert Barnard, eds. *A Brontë Encyclopedia*. Hoboken: Wiley-Blackwell, 2007.

Hoeveler, Diane Long, and Deborah Denenholz Morse, eds. *A Companion to the Brontes*. Hoboken: Wiley, 2016.

Journal Articles

Alexander, Christine. "Charlotte Brontë, Autobiography, and the Image of the Hero." *Brontë Studies* 36, no. 1 (2013): 1–19.

———. "Anecdotes of the Duke of Wellington." *Brontë Studies* 35, no. 3 (2010): 208–214.

Butcher, Emma. "Napoleonic Periodicals and the Childhood Imagination: The Influence of War Commentary on Charlotte and Branwell Brontë's Glass Town and Angria." *Victorian Periodicals Review* 48, no. 4 (2015): 469–486.

Cronin, R. "Wordsworth's Poems of 1807 and the War Against Napoleon." *The Review of English Studies* 48, no. 189 (1997): 33–50.

Duckett, Bob. "The Library at Ponden Hall." *Brontë Studies* 40, no. 2 (2015): 104–149.

———. "Where Did the Brontës Get Their Books?" *Brontë Studies* 32, no. 3 (2007): 193–206.

Favret, Mary A. "Coming Home: The Public Spaces of Romantic War." *Studies in Romanticism* 33, no. 4 (1994): 539–548.

Fermi, Sarah. "A Question of Colour." *Brontë Studies* 40, no. 4 (2015): 334–342.

Gash, N. "After Waterloo: British Society and the Legacy of the Napoleonic Wars." *Transactions of the Royal Historical Society* 28 (1978): 145–157.

Guimarãs, Paula. "Dramatizing the Conflicts of Nation and the Body: Displacement in Charlotte and Emily Brontë's Poetry of Home and Exile Dualities." *Miscelánea: A Journal of English and American Studies* 38 (2008): 63–77.

Hartman, Geoffrey. H. "On Traumatic Knowledge and Literary Studies." *New Literary History* 26, no. 3 (1995): 537–563.

Heywood, Christopher. "Africa and Slavery in the Bronte Children's Novels." *Hitotsubashi Journal of Arts and Sciences* 30, no. 1 (1989): 75–87.

Hiltner, Ken. "Shirley and the Luddites." *Brontë Studies* 33, no. 2 (2008): 148–158.

Jones, Edgar, and Simon Wessley. "Case of Chronic Fatigue Syndrome After Crimean War and Indian Mutiny." *British Medical Journal* 319 (1999): 1645–1647.

———. "Psychiatric Battle Casualties: An Intra- and Interwar Comparison." *The British Journal of Psychiatry* 178 (2001): 242–247.

Lamb, Jonathan. "Scorbutic Nostalgia." *Journal for Maritime Research* 15, no. 1 (2013): 27–36.

Longmuir, Anne. "'Reader, Perhaps You Were Never in Belgium?': Negotiating British Identity in Charlotte Brontë's *The Professor* and *Villette*." *Nineteenth-Century Literature* 64, no. 2 (2009): 163–188.

May, Chad. "The Horrors of my Tale: Trauma, the Historical Imagination, and Sir Walter Scott." *Pacific Coast Philology* 20, no. 1 (2005): 98–116.

Oda, Yukari. "Wuthering Heights and the Waverley Novels: Sir Walter Scott's Influence on Emily Brontë." *Brontë Studies* 32, no. 3 (2007): 217–226.

O'Sullivan, Lisa. "The Time and Place of Nostalgia: Re-situating a French Disease." *Journal of the History of Medicine and Allied Sciences* 67, no. 4 (2012): 626–649.

Pike, Judith. "Rochester's Bronze Scrag and Pearl Necklace: Bronzed Masculinity in Jane Eyre, Shirley, and Charlotte Brontë's Juvenilia." *Victorian Literature and Culture* 41, no. 2 (2013): 261–281.

Ramsey, Neil. "Romanticism and War." *Literature Compass* 3, no. 2 (2006): 117–126.

Rosen, George. "Nostalgia: A 'Forgotten' Psychological Disorder." *Psychological Medicine* 5, no. 4 (1975): 340–354.

Shaw, Philip. "Longing for Home: Robert Hamilton, Nostalgia, and the Emotional Life of the Eighteenth-Century Soldier." *Journal for Eighteenth-Century Studies* 39, no. 1 (2014): 25–40.

Willis, Martin. "*Silas Marner*, Catalepsy, and Mid-Victorian Medicine: George Eliot's Ethics of Care." *Journal of Victorian Culture* 20, no. 3 (2015): 326–340.

Web Sources

Alabed, Bana. *Twitter Feed of Bana Alabed*. Accessed 12 December 2016. https://twitter.com/alabedbana.

Bowen, John. "Melding Fantasy and Realism in Wuthering Heights." *British Library Discovering Literature: Romantics and Victorians*. Accessed 2 February 2014. https://www.bl.uk/romantics-and-victorians/articles/melding-of-fantasy-and-realism-in-wuthering-heights.

"Conflict." *Oxford English Dictionary Online*. Accessed 5 December 2016. https://en.oxforddictionaries.com/definition/conflict.

Crabtree, John. "Census Record of the Crabtree Family, 1851." Accessed 14 December 2014. https://www.myheritage.com/names/haworth_crabtree.

Cronin, R. "Magazines and Romantic Modernity." In *The British Periodical Text, 1797–1835*. Edited by Simon Hull. Accessed 13 April 2015. http://www.humanities-ebooks.co.uk/pdf/Pages_from_Hull_Periodicals.pdf.

Flood, Alison. "Unseen Charlotte Brontë Story and Poem Discovered." *The Guardian*. Accessed 12 November 2016. https://www.theguardian.com/books/2015/nov/12/unseen-charlotte-bronte-story-and-poem-discovered.

Goodwin, Gordon. "James MacQueen (1778–1870)." *Oxford Dictionary of National Biography*, Accessed 7 September 2015. http://www.oxforddnb.com/view/article/17736.

Shaw, Philip. "Childe Harold's Pilgrimage: Lord Byron and the Battle of Waterloo." *British Library Discovering Literature: Romantics and Victorians*. Accessed 2 February 2014. https://www.bl.uk/romantics-and-victorians/articles/childe-harolds-pilgrimage-lord-byron-and-the-battle-of-waterloo.

Mather, Ruth. "The Impact of the Napoleonic Wars in Britain." *British Library Discovering Literature: Romantics and Victorians*. Accessed 2 July 2014. https://www.bl.uk/romantics-and-victorians/articles/the-impact-of-the-napoleonic-wars-in-britain.

"The Reform Act 1832." *Living Heritage: UK Parliament Online*. Accessed 12 October 2016. http://www.parliament.uk/about/living-heritage/evolutionofparliament/houseofcommons/reformacts/overview/reformact1832/.

Index

© The Editor(s) (if applicable) and The Author(s) 2019
E. Butcher, *The Brontës and War*,
https://doi.org/10.1007/978-3-319-95636-7

Printed by Printforce, the Netherlands